Rand El Zein
Between Violence, Vulnerability, Resilience and Resistance

Editorial

The series is edited by Elke Grittmann, Elisabeth Klaus, Margreth Lünenborg, Jutta Röser, Tanja Thomas and Ulla Wischermann.

Rand El Zein, born in 1991, is a researcher from Beirut, Lebanon. She received her PhD in Communication Studies at Universität Salzburg and her MA in Media Studies at the American University of Beirut. Her research focuses on Arab media, feminist theory, and cultural studies.

Rand El Zein

Between Violence, Vulnerability, Resilience and Resistance

Arab Television News on the Experiences of Syrian Women
during the Syrian Conflict

Diese Publikation wurde im Rahmen des Fördervorhabens 16TOA002 mit Mitteln des Bundesministeriums für Bildung und Forschung im Open Access bereitgestellt.

Bibliographic information published by the Deutsche Nationalbibliothek
The Deutsche Nationalbibliothek lists this publication in the Deutsche National-bibliografie; detailed bibliographic data are available in the Internet at http://dnb.d-nb.de

First published in 2021 by transcript Verlag, Bielefeld
© **Rand El Zein**

Cover layout: Yara Abdallah, Beirut, and Maria Arndt, Bielefeld
Proofread: Marie Frohling

Print-ISBN 978-3-8376-5959-7
PDF-ISBN 978-3-8394-5959-1
EPUB-ISBN 978-3-7328-5959-7
https://doi.org/10.14361/9783839459591
ISSN of series: 2512-4188
eISSN of series: 2747-3937

Contents

*Dedicated to every woman who is grappling through life and refuses to kneel down.
Thank you for your strength, thank you for your resistance, but more importantly,
thank you for embracing your vulnerability.*

"I am my mother's daughter, which means on days when the world hurts, but I have things to do, I tell it to come back tomorrow." – Maysan Nasser

List of Tables

Acknowledgements

I would like to first of all thank my mentor, Prof. Dr. Elisabeth Klaus, for her guidance, advise, expertise, and ecouragement throughout this project as well as my entire PhD experience. Watching her build and lead the doctorate school (DSP) for geschlecht_transkulturell at Universität Salzburg has been one of my best learning experiences. Her mentorship has helped lead me to an area of scholarship that I am genuinely looking forward to continue working in.

I would like to thank the members of my committee, Prof. Dr. Sigrid Kannengieße, Prof. Dr. Kyoko Shinozaki, and Prof. Dr. Rudolf Renger, for their interest, contribution and input. I would also like to acknowledge the support I've received from the gendup (Zentrum für Gender Studies and Frauenförderung) and especially the Marie Andeßner Stipendien, as well as the One World Scholarshop at the Afro-Asiatisches Institut. A great thank you to the editors at Transcript Verlag for suggesting to publish my work, and to every person that helped make this publication possible. . My deepest gratitude goes to my mother, my late father and Patrick for their unconditional support, constant care and their belief in me.

1. Introduction

1.1 Context and Significance

This book brings together two main fields of interest: communication studies and gender studies. It explores the relationship between power structures and the notion of agency among Syrian women during the recent conflict in Syria. The book poses questions on gender politics in the context of displacement, conflict, the body, and the nation. Its significance lies in its attempt to reconcile critical media theory as myriad and productive with the theoretical concepts on subjectivity, power, performativity, neoliberalism, and humanitarian governance.

Methodologically, the book introduces a research project that employs an inductive approach and uses a critical discourse analysis of Arab television news. Considering each television station's sociopolitical views and media ownership structures, I examine 32 television news reports aired between Jan 9, 2012 and Sept 27, 2018, from seven leading Arab television news stations: *SAMA, SANA, Syria Al Ikhbariah, Al Jazeera, Al Arabiya, Al Aan,* and *RT Arabic.* I explore how the dominant media discourses in the news discursively represented the experiences of women during the Syrian conflict. In the Arab television news, these experiences are frequently addressed in the context of the four main concepts: *violence, vulnerability, resilience,* and *resistance.* Therefore, in order to recover the meanings, the news producers give to the practices of representation, I propose a theoretical framework that provides a thorough understanding of the four main concepts and the social, political and cultural meanings they have in the context of the Syrian conflict.

By tracing the practices of representations in the news reports, the book exposes how the figure of the Syrian woman in television news was constructed in five dominant media frames:

a) Women as a source of shame
b) Women as victims of their previous imprisonment
c) Females as destined child brides
d) Women as the neoliberal subject
e) Women as mothers of the nation

I draw a connection between the television media frames and the cultural meanings and language disseminated in the media narratives; I then use this connection to trace the hegemonic discourse in the news reporting.

The hegemonic discourse is traced by examining how the production of the message was carried out by seven different procedures of media reporting:

a) The circulation of shame
b) Stigmatizing the female victim
c) De-humanization by misrecognized female desire,
d) Sentimental de-politization,
e) Strategic silencing
f) De-historicization
g) Nationalizing the female body

By presenting these findings, I expose how the Arab television news naturalized the suffering and precariousness of Syrian women during the conflict, on the one hand, and misrepresented and/or ignored their agentive attempts, on the other hand. The findings also show how the Arab television news either glorified the Syrian women's agency by depicting them as strong and resisting subjects fighting in the war or represented them as hopeless victims to the widespread outbreaks of violence and social and economic injustice during the conflict. I tackle those dichotomous images by situating this work in relation to previous work from the media, gender, and cultural studies disciplines. I use Judith Butler's concept of vulnerability and resistance as a main starting point for my research and borrow Michel Foucault's ideas on discourse, power, governmentality, and the subject, as well as Saba Mahmoud's thoughts on reading agency beyond liberal politics.

In defining a conception of vulnerability, Judith Butler (2016) compares masculine and feminine ideals. She observes how the 'masculinist' model of acquiring agency is implied and practiced when one attempts to overcome a perceived vulnerability. Butler asserts that this 'masculinist' model should be challenged, positing that effective resistance comes from mobilizing vulnerability rather than overcoming it. By way of example, mobilizing vulnerability could take the form of a vulnerable subject purposefully walking through dark streets, thereby acknowledging and confronting the possibility of harm. This exposes the subject to risks, biopolitical threats, and violence. Despite this, the subject insists on moving, crossing borders, and defying checkpoints and controls. In this way, mere existence becomes a manifest act of resistance.

This same conceptualization explicates how, during times of conflict, vulnerability is directly tied to infrastructure. Both infrastructure itself and resistance to infrastructural challenges may take myriad forms: In the case of a single mother who has become displaced in a foreign country along with her children, resistance may include demands for clean water, the right to work, a safe shelter with a locking door, a running toilet, or education for her or her children.

The representations of these realities within the context of the Syrian conflict were vastly perpetuated by Arab television news. Given this context, what captures my interest is the manner in which Arab television news construct the subjects' experiences or struggles during this violent conflict and how they were represented, framed and communicated in relationship to power, gender, and class. Throughout the scope of this research project, I have looked at what has been perpetuated and reproduced in the Arab television news and what has been left unreported and decontextualized from the socio-political circumstances the subjects inhabit.

I address these questions and challenges by pointing towards the complexity of the notion of agency among different groups of Syrian women and how it has been articulated in the dominant media discourses through the intersection of media logic, gender logic, and war logic. Rather than limiting the analysis to whether the news reports represented the figure of the Syrian women through stereotypical gender roles or provided realistic depictions of their experiences, this book complicates notions of power, subjectivity, and agency circulating within and around the television images. Thus, the question of the subject's agency is always at the center of the news report analysis, as I examine how relations of power operate through the television representations of the subjects.

1.2   A Brief History of Television News in the Arab World

A significant factor to consider when analyzing news coverage from Arab television news is the presence of a unique television media landscape that involves diverse media ownership structures.

Until the 1990's, "mass media in the Arab world were still vastly censored by authoritarian regimes. Arab television stations suffered from a lack of credibility among viewers, who perceived broadcasting as a 'mere' propaganda machine for the ruling elite" (Sakr, 2007, p. 10). In this context, the ruling elites are the Arab regimes. Gunter and Dickson (2013) asserted that:

> "[Arab Television] broadcasters were subservient to government information ministries... TV was conceived as a national resource that could be utilized for the betterment of the nation. Most TV services were funded entirely by governments and were in consequence seen as an extension of them" (p. 4).

Today, the television media landscape looks different; it is now characterized by a more diversified range of television broadcasters that operate outside or with less government control. Although government-controlled television broadcasting services remain in operation, the launch of *Al Jazeera* in 1996 changed the entire television media landscape (Kraidy, 1998). Financed by Sheikh Hamad bin Khalida Al Thani, *Al Jazeera* was the first pan-Arab television station to bring "proper investigative journalism" in the Arab world (Sakr, 2007). It was considered a pioneer for introducing "concepts like democracy and human rights...and demolishing social, political and religious taboos" (Miles, 2017). It also "drastically pushed back the boundaries of free speech" (Miles, 2017). With the motto "The opinion and the counter-opinion," *Al Jazeera* is known for its vast coverage of wars and its criticism of Arab regimes (Kraidy, 2002).

For instance, when the war in Iraq broke out in 2003, Arab audiences across nation states were able to watch the bombing of Baghdad and the live portrayal of human causalities through the lens of *Al-Jazeera* rather than those of *CNN*.[1] For the first time, 24-hour coverage of the war was being provided from a pan-Arab perspective, and Arab audiences did not have to rely on

---

1   English-speaking television news outlets from foreign countries, such as CNN (USA), BBC (UK), and RT (Russia) have all created an Arabic-speaking version of their news services to appeal to Arab audiences.

Western television broadcasting to get live updates on the escalating events (Mauer, 2013). *Al Jazeera* became a game-changer, as Arab audiences became acclimatized to a different type of news coverage. This eventually led to the emergence of more privately owned as well as transnationally operated Arab television stations (Gunter & Dickson, 2013, p. 5). For instance, pan-Arab television stations, such as *Al Arabiya* and *Al Aan*, were founded after Arab Gulf States "recognized these wider audiences' needs and relaxed some editorial controls allowing these services to enjoy greater freedom" (Gunter & Dickson, 2013, p. 6).

Another significance of *Al Jazeera* was its introduction of political and social talk shows that discussed a wide range of topics such as social taboos and women's rights in the Arab world. The station's "given financial resources and regulatory freedom" made it possible to "foster an open debate of difficult issues [and] enhance civil society in the Arab world" (Gunter & Dickson, 2013, p. 11). This gave *Al Jazeera* global recognition, as it was able to compete with other major western news broadcasters.

However, after the outbreak of the Syrian conflict, *Al Jazeera* received criticism from journalists and its former employees for providing unfair and biased coverage of the conflict. Its political agenda became fundamentally supportive of the Free Syrian Army. It also started providing a biased coverage of the war, favoring the Islamists in Syria while demonizing the Syrian government. This led many *Al Jazeera* staff member to resign (RT News, 2012).

A number of academic studies have shown that *Al Jazeera's* news production tends to "embrace sensationalism," as it "uses glossy production formats to stand out from other Arab news broadcasters" (Ayish, 2002; Falk, 2003; Gunter & Dickson, 2013 p. 12). However, the same holds true for *Al Arabiya*, a for-profit news network that partly relies on advertising revenue to operate (Pavlik, 2016). *Al Arabiya*, a major competitor of *Al Jazeera* (Cablegate, 2012), operates from Dubai and is funded by "the brother-in-law of Saudi Arabia's King Fahd, with additional investment from Lebanon's Hariri Group and investors from Saudi Arabia, Kuwait, and other Gulf countries" (Najjar, 2018). This indicates that different political elites finance the pan-Arab television station.

Another Arab news station is *Al Aan*, which is based in Dubai Media City. The station is under the ownership of a holding group called Tower Media, and it is known to be targeted to Arab women. It is politically leaning against the Syrian regime and is supportive of the United Arab Emirates government (Sakr, 2007). With the start of the Syrian conflict, the UAE became a vocal opponent of Hezbollah and Iranian leaders (the political allies of the Syrian regime), as it stood "firm with the Kingdom of Saudi Arabia against Iranian attempts to interfere in the internal affairs of the Arab States' (United States Institute of Peace, 2015; from Almezaini & Rickli, 2017).

Al Jazeera, Al Arabiya, and *Al Aan* are not predominantly perceived as government propaganda mouthpieces for the Qatar, Saudi Arabia, and UAE governments respectively, but rather as pan-Arab television stations that try to appeal to diverse set of Arab-speaking audiences. Arab news stations, such as *SANA, Syria Al Ikhbariya,* and *SAMA,* are considered less pan-Arab television stations and more regime propaganda tools. For instance, the television station *SANA (the Syrian Arab News Agency)* is the state-owned Syrian television station operated by the Assad regime. It was established in Damascus in 1965 and "is linked to the Ministry of Information" in Syria (Web.archive.org, 2011). *SAMA* and *Syria Al Ikhbariyah* are regime-controlled and essentially reinforce regime policies and report positively on the government performances. *Syria Al Ikhbariya* is known to be loyal to the Syrian president Bashar al-Assad (Herald Sun, 2012). As for *SAMA,* this television station started broadcasting in Damascus in 2012 and is the "sister channel of *Addounia TV,*" a "mouthpiece of the Syrian government" (Dunham, 2011).

Another Arabic-speaking television news station relevant to this research project is *RT Arabic.* It is a television station "controlled by the Russian state and funded by the federal tax budget of the Russian government" (Atlantic Council's Digital Forensic Research Lab, 2018). It was launched in 2005 under the name of *Russia Today* and reports on international news in English, Spanish, French, German, Arabic, and Russian. Due to its funding source, *RT* reports with biased journalistic standards of Russian government narratives (Benkler, Roberts & Faris, 2018). Throughout the Syrian conflict, the Russian government has supported the Assad regime politically, contributing with military aid, as well as launching a direct military involvement in the proxy war in Syria (Charap, Treyger, & Geist, 2019). This gives *RT Arabic's* news coverages of the Syrian conflict greater significant to the research topic at hand.

Furthermore, it is important to note that the financing source is not the only factor that influences news production. Recent studies have shown that television media discourses on armed conflict are heavily relying on non-governmental organizations (NGOs) for news sources. This gives humanitarian workers present on the ground the role of the reputable experts who are able to provide immediate updates on the situation. At the same time, news outlets are able to receive information without having to send their own journalists to dangerous war zones. The increased dependency on humanitarian organizations to acquire information on the latest events in war zones and refugee camps may influence and shape the public media discourses (Meyer, Sanger, & Michaels, 2017).

Therefore, this research project not only looks the at media ownership of the television stations: it also acknowledges how the growing reliance on NGOs and other experts has influenced the television news coverage of the Syrian conflict.

1.3   The Syrian Conflict as a Case Study

What renders the case study of the Syrian conflict a significant one to tackle is the plurality of international actors and regional interests within it, as well as the changing gender realities lived by the internally and externally displaced Syrian communities.

The Syrian conflict began with the 2011 uprising. By late summer 2012, it had escalated into a violent proxy war (Rogers, 2012). The conflict is considered one of the most devastating battles in recent history. Between 2012 and 2013, it caused "about half of all war casualties around the world" (Dupuy & Rustad, 2018). Many powerful regional and international players are involved. The main national fighting actors are the Syrian regime, the Islamic State of Iraq and Syria (ISIS), as well as the Syrian Opposition armed groups that include the Free Syrian Army (FSA), and Islamic brigades, such as Harakat Ahrar al-Sham al-Islamiyya, Jeish Al-Islam, Liwa al- Tawhid, Al Nusra Front (Alsaba & Kapilashrami, 2016). Each actor, unique in its military structure, holds different political views and goals. Moreover, each actor has a different coalition with an international player, who is also a regional power in the proxy war. Alsaba and Kapilashrami (2016) explain the complexity and plurality of these coalitions:

"... Turkey, Qatar, and Saudi Arabia, ... continue to be main sponsors of the fighting actors and [they] use substantial religious and sectarian discourses to justify political involvement. This intersection between ideologies is resulting in a fanatic discourse, which impacts trends of violence in general and against women in particular. In addition to the regional support to the Opposition armed groups, international support comes from the USA,

France and the UK... In addition, the Syrian government depends on regional parties like Hezbollah, and Iraqi and Iranian militias, and internationally mainly on Russia... The Kurdish Democratic Union Party (PYD), and the Islamic State of Iraq and Syria (ISIS) have entered the conflict scene more recently..." (p. 6).

This demonstrates how the Syrian conflict is unstructured in nature and has a plurality of international actors and regional interests acting within it.

Granted, the conflict led to intensified levels of violence and a huge number of displacements in the Syrian population (Roger, 2012). "More than 95,000 Syrians have disappeared since March 2011" (The Independent, 2018), while many Syrian women and men continue to flee from areas that were and continue to be dominated by violence. There has been an increase in "torture and acts of sexualized violence committed against women, men, and children in Syria" (Unmüßig, 2016). These "systematic acts of torture are committed inside prisons" by the Assad regime, while anti-regime groups and ISIS members have committed "sexualized violence against women...as one of the main forms of torture" (Unmüßig, 2016). Other brutal war tactics of gender-based violence include "military sexual slavery and forced prostitution" (Alsaba & Kapilashrami, 2016, p. 5). These tactics are used as tools of political repression. Hence, violence against women is being normalized in Syria, along with forced recruitments by militias, forced early marriages, and forced detentions (Alsaba & Kapilashrami, 2016, p. 7).

The mainstream media tend to represent these forms of violence as a uniform experience among all women in Syria. In reality, however, women living across diverse Syrian regions controlled by different fighting groups such as the Syrian regime, the Islamic State of Iraq and Syria (ISIS), and the Syrian Opposition armed groups, are experiencing violence differently (Szanto, 2016). For example, women living in geographical areas controlled by ISIS are facing enforced disappearance, abduction, and enslavement (Alsaba & Kapilashrami, 2016, p.10). On the other hand, women living in Kurdish controlled areas are forced into military recruitments, while women living in those controlled by Syrian opposition have to live under the oppressive ideological doctrines of certain militant groups and are forced into marriages and other arrangements (Alsaba & Kapilashrami, 2016, p. 12). In general, Syrian women caught in the conflict continue to be perceived as assets and treated as commodities in conflict zones, at checkpoints, and in detention centers (Alsaba & Kapilashrami, 2016, p.10).

After many Syrian communities became displaced in the countries bordering Syria, an increase in child marriage cases has been recorded (El Arab & Sagbakken, 2018). A study by the Norwegian Refugee Council (2019) showed that:

> "In Jordan...12 per cent of registered marriages involved a girl under the age of 18. This figure had risen to 18 per cent in 2012, 25 per cent in 2013 and 32 per cent by early 2014. In Lebanon ...41 per cent of young displaced Syrian women between 20 and 24 years were married before they turned 18. Given that many marriages are unregistered, these figures may, in fact, be understating the actual rates" (Høvring, 2019).

Moreover, internally displaced Syrian girls inside Syria are very likely facing the same problems; however there has been "limited data about the situation inside the country" (Høvring, 2019). All these changes have heightened the vulnerability of Syrian women and girls.

With more violence and ambiguity shaping the daily lives of displaced Syrian women, everyday forms of resilience emerged. For instance, entering a polygynous marriage has become a survival strategy among displaced Syrian women living in refugee camps (Herwig, 2017). Herwig (2017) asserted that,

> "... we should not simplify the decision to enter a religious polygynous marriage by always labelling it ›forced‹, thereby leaving no room for agency or resistance. This simplification diminishes the actions that some women take to secure the welfare of their family and improve their situation... Although some women enter very consciously in a polygynous marriage to support themselves and their family or to be less targeted by other men, one should not hold them responsible for the possible negative consequences: an agent can be a victim; a victim can be an agent" (p. 188).

In other words, even though this survival strategy can prove effective, polygynous marriages undoubtedly reproduce patriarchal structures of normativity. Nonetheless, this does not necessarily indicate that women who enter those marriages are entirely lacking agency.

Furthermore, with more severely injured Syrian men and others being imprisoned or disappearing, more Syrian women have taken up jobs that were predominantly reserved for men in pre-conflict Syria. Thus, many Syrian women have become the main breadwinners of their households, shifting many traditional gender roles in Syrian culture. However, the shift to a female-led household does not necessarily translate to more equal opportunity among the men and women (Hilton, 2019).

Because a large part of Syria's population is currently displaced in refugee camps in countries bordering Syria, namely Lebanon, Jordan and Turkey, humanitarian organizations have implemented many resilience-building projects to help Syrian women generate income and financially support their families. These so-called entrepreneurship and skill-building programs are usually tailored to specific purposes, such as women's empowerment and poverty alleviation, particularly for displaced Syrian women, who find difficulty obtaining a work permit in the host country.

Although these programs can help displaced Syrian women find a job opportunity, they nevertheless have several disadvantages. Alkhaled (2018) writes:

> "Historically, feminized industries have been illustrated as a vehicle for women's empowerment and an alleviator of socioeconomic constraints, both domestically and within their community in the Arab region. However, reflecting on the literature, which emphasizes the "darker sides" of women's entrepreneurship in contexts of inferiority, it becomes evident that [displaced Syrian women] [are] caught in an entrepreneurial ecosystem that may offer survival, but is not sustainable in the current climate" (p. 250).

Thus, even when programs are successful at integrating displaced Syrian women in the local labor market and perhaps boost the local economy on the long run, many displaced Syrian women still face many constrains in obtaining a decent and sustainable living through such blue-collar jobs and resilience-building projects (Alkhaled, 2018). Furthermore, they tend to reinforce the normative gender division of labor as opposed to shifting them.

The formation of an all-female military force by the Syrian regime and the Kurdish militias has also contributed to the ever-changing gender realities during the conflict (Kajjo, 2017). The recruitment of women soldiers is being used as a tactical approach by the Syrian Arab Army as well as the opposition armed forces. Alsaba and Kapilashrami (2016) stated that recruiting women soldiers:

> "...draws extensively on religious beliefs and social constructs of sexuality to shame and emasculates Muslim male fighters. For example, women fighters are recruited by Kurdish militia against ISIS given the belief that being killed by a woman would deny one a place in heaven" (p.10).

Mainstream media outlets have framed the recruitments of women in Kurdish territories as a challenge towards gender norms in traditional Syrian society and have disregarded the fact that most Syrian women who join military forces usually come from low-income families (Szanto 2016). Alsaba and Kapilashrami (2016) asserted that,

> "Such recruitments (and involvement of women in military forces) are often hailed by the Western media as challenging gender frames within traditional Syrian society, and showing women as active participants fighting alongside their male counterparts (for instance, Zulver, Aljazeera 2014 focus on Kurdish female fighters). However, the circumstances in which those women soldiers are recruited remain largely undocumented" (p.10).

A study by Szanto (2016) explained how English-speaking mainstream media outlets have overlooked the socioeconomic backgrounds and conditions the female fighters inhabit during the Syrian conflict. At the same time, they glorified the role of female fighters in Syria, as though they are challenging male domination and breaking free from social and governmental control (Szanto, 2016, p. 308).

All these factors point to a predetermined understanding of how women active in armed conflicts are challenging gender norms and how women affected by political violence are lacking agency. This research project challenges this understanding by using the Syrian conflict as a case study. It examines the relationship between violent conflicts and the notion of agency among different groups of Syrian women by focusing on their representations in the Arab television news. The main research questions asked along the way are:

1. How do Arab television stations disseminate, maintain, and normalize the experiences of different groups of Syrian women throughout the conflict?
2. How did each television station frame the visibility of different groups of Syrian women in the context of violence, vulnerability, resilience, and resistance?
3. How do the socio-political views and media ownership structures of each Arab television station and the growing reliance on NGOs and other experts influence the dominant media frames and the procedures of the media reporting?
4. How were the agentive attempts of different groups of Syrian women framed in the Arab television news?

1.4   Structure of the Book

Chapter 2 provides the theoretical framework for the research project. I explore the ideas and theories of different critical cultural theorists. In *Section 2.1*, I describe how Judith Butler's theory of vulnerability was used as a starting point for my research and how I contextualize the notion of 'dependency of infrastructure' to the topic of this research. In *Section 2.2*, I explore the concept of power and the different modes of violence that appear in the news reporting. I borrow ideas from various scholars to explain the different and nuanced meanings of the notion of violence. *Section 2.3* focuses on defining the notion of resilience, specifically in a neoliberal context. I borrow ideas from Judith Butler (2003, 2009) and Sara Bracke (2016) to describe how resilience can be understood in relationship to biopolitics. *Section 2.4* deals with the notion of agency and how it can be read through the television reporting related to the context of resistance. I refer to Saba Mahmoud's (2006) concepts from *Politics of Piety* and draw on her framework that understands the notion of agency beyond liberal politics and in other contexts, such as the Arab Muslim world.

Chapter 3 describes the methodology used in the research project. In *Section 3.1*, I provide an overview on the meaning of language and discourse and refer to concepts from Michel Foucault and Stuart Hall. In *Section 3.2*, I describe the type of discourse analysis this book adopts, which includes the three-dimensional framework provided by Norman Fairclough. In *Section 3.3*, I give a detailed description of the units of analysis and how I collected the sample of news reports. In the same section, I talk about the selection of dominant themes and how the four main concepts (violence, vulnerability, resilience and resistance) were categorized under those themes. In *Section 3.4*, I address the methodological limitations and pose methodological questions on the Foucauldian understanding of power relations and the points of reversibility.

Chapter 4 is the first data analysis chapter. I examine news reports related to the context of violence. I analyze seven news reports from *Al Jazeera*, *Al Arabiya*, and *Al Aan*, and explore how the news reports generated and naturalized the prevailing images of the violation, assault, and detainment of Syrian women in different physical spaces, such as prisons, checkpoints, detainment centers, bakeries, and homes. I question and interpret the roles these spaces play in relation to the shaming of the victim. The general purpose of the chapter is to propose alternative ways of thinking about the dominant social structures the Syrian women inhabit. I question whether the agentive attempts of the subjects represented in the news have been rendered non-existent, specifically among the groups of Syrian women who faced social stigma and chose or were forced into exile.

Chapter 5 focuses on the concept of vulnerability and analyzes eight news reports from *Al Jazeera*, *Al Arabiya*, and *Al Aan*. In this chapter, I propose rethinking the relationship between the increase in child marriage cases among members of the displaced Syrian communities in Lebanon and Jordan and the deterioration of refugee makeshift shelters that continue to exist on an ad-hoc basis despite their long presence. I examine how the news reports represented child marriage cases in relationship to the states of impoverishment that shape the daily life experiences of the displaced Syrian communities. Throughout the analysis, I question whether the news reports perceived child marriage as a standalone issue that remains *de*contextualized from the general widespread socio-economic injustice.

Chapter 6 explores the concept of resilience by examining Arab television media news images of Syrian women at work. I survey nine news stories from *SANA*, *Al Aan*, *Al Jazeera*, and *Al Arabiya*, which, internally and externally, have depicted displaced Syrian women in (post)war adjustment settings. The groups of displaced Syrian women who appear in the news are, internally and externally, displaced Syrian women working in Syria, Lebanon, Iraq, Jordan, and Turkey. A number of these women are depicted participating in vocational and cash-for-work programs funded by the UN and other NGOs. Other groups of displaced Syrian women are shown participating in other types of blue-collar jobs such as tailoring, plumbing, housecleaning, etc. The analysis focuses on the symbolic function of resilience among these different groups of displaced Syrian women, who, I argue, have been rendered neoliberal subjects by the Arab television news. Throughout the chapter, I question whether the prevalent media frames concerning resilience reinforce neoliberal ideals and humanitarian reasoning in the television media narratives.

Chapter 7 explores the representations of Syrian women in the context of resistance. I examine eight news reports from the television stations supportive of the Syrian regime: *SAMA*, *SANA*, *RT Arabic*, and *Syria Al Ikhbariyya*. The chapter demonstrates how the notion of 'mothers of the nation' has prevailed in news reports that represented Syrian women as the "resisting subject" during the war. I explore how the news reports perpetuated the ideological/political views of the Ba'ath Party concerning the role of Syrian women during the conflict and the Syrian women's duties towards the nation. In the last part of the chapter, I contextualize the main findings and juxtapose them with the notion of agency.

Chapter 8 provides a deeper analysis of the main findings and looks at how displaced Syrian women were portrayed in Arab television news. In *Section 8.1*, I explain how violence against women has been normalized in the news reports. In *Section 8.2*, I discuss the role of the expert in the news by referring to the two Latin terms for witnessing an act: *testis* and *superstes*. I explain how the humanitarian and personal testimonies in the television reporting were constructed under the aesthetic dimension of the camera. In *Section 8.3*, I explore the notion of agency among displaced Syrian women during the conflict and voice the need to move beyond liberal and post-structuralist perspectives. I look at the theoretical concept of performativity among the subaltern and use Saba Mahmoud's ethnographic study on the women's piety movement in the mosques of Cairo as an exemplary analogy. By posing questions on the displaced Syrian women's daily struggles, I explore the significance of the power dynamics of shame, dignity, and fear, which were established in the television news.

Chapter 9 summarizes the main findings of the research project and places these in the context of recent scholarship. In *Section 9.1*, I reflect on the biases and blind spots that have appeared in the reporting in relation to the sociopolitical context of the Syrian conflict. I link these factors to the ownership of each the television station. In *Section 9.2*, I summarize the dominant media frames that have appeared throughout the news report analysis and reflect on the procedures of media reporting. In *Section 9.3*, I explore how the figure of the Syrian woman in the Arab television news has appeared as a foreground for the mediated representation situated against the background of the geopolitical tensions during the Syrian conflict. In *Section 9.4*, I summarize the main findings of the research project according to the concepts of media logic, gender logic, and war logic. In *Section 9.5*, I propose a feminist logic in the context of the media representations by discussing the notion of 'spaces of appearance.'[2]

Chapter 10 provides a conclusion and a brief summary of the findings. I discuss the limitations of this research project and provide insights into how it could be developed in future research.

---

2   The term 'spaces of appearance' was coined by Hannah Arendt. In the context of this research, it refers to spaces of agency, or spaces where the subject's voice is heard.

This introductory chapter has listed the preliminary points of this research project. I gave a brief overview of the Syrian conflict and a brief history of television news in the Arab world, and I outlined why the television depictions of the experiences of Syrian women during the conflict provide an insightful case study on topics and themes related to media, gender, and conflict. In the following chapter, I present the theoretical framework of this research project.

2. Theoretical Framework

2.1 Vulnerability, Resistance, and the Dependency on Infrastructure

This research project aims to understand vulnerability in the context of violent conflicts. The term 'vulnerable' is "derived from the Latin noun *"vulnus,"* meaning 'wound.' A vulnerable person is someone who is "capable of being physically or emotionally wounded." In contexts of war and displacement, being vulnerable denotes to being "open to attack or damage" (Merriam-Webster, 2011). In other words, such a person is vulnerable because he or she is exposed to violence. Both Judith Butler and Julia Kristeva suggest that "we need to accept our own vulnerability rather than try to deny it" (Oliver, 2007, p. 8). Kristeva (2014) proposes a positive ontology of vulnerability, asserting that it is an integral part of human existence and should thus be included "with liberty, equality, and fraternity as a key principle of humanism" (Bunch 2017, p. 142; Kristeva 2014). In her essay *Rethinking Vulnerability and Resistance*, Butler (2016) proposes a reconceptualization of the relationship between vulnerability and resistance. Suggesting that vulnerability appears at a different stage than is commonly understood, Butler places it alongside and in relation to precarity. She asserts that this vulnerability is born in relationship to precarity. Graphic images of refugees settling in camps with dire living conditions, which Butler labelled as "failed infrastructures," expose the precarity of the subject. Butler (2016) writes:

> "Without shelter, we are vulnerable to weather, cold, heat, and disease, perhaps also to assault, hunger, and violence. It was not as if we were, as creatures, not vulnerable before when infrastructure was working, and then when infrastructure fails, our vulnerability comes to the fore" (p.13).

At this point, Butler (2016) asserts that vulnerability is a fundamental condition of humanity, and we cannot negate its existence. However, precarity appears when this vulnerability is exploited, and, as a result, basic aspects of life become impossible to bear.

Butler (2016) refers to the exploitation of people by the state. The television news reports examined in this research project depict displaced Syrian women living in ad hoc refugee camps and makeshift shelters in Syria's neighboring countries. In this setting, the most basic and essential needs and utilities for a decent life are lacking or difficult to acquire. Butler (2016) described these realities as a 'dependency on infrastructure.' She described such conditions as the continued failure of infrastructure; here the failure becomes the normal state of affairs. Examples of failed infrastructures could entail the struggle for running or clean water, living in a shelter without a door, unpaved streets or the lack of transportation, the struggle to find paid work, no access to medical care, or any necessary provisions that are essential to living. Because there is a 'dependency on infrastructure,' and one's survival and attempts of making one's life livable depend on this same infrastructure, acts of resistance emerge as a consequence.

Butler describes this type of resistance as an act of mobilizing states of vulnerability. She asserts that this resistance appears as a way of combating the precariousness that has taken over people's lives and living conditions. These states of precarity, which embody a sense of exploitation can come in the form of economic, social, or political exploitation. For instance, in the context of the Syrian conflict, social exploitation appears when Syrian women and girls enter child marriages or forced marriages, as a way to ease the economic hardship of the family. Political exploitation appears when Syrian women become the target of state violence, and are sexually assaulted as a way to put pressure on the opposition or the rebels fighting the Syrian Arab Army. As for economic exploitation, this form of exploitation appears when displaced Syrian families live in makeshift shelters or states of impoverishment and take on unpaid or poorly jobs to make ends meet.

Butler (2016) considers these the acts of exploitation–whether those practiced by the state emerge as a result of discriminatory laws, or neoliberal governing systems that produce economic inequality – and "rejects the fundamental reality of vulnerability, which further feeds [the] ability to exploit." When the exploited subject resists this exploitation through action, resistance is pursued by acknowledging one's own state of vulnerability. In other words, this acknowledgment of vulnerability becomes fundamental to one's ability to resist forms of exploitation and the forces that fuel this exploitation.

At this point, Butler (2016) proposes that masculinist politics, which heroizes overcoming one's vulnerability, should be criticized and reconceptualized in feminist theory. She asserts that mobilizing one's vulnerability is a tactical deployment of the state of vulnerability, and this mobilization is essential for acts of resistance. The deployment of this mobilization is also connected to infrastructure. The definition of infrastructure in this particular case extends between (1) a public street, as an infrastructural good which functions as a platform to stage one's political demand, or (2) a mobile phone or any public media in which the subject or the exploited may appear, e.g., a media outlet that brings the subjects' voices into the public sphere. Butler (2016) writes:

> "The very term "mobilization" depends on an operative sense of mobility, itself a right, one that many people cannot take for granted. For the body to move, it must usually have a surface of some kind, and it must have at its disposal whatever technical supports allow for movement to take place. So, the pavement and the street are already to be understood as requirements of the body as it exercises its rights of mobility. No one moves without a supportive environment and set of technologies. And when those environments start to fall apart or are emphatically unsupportive, we are left to "fall" in some ways, and our very capacity to exercise most basic rights is imperiled" (p. 15).

Moreover, one cannot take for granted the idea of freedom that can be exercised by the subjects when they decide to mobilize their political action or move physically from point A to point B. For example, Sophie Richter-Devroe (2011) observed the daily struggle of women living in the West Bank and East Jerusalem. The author affirmed that Palestinian women living under occupation found ways to get on with their daily life. In these circumstances, travelling from the West Bank to Jerusalem is not just an act to reaffirm their right to "enjoy life and have fun;" it also a form of defiance and resistance against the Israeli control of Palestinian people. In this setting, travelling, as a daily struggle, under the occupation in order to run errands and get on with one's daily life, becomes a form of resistance that is complementary with the concept of *sumud*[1] (Richter-Devroe, 2011). By employing their acts of *sumud*, ordinary unarmed Palestinian women are able to sustain daily life under the Israeli occupation (Bourbeau & Ryan, 2017).

---

1   *Sumud* (صمود) is the Arabic word for resilience.

In the context of the Syrian conflict, a Syrian woman's survival is dependent on simple physical movements. A physical movement may simply be a way to commute to work in order to make a living, despite the fact that the woman's daily commute places her in danger of being exposed to sexual harassment or put in vulnerable positions, such as when she is caught at checkpoints or put under police surveillance. In this case, the subject exposes her precarity in the public space. Butler (2015) asserts that "these bodies, in showing this precarity, are also resisting these very powers; they enact a form of resistance that presupposes vulnerability of a specific kind, and opposes precarity" (p.22).

This line of argumentation does not position vulnerability outside of agency or as something opposed to it; instead, it proposes a feminist model, which rejects the masculinist ideals that perceive agency in a binary opposition to precarity or vulnerability. Butler (2016) affirms that it is a feminist task to undo this binary model, and I follow her affirmation throughout this research project.

2.2   Power and Different Modes of Violence

This research project attempts to understand power in its conceptual capacities and how violence, beyond its general definition of "bodily harm," appears in the media discourses. The research draws on theories by Michel Foucault, Hannah Arendt, and Slavoj Žižek to establish a theoretical framework which enables the exploration of the media discourses on power and different modes of violence that appear in the news reports. Through a critical media studies lens, I explore the concept of violence and how it appears in the television reporting by looking at the different capacities of power.

Foucault (1990) challenged the traditional understanding of power as "top-down substantive phenomenon," which was seen by many conventional scholars as a force that is restraining and oppressive by nature. He did not see it as a synonym to the word 'violence.' Instead, Foucault (1990) contended to understand power and power relations through their ability to enable action and other human capacities. He asserted that power has many facets and can only function when it is brought into action through individual interaction and relationships. Foucault (1980) argued that "power exists only when it is put into action, even if, of course, it is integrated into a disparate field of possibilities brought to bear upon permanent structures" (p. 210). Within this framework, the notion of power is open, allowing the reader to ask questions about "how" and "why" certain subjects exposed to power relations act as they do.

It is within this frame of reference that Arab television news portrayed Syrian women who have been exposed to incidents of rape, public shaming, and sexual assault throughout the conflict. Such women were depicted as either weak subjects, who were dismissed by their own communities, or as displaced women living in exile. In so doing, they provided a way to escape the societal norms that stigmatized them as victims of torture and gender-based violence. The idea of 'choosing exile' to escape stigmatization can, on the one hand, be seen as an example of one's 'failure' to face the norms that made them victims of their victimhood. At the same time, however, this 'failure' can also be perceived as a choice made by the victim as a way of refusing the status of victimhood subjected upon them by society. Hence, through a Foucauldian understanding, power here is understood as a 'force relation' that can result in (un)intentional behaviors. Foucault wrote:

> "There is no power that is exercised without a series of aims and objectives. But this does not mean that it results from the choice or decision of an individual subject. Subjects try to control the acts of others (or one's own) but lack the ultimate ability to foresee or govern the outcome, i.e., the subject is only ever partially autonomous" (Maze 2018; from Foucault 1990, p. 95).

This sheds light on how power is multifaceted, as it creates an arena where acts always occur unexpectedly within the power relationship. Moreover, these acts taken on by the subject, shape the different uses of power as well as exemplifies how power creates as well as *enables* subjects.

In defining the notion of 'punishment', Foucault (1984) explained how:

> "The individual is an effect of power, and at the same time, or precisely to the extent to which it is that effect, it is the element of its articulation. The individual which power has constituted is at the same time its vehicle" (p. 26).

On this basis, the subject comes into being in relationship to power. This power construct defines the way ethnicity, social class, and sexuality define the subject's subjugation. Without the notion of power, these terms do not hold any true meaning. Furthermore, in the context of power relations, subjectivity is not limited to simply action, but also other possibilities and conditions present "at any given time as well as the space in which acts (and speech) are carried out" (Maze, 2018, p. 123). This demonstrates how power is not a human possession; rather, "it only exists in its exercise, and is not something that is acquired, seized, or shared" (Foucault, 1990, p. 94). Hence, one can only employ power in a certain time and space, but it can never be possessed (Maze, 2018). In this regard, it is very unlikely that a woman from Syria could join a local refugee community based in Lebanon and work on empowering other Syrian refugee women like herself if she were not displaced and labelled as a refugee herself. Foucault would argue that power has a dual effect. It both enables and confines subjects and it is only through this duality that the subjects recognize their capacities and possibilities to act (Maze, 2018).

Hannah Arendt described this relationship between the power and the subject through the understanding of 'doing' and 'suffering.' She explained:

> "Because the actor always moves among and in relation to other acting beings, he is never merely a 'doer' but always at the same time a sufferer. To do and to suffer are like opposite sides of the same coin" (Arendt, 1958, p. 190).

Through this duality, the possibility of the subject to resist this form of power comes into play. According to Foucault (1984), this possibility is inevitable, because without the subject's attempt to resist, the power relationship cannot come into existence. This explains how "power does not occur *beyond* but *between* subjects" (Maze, 2018, p. 125).

If power is pluralistic and not individualistic, as it exists between subjects rather than over them, what is the role of violence in this particular setting and how can we understand it vis-à-vis power? Arendt (1970) asserted that violence is always perceived as something individualistic even when it is employed in a collective manner. Thus, violence needs to be deployed in order to function, and this deployment requires tools. Arendt (1970) wrote:

> "The extreme form of power is All against One; the extreme form of violence is One against All. And this latter is never possible without instruments...Instruments of violence are the manners in which violence exerts itself, and, unlike power, they *can* be owned" (p. 42).

By referring to Arendt (1970), I do not use terms such as "force, power, strength, and violence" interchangeably or as synonyms. Moreover, in the news report analysis, I do not intend to compare these incidents of violence (e.g., rape and sexual assault) to other incidents of gender-based-violence that take place in other contexts of war and conflict. Rather, I am interested in linking these examples of violence to other forms of violence to which Syrian women are exposed or have experienced throughout the Syrian conflict, even when these forms of violence are not viewed as 'gendered' in nature. I allow myself to discover the power relations existing in this context and how they take form in these specific settings. Thus, I do not limit my understanding of violence to only its physical forms. I also acknowledge that violence is exercised in different appearances.

Slavoj Žižek (2008) explored how violence takes place in modern times, especially how it is represented in society in relationship to economic interests. He asserted that the reader ought to differentiate between *subjective* and *objective* violence. The former appears when incidents of violence are implemented by an identifiable agent, such as rapists or soldiers, who torture prisoners. In the latter case, objective violence is implemented by an unidentifiable agent; the doer of the violent act is not always present in the narrative. Thus, when objective violence appears in news, the perpetrator usually goes unnoticed by the reader or viewer. Objective violence is "often overlooked in the background of subjective violence outbreaks" (Weiss, 2015).

For example, Arab television news reports depicted displaced Syrian families living in poverty-stricken neighborhoods or 'slums' with failed infrastructure, alongside their daughters, who were entering child/early marriages. The dominant discourse in the news may frame the issue of child marriage as a consequence of 'bad parenting.' By applying Žižek's (2008) theorization of objective violence, the constructed image of the 'bad' parents in the television news could be read differently. The researcher may argue that the 'bad' parents may be (partially) exonerated because their subjugation to a neoliberal economic system, one which forces poverty-stricken families to resort to desperate (and sometimes hurtful) forms of resilience. In this context, the agent of violence is unclear because the form of *objective* violence is enabled by more than one factor: a lack of laws protecting girls from early marriages – an unfair economic system that gives rise to poverty – and patriarchal norms that turn daughters into objects of sacrifice.

At this point, the acts of resilience become a significant factor to be examined in relationship to power and violence. In the following section, I discuss the concept of resilience in more detail.

2.3   Defining Resilience in Neoliberal Times

Although resilience and resistance are not mutually exclusive, the former can contribute to the latter. Philippe Bourbeau and Caitlin Ryan (2017) define resilience as follows:

> "Resilience is the process of seeking to maintain the status quo in the face of shocks, but it also refers to the idea of transforming a referent object. As such, communities developing strategies to adjust to difficulties are also potential sites of resistance to the structures, inequalities or injustices that have necessitated these adjustments. Enacting resilience can mean that you find a way to 'get on' with daily life without acquiescing to the political, economic or social situation that you are in" (p. 9).

In other words, resilience represents the ability of an individual to recover in certain violent or unjust situations and to regain the freedom of acting and deciding. It is an individual's attempt to make daily life bearable (or possible) by adjusting to disruptions. For instance, in times of conflict, an adversary may employ tactics designed to make living conditions intolerable for individuals or communities. Modes of resilience may appear as the adversary heightens subjugation, while the subject tries to maintain a "normal" life by remaining in place or by seeking and adjusting to the failures of infrastructure. These acts are directly tied to the existing relations of power. They are heterogeneous among women and are dynamic by nature (Bourbeau & Ryan, 2017).

Within the framework of this research, resistance embodies a stage when the subject's state of existence is barely or minimally impacted by disturbances of failed infrastructure or outbreaks of violence. In other words, resistance is achieved when common acts of resilience become the norm in a given situation. As such, the spectrum of resilience and resistance comprises: (1) coping mechanisms, which can be seen as acts of resilience, (2) other symbolic acts that are not necessarily identified as belonging to a political struggle (e.g., infrapolitics[2]), and (3) political actions practiced in a structured environment. Nonetheless, the prevalence of resilience—as a desired good or prize the

---

2   Alberto Moreiras (2010) identifies infrapolitics as an autonomous practice. "[Infrapolitics] enacts a rupture from the political, not in the name of the political, but rather in the name of an essential affirmation that, while involving the ethical, cannot confine itself to the ethical... Infrapolitical action exceeds the political and it exceeds the ethi-

subject seeks in their daily life in order to recover from misfortune, shock, or illness—may also function as a tool that reinforces the modes of political economy and cultural hegemony (Butler, 2003; 2009).

In the chapter *Bouncing Back: Vulnerability and Resistance in times of Resilience*, Sarah Bracke (2016) makes a distinction between the terms 'social resilience' and the 'resilient self.' The terms do not hold opposite meanings, but rather create different nuances to the meaning of 'resilience.' The former, which includes the word 'social,' establishes an understanding that the concept of resilience demands the collective ability of individuals present within the same nation, community, racial group, or class, to bear and enhance their state of well-being against all odds and challenges that come in the way (e.g., natural disasters, threats from terrorism, health epidemics, and other disruptive encounters). Therefore, the term social, as an adjective, brings emphasis to how the capacity to overcome a certain struggle is not placed solely on one person, but rather on a group of people that make use of institutional, social, and cultural resources to mobilize their well- being.

On the other hand, the latter has a slightly different connotation. Bracke (2016) stated that the 'resilient self' alludes to a specific bio-political power at work, where the act of resilience "produces a new regime of subjectivity, that is to say, new resilient subjects" (p. 63). By employing the word 'self,' resilience, as a new regime of subjectivity within a neoliberal political economy, goes beyond its dictionary definition of "rebounding; recoiling; returning to the original position" (The Oxford English Dictionary, 2019). The term somewhat becomes part of wider neoliberal discourse, one in which "the good subjects" are represented. The "good subjects, according to Neocleous (2007), are the individuals who constantly respond to any situation in resilient ways. Hence, their ability to bounce back becomes the norm, and their attempts to exercise their agency becomes highly tied to their everyday forms of resilience. Bracke (2016) writes:

> "In a neoliberal political economy, resilience has become part of the "moral code": the "good subjects" of neoliberal times are the ones who are able to act, to exercise their agency, in resilient ways. Good subjects...will 'survive and thrive in any situation,' they will 'achieve balance' across the several insecure and part-time jobs they have, 'overcome life's hurdles' such as fac-

---

cal, but it is still a practical action oriented to the relation between people" (Moreiras 2010, p. 190 - 191).

ing retirement without a pension to speak of, and just 'bounce back' from whatever life throws, whether it be cuts to benefits, wage freezes or global economic meltdown. Neoliberal citizenship is nothing if not a training in resilience as the new technology of the self: a training to withstand whatever crisis capital undergoes and whatever political measures the state carries out to save it" (p. 61).

In other words, the term 'self-resilience' is perceived as a commodity of neoliberal citizenship. Resilience, as a property of an individual, is transformed to a property of a system; a system that relies on resilience to remain in operation. This brings the conversation to the question of security: When does resilience start to function as part of a new security apparatus?

Bracke (2016) argues that in a neoliberal society, self-resilience becomes the main, if not the only, source of security. The persistence of resilient practices or the ability to adapt and protect oneself from threat, crisis, or disaster while maintaining structure and function, hinders the ability or the chances to mobilize one's vulnerability. Under neoliberal ideals, vulnerability is deemed shameful, while the presence of threat, crisis, and disaster becomes the norm, and the possibility of their occurrence becomes permanent. In these circumstances, resilience starts functioning as an abundant 'raw material' of the neoliberal system. The individual's persistent ability to adapt to such circumstances or be prepared to cultivate disciplines of resilience on a daily basis in the face of odds, may result in the denial of the state of vulnerability and the reinforcement of neoliberal governmentality. Perhaps the raw material of self-resilience "is arguably fetishized by the economic and political institutions that bear great responsibility for the contemporary conditions of precarity that are (designed to be) met with resilience" (Bracke, 2016, p. 60). Therefore, within the framework of this book, the definition and function of resilience is not limited to an individuals' ability to deal with challenges and obstacles, but also involves the ways in which neoliberal governmentality operates its powers within a society – a society in which individuals automatically cultivate a sense of preparedness to the accumulation of crisis, threat, or disasters.

In the context of the Syrian conflict, the resilient subaltern subjects emerge as the displaced Syrian women who have survived the war and are fighting racism, poverty, gender-based violence and discrimination. These subjects, who have lost their possessions, their home and sense of belonging, attempt to rebuild everything or simply to survive. These realities are largely constructed in the television news through images of externally displaced Syrian women participating in vocational and cash-for-work programs. These programs are basically poverty alleviation programs funded by the UNHCR and other NGOs, the main purpose of which is to illustrate the importance of resilience and how to acquire it. Neocleous (2013) sheds light on the nature of these so-called "training programs." He writes:

> "The beauty of the idea that resilience is what the world's poor need is that it turns out to be something that the world's poor already possess; all they require is a little training in how to realize it. Hence the motif of building, nurturing, and developing that runs through so much of the IMF literature" (p. 4-5).

In examining how the Arab television news depicted Syrian women practicing everyday forms of resilience, I draw on Neocleous' (2013) understanding of the concept, as well as Bracke's (2016) work to reflect on the following question: When is resilience detached from the context of vulnerability, and when are the subjects' agentive attempts "hindered or rendered virtually impossible through disciplines of resilience?" (p. 63).

In the section below, I explore concepts by Judith Butler and Saba Mahmoud on the notion of resistance and its relationship to agency.

2.4   Resistance, Agency, and the Non-liberatory Subject

I trace the concept of resistance and how it appears in the representations of different groups of Syrian women in the television news by drawing on Judith Butler's theory of performativity and her understanding of the notion of subjectivity. In *Undoing Gender*, Butler (2004) establishes a theory of signification through the notion performativity. Butler (2004) does not limit her understanding of performativity to gender alone. She provides a general model of the subject based on how actions create meaning through power relations. In Butler's understanding:

> "The subject comes into being through action. Next, the subject desires recognition from another and is constituted through this recognition. Finally, recognition occurs only when a performance is read in relation to a norm. This means that the subject, who desires recognition, comes into being through the ritualized repetition of acts, gestures, or desires, which,

upon recognition, create the illusion of an essential identity" (Clare 2009, p. 51).

The subject's performance, in acts of speech that appear in the news reports, acquire meaning in the dominant discourses when they become acknowledged in relation to social norms. For instance, Syrian female fighters are depicted in the television news as defenders of the homeland. Their act of defense, which are forms of armed resistance, are represented in relation to their roles as mothers of the homeland. In this setting, their role as fighters is framed in relation to (stereotypical) gender norms, such as 'mothers of Syria.' Thus, by drawing on Butler's concept of performativity, I examine the relations of power present in the television representations, and how the (re)production of gender binaries and "norms are consolidated or re-signified through their citation" (Clare, 2009, p. 52).

Furthermore, in order to trace the "possibilities of resistance to the regulating power of normativity" and the agentive attempts of the subject, I refer to Mahmoud's (2005) theory of agency. Mahmoud posits agency "outside discourse within discourse" (Clare, 2009) by asking the reader to think beyond the "dualistic structure of consolidation/resignification, doing/undoing, of norms" (Mahmood, 2005, p. 22). Although Butler's model of performativity is essential to trace how the notion of 'resistance' is represented in the news reports, especially in relationship to power relations and normativity. Nevertheless, I do not regard Butler's theory of agency as universally translatable to all contexts and cultures, especially not in the context of this research project.[3] Thus, I firstly conduct the news report analysis on the concept of resistance by using Butler's theory and then contextualize the findings with Mahmoud's ideas on agency.

Following Mahmoud's rational, as a reader I ask myself to consider the subject's agentive attempts beyond the "subversion or resignification of social norms" (Mahmood, 2005, p. 14). Clare (2009) writes:

"When agency is understood in terms of performativity, one can too readily slide into a troubling yet formulaic model of academic study: someone acts, another watches and interprets. A theory of agency articulated in terms of signification and performativity may naturalize the position of the academic

---

3   Mahmoud (2005) pointed out that Butler's version of understanding agency is more
     productive when applied in contexts dealing with queer politics.

within an international division of labor as she who holds the normative, interpretive gaze over her objects of study because she judges whether an action is an instance of agency or not. In contrast, a model of agency concerned with the practices through which norms are embodied destabilizes the position of the academic. In this model, agency is not identified by the academic through her interpretation of an action. Instead, the academic must attempt to understand the multiple effects, sensations, and desires that emerge from a practice *for* the subject enacting it, to the extent this is possible. The academic, in this model, is no longer positioned as the audience for action" (Clare, 2009, p. 53-54).

By using Mahmoud's concepts on agency, I allow myself to understand the agentive attempts of the subject beyond the "practices of signification but also within registers of corporeality"[4] (Clare, 2009, p. 54). The registers of corporeality entail that "transgressing gender norms . . . might well require the retraining of sensibilities, affect, desire, and sentiments — those registers of corporeality often escape the logic of representation and symbolic articulation" (Mahmood, 2005, p. 188).

Therefore, within the framework of this book, I trace the concept of agency in the context of the subject by thinking beyond the model of language.[5] In the analysis, I assert how the body can function as "a medium for, rather than a sign of, the self" (Mahmood, 2005, p. 165). This places desire at the center of the discussion and considers it "part of the subject-formation" (Clare, 2009, p.53). This also allows me to regard the agency of the subject not just through to transgression of social norms but also through the inhabitation of social norms.

A theoretical framework that unites concepts from both Butler and Mahmoud is significant to the context of this research project, as it provides a theoretical model that contributes to feminist critical theory and opens up a space to read agency beyond liberal politics. In this way, I am no longer positioned to quickly deem subjects that do not adopt liberal feminist ideals as simply lacking in agency.

---

4   Signification refers to the sensation of language, or how the dominant discourses create meanings through the body of the subject.

5   Butler and Foucault adopted the model of language that perceives the body as a source of material, in which language and signification are created, hence as a 'site of performativity.' In this context, the body "is treated as a sign that becomes meaningful" to the relations of power (Clare 2009).

3. Methodology

3.1 Perspective on Language and Discourse

I conduct a discourse analysis that focuses on four different aspects: (a) the linguistic statements in the news reports; (b) the socio-political context of the news story; (c) the images that appear in the reporting; (d) and the ownership of the television stations. I evaluate the language in the television reports and examine how media ownership influences the socio-political views of the news television station. I look at television news reports and consider the speech acts[1], images, and videos as forms of language present in the dominant media discourse.

I draw on Stuart Hall's (1997) understanding of the difference between connotative and denotative meanings behind messages. Hall (1997) argues that it is only by understanding the connotative that can one analyze the cultural codes and the power embedded in the meaning. I refer to Foucault's concept of "object of knowledge" presented in his book *Archeology of Knowledge* (1969) in order to understand discourse in relation to the manufacturing of knowledge. Foucault saw discourse as a structure that characterizes prevalent societal conversations and discussions about fields of knowledge within social sciences (Fairclough 1992). Stuart Hall (1992) also described the Foucauldian understanding of discourse using the following definition:

"A discourse is a group of statements which provides a language for talking about – a way of representing the knowledge about – a particular topic at a particular historical moment... Discourse is about the production of knowledge through language. But... since all social practices entail meaning, and

---

1   Speech acts are requests, warnings, promises, apologies, greetings, or any number of declarations made by the person interviewed in the news reports.

meanings shape and influence what we do – our conduct – all practices have a discursive aspect." (p. 291)

Therefore, this research project examines discourse by looking at the *knowledge* and *language* produced in the news reports as *social practices*, which are understood by what Foucault termed as 'discursive construction.' I look at how these social practices are presented in a set of statements that are articulated in the news reports, and I examine their emergence and transformation. By examining knowledge, language, and statements, I am able to trace how the discourse is present in the news reports and how this discourse constructs subjects and events, which, at times, allows or limits the possibilities of the viewer to understand them.

In the context of this research, the subject refers to the different groups of Syrian women, whereas the events refer to the incidents the subjects' experienced. Examples of these events and incidents include sexual violation, sexual harassment, imprisonment, detainment, snowstorms, child marriages, entering the workforce, and fighting in the military. Throughout the analysis, I perceive the dominant discourse present in the news stories as a force that facilities, enables, and constrains the language and knowledge produced about the subjects and events.

I analyze semantics by looking beyond the linguistic structure of the text. I focus on examining the discourse through the meaning of words and the relationships between them (Van Dijk, 1983). According to Fairclough (1992), applying a discourse analysis in a traditional manner includes an intertextual analysis of the language within the text. Therefore, I examine "the grammar, vocabulary, sentence structure, structure cohesion, and dialogue dynamics" (Fairclough, 1992) of the analyzed text. I then try to place the linguistic body in discussion using the chosen concepts, which supply my analysis with the needed socio-economic context (Fairclough, 1996).

I look at the language or speech used by the television reports depicting the subject and at the simple speech acts performed by the subject. Butler (1990) wrote: "Does speech continue to act on us at the very moment in which we speak, so that we may well think we are acting, but we are also acted on at that very same time?" (p. 16). Thus, throughout my analysis of the speech acts performed by the subject in the news reports, I always bear in mind that these speeches do not exist independently from prevailing social, economic, political, and environmental conditions.

Furthermore, because this research project conducts a discourse analysis of television news—a form of visual media—I examine the semiotic modalities that appear in the news reports, such as images, gestures and sounds (Lazar, 2007). I focus on how the subjects in the television news are given 'visibility' and how they are 'viewed' (Wang, 2014). Gillian Rose (2001) emphasized the importance of differentiating between 'visibility' and 'visuality.' "Visibility is embedded in the notion of vision, what the human eye is capable of seeing, while visuality is the construct of the vision, the notions of how and what we see" (Rose 2001; quoted from Najem 2016). Visibility influences visuality and vice versa. Nevertheless, by drawing differences between the two, I am able to question not just the regularity of the Syrian women's visibility in the news, but also *how* they are made visible in the context of the power relations inherited in the media message.

3.2   A Critical Approach to Discourse Analysis

To understand the dominant media discourses concerning gender and agency and how the visibilities of different groups of Syrian women were constructed in Arab television news, it is essential to apply a critical approach during the analysis process and not to limit the understanding based on the obvious message. Therefore, this research implements a critical discourse analysis, which focuses specifically on the relations of power and inequality in language (Blommaert & Bulcaen, 2000). The purpose of critical discourse analysis (CDA) is to examine "the way social power abuse, dominance, and inequality are enacted, reproduced, and resisted by text and talk in the social and political context" (Van Dijk, 2001 p. 352). It is best used to study the "opaque as well as transparent structural relationships of dominance, discrimination, power and control as manifested in language" (Wodak, 1995, p. 204).

This research project concerns itself with the three-dimensional framework for critically analyzing discourse. According to Fairclough (1992), the first-dimension deals with discourse as a form of text. The second dimension focuses on discursive practices within the discourse, which requires the researcher to regard the discourse as "something that is produced, circulated, distributed, [and] consumed in society" (Blommaert & Bulcaen, 2000, p. 448). In other words, when analyzing vocabulary, text structure, grammar, and word cohesion, the focus should be on "speech acts, coherence, and intertextuality – three aspects that link a text to its context" (Blommaert & Bulcaen,

2000). Within the second-dimension, I refer to two types of intertextuality, 'manifest intertextuality,' and 'constitutive intertextuality.' Because the former constitutes the process of drawing on other texts to analyze the discursive practices, I refer to journalistic and newspaper articles as well as humanitarian reports to further explore the text within the given context. As for the latter, it constitutes the process of drawing similarities between texts, and outlining the heterogenous elements within the discourses. One important aspect of the second-dimension is the attention given to the quoted statements that appear throughout the news reports and how they are selected, altered, and contextualized in the news story.

The last and third-dimension of discourse analysis focuses on the social practice of the dominant discourse and how it influences representations in the television reports. In the context of this research, the social practice is specifically tied to the sociopolitical agenda of the television station, which dictates the agenda and gatekeeping in the reporting, and the knowledge the experts inherit and reproduce through their speech acts in the news stories, e.g., the experts interviewed in the news are the lawyers, humanitarian workers, government representatives, and other specialist or professionals who claim to provide objective reporting, and who speak from a position of authority. Thus, the third-dimension is primarily concerned with the power practice and how it is achieved and articulated in the media representations. The analysis of the third-dimension appears when I, for example, criticize the television media for having an elitist or bias viewpoint on the issues at hand. By analyzing the speech acts or utterances performed by the subjects in the television news, I expose the reproduction of the dominant discourse or an emergence of new orders of discourse. The reproduction of a dominant discourse is read as a reinforcement of the hegemonic discourse articulated in the television media, whereas an emergence of new orders of discourse is perceived as a counter-discourse or a struggle to resist the dominant discourse. If the subject speaks in a manner that challenges the dominant discourse, her speech act is seen as a 'hegemonic struggle' (Fairclough, 1992). Blommaert and Bulcaen (2000) described the hegemonic struggle as a speech act that "struggles over normativity, attempts at control, and [resists] regimes of power" (p. 449). On the other hand, if the subject is represented (re)speaking or (re)articulating orders of the dominant discourses, the reinforcement of the dominant discourse is thus achieved.

Therefore, my analysis focuses on how news reporters, as well as the interviewees featured in the news story, create meaning through the use of particular words and phrases and how their speech contributes to the representations of the subject. Kenney (2009) explains that discourse analysis is used most effectively when the researcher aims to focus on "authoritative texts" from the media that claim to be demonstrating the "truth." Television news media match these criteria, as the television stations usually have a preferred sociopolitical agenda, which is directly tied to their media ownership. Hence, when they represent certain events, the version of the reality they display is framed within this preferred sociopolitical agenda. Thus, the discourse analysis used in this research project aims to appropriately examine the patterns of language, and the common or opposing rhetoric within the news reports. This rhetoric most likely reinforces the television stations' viewpoints on the Syrian conflict.

Furthermore, I explore the nuances in the language used, in order to examine the type of literary or rhetorical conventions, as well as the overarching themes that appear in the news reports. Additionally, I highlight the similarities and differences between the subjects' representations on the different television stations. (Kenney, 2009; Long & Wall 2009; Fairclough, 2003).

3.3   Units of Analysis

To examine the representations of Syrian women and their experiences during the conflict in Arab television news, a sample of news reports was chosen for this case study. The coverage of the Syrian conflict has brought intensified levels of media coverage between different Arab television stations. Majalla (2012) asserts that there are roughly two opposing sides of news coverage in the Arab region: "The so-called moderate Arab states and the resistance axis." The Arab television stations that are critical of the Syrian regime and are supportive of the uprising in Syria, are financed by Arab Gulf States. On the other hand, the Arab television stations supportive of the Syrian regime are either owned and controlled by the Syrian regime or are funded/owned by the allies of the Syrian regime, such as Russia and Iran (Majalla, 2012).

Therefore, this research project chose seven television stations, which are owned or act as mouthpieces for the political actors and regional powers involved in the conflict. The list of television stations consists of four Arabic-speaking television stations owned by or supportive of the Syrian regime, and three Arabic- television stations critical of the Syrian regime. The television stations that are politically aligned with Syrian regime are: *Syria Al-Ikhbariya*,

SANA, RT Arabic, and *SAMA.* The television stations that are politically opposed the Syrian regime are: *Al-Arabiya, Al-Jazeera,* and *Al-Aan.*

3.3.1   The Sample Selection

To explore how the experiences of different groups of Syrian women during the Syrian conflict were portrayed in the news in relation to the four concepts of *violence, vulnerability, resilience,* and *resistance,* I proposed a purposeful selection of television news reports, which was compiled in a non-random manner, as I viewed the reports as insightful and discursively in the context of this research. I followed three main steps.

Step One - Keywords: I noted keywords I deemed relevant to the case study. Drawing on my cultural knowledge, as well as political and social understanding of the Syrian conflict, I created a list of keywords for each concept. They are listed in the table below:

Table 1. Keywords for the main concepts

Concepts	Keywords
Violence	Violence, rape, torture, gender-based violence, sexual harassment, detention, imprisonment, shame, stigma, suffering, checkpoint, and prison.
Vulnerability	Vulnerability, child marriage, early marriage, poverty, domestic abuse, suffering, humanitarian crisis, impoverishment, infrastructure, gender-based violence, sexual harassment, and refugee camps.
Resilience	Resilience, work, cash-for-work, humanitarian aid, vocational programs, survival techniques, coping mechanisms, protection, and refugee camps.
Resistance	Armed resistance, unarmed resistance, rebellion, fight, battle, struggle, military, sacrifice, weapons, defense, and opposition.

Certain keywords for each concept overlap with other keywords listed under a different concept. For instance, the keywords 'gender-based violence' and 'sexual harassment' are listed under the two concepts, *violence* and *vulner-*

ability. However, other keywords such as 'shame' and 'stigma,' were exclusive to the concept of *violence*.

Step Two - Sampling from YouTube: I visited the YouTube channels of each television station and typed in the keywords for each concept in order to obtain the available news reports published online. Not all news reports created by the television stations are downloaded online, especially not on YouTube. Hence, referring to the television stations' YouTube channels was a limiting factor in the sampling process. Because I do have no access to any other source that allows me to acquire the news stories, I had to rely entirely on YouTube. The table below demonstrates all the news reports that were found:

Table 2. Initial sample of news reports

Arab Television Stations	Main Concepts				
Critical of the Syrian Regime	Violence	Vulnera-bility	Resilience	Resis-tance	Sub-Total
Al Jazeera	8	5	16	0	29
Al Arabiya	8	7	9	0	24
Al Aan	7	4	14	0	25
Sub-Total	**23**	**16**	**39**	**0**	78
Supportive of the Syrian Regime					
SANA	0	0	1	5	6
SAMA	1	0	0	4	5
Syria Al Ikhbariya	2	0	0	1	3
RT Arabic	1	0	0	2	3
Sub-Total	**4**	**0**	**1**	**12**	17
Total					**95**

I found 95 news reports, 78 of which were from the television stations with a sociopolitical agenda critical of the Syrian regime, and 17 were from television stations supportive of the Syrian regime.

Step Three - Final Sample Selection: I selected the most relevant news reports from the group. The objective here was to ignore any news reports with redundant content and to ensure that all news reports are relevant to the purpose of this research. I accomplished this step by watching each news story three times. The relevance of the news report's content was measured in terms of context and the date of publication. The news story had to cover topics related to the experiences of Syrian women during the Syrian conflict. The events shown in the news reports had to have either taken place in Syria or its the neighboring countries. Furthermore, the news stories had to have been published between 2013 and 2018. The final sample selection contained 32 news reports. See the table below for more details.

Table 3. Final sample of news reports

Arab Television Stations	Main Concepts				
Critical of the Syrian Regime	Violence	Vulnera-bility	Resilience	Resis-tance	Sub-Total
Al Jazeera	3	2	1	0	6
Al Arabiya	2	3	2	0	7
Al Aan	2	3	4	0	9
Sub-Total	**7**	**8**	**8**	**0**	23
Supportive of the Syrian Regime					
SANA	0	0	1	5	4
SAMA	0	0	0	4	3
Syria Al Ikhbariya	0	0	0	1	1
RT Arabic	0	0	0	2	1
Sub-Total	**0**	**0**	**1**	**12**	9
Total	7	8	9	8	**32**

Lastly, because this research looks at Arabic-speaking television stations, all of the examined news reports were in Arabic. Thus, I translated the text of the news reports from Arabic to English.

3.3.2   The Selection of Dominant Themes

After the selection was finalized, I categorized the four main concepts under the dominant themes present in the news reports sample.

Themes in the category of Violence: Seven news reports were selected for the category of violence; two news reports were published by *Al Aan*, three by *Al Jazeera*, and two by *Al Arabiya*. They were published between Jan 9, 2012 and Mar 7, 2018, and focused on a specific group of Syrian women who were internally displaced or were (un)willingly living under the Bashar Al-Assad regime. The two main themes that regularly appeared in the news stories were: (a) Syrian women discussing how the Assad regime had committed crimes of rape, torture, and gender-based violence in different physical spaces (e.g., checkpoints, bakeries, and homes), as a way to publicly shame the female victims; and (b) Syrian female victims who were previously held captive and choose to remain silent with regards to their experience of gender-based violence, while others fled Syria and started a new life in exile.

Themes in the category of Vulnerability: Eight news reports were selected for the category of vulnerability. Three news reports were published by *Al Aan*, two by *Al Jazeera*, and three by *Al Arabiya*. The news reports were published between Jan 4, 2014 and Aug 8, 2017. The two main recurring themes in selected news reports were: (1) The increase in child marriage cases in the informal refugee settlements in Lebanon and Jordan; (2) the deterioration of refugee makeshift shelters in Lebanon's Beqaa valley during snowstorms.

Themes in the category of Resilience: Nine news reports were selected for the category of resilience. One news report was published by *SANA*, one by *Al Jazeera*, two by *Al Arabiya* and five by *Al Aan*. The news reports were published between Nov 13, 2013 and April 7, 2016. The news report from *SANA*, an Arab television station that is politically sympathetic towards the Syrian regime, included an interview with an internally displaced Syrian woman working as a tailor in Syria. The news reports published by *Al Aan*, *Al Jazeera*, and *Al Arabiya*, which are pan-Arab television stations with a political agenda critical of the Syrian regime, mainly focused on externally displaced Syrian women living in Lebanon, Iraq, Jordan, and Turkey. In the news reports, these groups of Syrian women are shown taking part of vocational and cash-for-work programs funded by the United Nations and other NGOs.

Themes in the category of Resistance: Eight news reports were selected for the category of resistance. Three by *SAMA*, three by *SANA*, one by *RT Arabic*, and one by *Syria Al Ikhbariyya*. *RT Arabic* sympathizes with the Syrian regime;

SANA, SAMA, and *Syria Al Ikhbariyya* are controlled by the Syrian regime. Eight of the fourteen videos were selected for the research sample and were published between April 2, 2013 and Sep 27, 2018. In the news reports, different Syrian women were depicted in diverse contexts and situations: Syrian women serving in the Syrian Arab Army, Syrian women serving food for the men of the Syrian Arab Army, Syrian women marrying men from the Syrian Arab Army, and Syrian women taking part of social and cultural events promoting women's rights organized by the GUSW. Although these women come from different demographical backgrounds and socio-economic groups, the notion of the 'mother of the nation' appeared in the speech acts and in the television images regardless of whether or not the Syrian women represented were actual mothers.

The table below lists the main themes under the four main concept:

Table 4. Main Concepts and Manifestations

Main Concepts	Main Manifestations
Violence	Female Syrian Ex-Prisoners in Exile: - Imprisonment, Sexual Assault, and Deterring Mobility - Being Shamed to Being Silenced - Intersection of Shame, Violence, and Stigma
Vulnerability	Syrian Mothers and Child Brides in Exile: - Child Marriage - Failed Infrastructure during Harsh Weather Conditions
Resilience	Displaced Syrian Women at Work: - Training the Good Resilient Subject - Erasing the Past or Painting it through their Work - News Reports on Vocational and Cash-for-Work Programs
Resistance	Syrian women in Assad Syria: - Ambivalent Role of Motherhood in Assad Syria - From Masculine Female Fighters to Ornamented Flowers - Motherhood as a National Duty

3.3.3 The Analysis Process

I apply a non-linear model of discourse analysis by examining the images, captions, and spoken texts that appear in the news reports. During my analysis process, I underline statements related to the research themes. I highlight certain phrases and images featured in each of the news report, and make written detailed notes on the content. My notes include comments on the language used and on the images that appear in the news report. I note the potential meaning behind the content and the possible ways to interpret the text and image.

As suggested by Fairclough (2001), I then begin the discourse analysis by examining the production of text. During this step, I draw on the media ownership of every television station and consider its socio-political views. This provides a clearer understanding of the partisan entity embedded in reporting. The research draws attention to the producer of those images and videos and, how the reporting references and interviews 'experts' as a way to reinforce the socio-political views of the television station. This step connects the functions of the dominant discourse to the institutional practices of the television media that organize, regulate, and administer social life (Foucault, 1980); other institutional practices could be directed by family, social, health, political, and government organizations, etc. Here, the analysis reveals how the subjects and events are being positioned in the television media discourse.

To do so, I focus on the prevalent themes that appeared under each of the four main concepts. These themes are considered examples of "sociocultural practice." This step advances the analysis and examines the media discourse in greater depth. It places the analyzed text in discussion with the partisan inclinations of the television stations and the socio-political context of the Syrian conflict (Fairclough, 2001). Examples of the questions asked at this stage of analysis is: How can the research draw a connection between the news reports' representation of child marriage in decaying refugee settlements and the television station's socio-political position on poverty, gender equality, and public health in the context of the Syrian conflict? In other words, what is the television station's political agenda regarding the advocacy of displaced Syrian women and girls living in vulnerable states and how does this affect the distribution of the media images representing these particular women?

Because this research project is immersed in questions related to discourse, language, and power in the news reports, I draw on a Foucauldian discourse analysis model to further guide the analysis. Graham Gibbs (2015) provides a methodological explanation of this model, by suggesting 16 main questions to explore:

1. What are the hidden relations of power present in the text?
2. Who is exercising the power; whose discourse is being presented, the discourse of any specific institution such as humanitarian aid organizations or government, etc.?
3. "Who is the 'ideal subject' or audience for the text?"
4. Who is the text aimed at?
5. Who is meant to be listening to it, or responding to it?
6. What is left unspecified or unsaid (not mentioned by the discourse)?
7. "Is there a use of passive voice or processes expressed as (things, reification), such as things rather than people?"
8. Is there a use of colorful description language (adjectives) to indicate a strong discourse? – metaphors, other descriptive indicators, etc.
9. "What alternative wording of the same information have resulted in different discourses?"
10. How are the events presented?
11. How are people – individuals involved in those events, certain kinds of individuals, certain kinds of subject behavior, etc. – characterized in the text?
12. "What message does the author intend you to get from the text?"
13. "What are they trying to say to you?"
14. Why is this particular image chosen or chosen to accompany the text (if applicable)?
15. What repetition exists within the text and between different texts on the same topic?
16. What professional media practices assist with the presentation of dominant discourses?

3.4   Methodological Questions on Agency and Points of Reversibility

Because this book addresses the agentive attempts of the different groups of displaced Syrian women throughout the conflict, I draw on a Foucault's methodological approach to power and its points of reversibility. According to Foucault (1980), knowledge is directly tied to power, and power itself is reversable. In other words, the idea of power as something that constrains– in the sense of a force that controls, prevents, represses, censors, and conceals– is rejected. I pursue Foucault's understanding of power to further investigate how power operates throughout the dominant media discourses, as well as how subjects react to these discourses through language, speech acts, etc. I explore the reality, the domains of object, and the rituals of truths represented in the television news, which, according to Foucault (1980), are produced by the dominant discourse itself.

While power may construct a reality and produce ways that restrict the subject's behavior within this constructed reality, Foucault (1980) claimed that this constraining power has points of reversibility that also enable, conversely, certain behaviors; this is the point where the subject's agentive attempts are questioned. Therefore, throughout my analysis, I do not take the complexities of the discourse for granted. I endeavor to see other ways of seeing how the notion of power in the dominant discourse has an *enabling*, and not just a constraining, quality.

3.5   Methodological Reflections

This research project applies a Foucauldian discourse analysis to examine the news reports. Thus, the authorial intention behind the media message is not addressed. Rather, the news report analysis r focuses on the rhetorical force behind the television news. In other words, the intention of the journalists and news producers is largely ignored. Moreover, this research project does not concede how most television news reports are limited to a certain time duration; this is usually a result of the editorial standards to which the news production team must abide. This suggests that the journalists may have acquired information and may have intended to include more (investigative) content and (critical) perspectives in the news story, irrespective of the brief duration[2] of the news reports to which the editorial team had to abide, which may have hindered these possibilities.

Moreover, because this research focuses on the *encoding* stage of the news reports, it does not explore how viewer audiences are *decoding* the messages. This research does not analyze whether the media messages are being accepted, resisted, or rejected by the viewers. Stuart Hall (1974) asserted that, in

---

2   Most of the analyzed news reports that were two to four minutes long.

the decoding stage, the viewer could either challenge the "dominant preferred reading" or possibly accept or interpret it differently than the dominant culture intended it to be. Hall also claimed that the "dominant preferred reading" would continue to exist in larger forms and will possibly prevail.

In the following chapter, I start the discourse analysis by examining the news reports in the context of violence.

4. Arab Television News Coverage of Former Female Syrian Prisoners in Exile:
The Intersection of Shame, Violence, and Stigma

4.1 Introduction

Millions have fled Syria and settled in neighboring countries since the outbreak of the Syrian conflict in 2011, while others have been detained and imprisoned. The Arab television coverage of the imprisonment and humiliation of Syrians aroused outrage and pity among viewers. Images of Syrian women being exposed to police brutality and sexual violence were widely presented on Arab television news. A study published by SNHR, the Syrian Network for Human Rights, revealed that:

> "Almost 14,000 people have died in Syrian regime prisons since March 2011 when the civil war first erupted, while about 128,000 others still remain in detention. Torture by the Bashar Assad regime forces made up 14,070 of this number, including 173 children and 45 women. Some 14,227 individuals [including 177 children, 62 women] have died due to torture at the hands of main parties to the conflict in Syria from March 2011 to June 2019" (Daily Sabah, 2019).

The listed number of victims are among those that were identified by SNHR. In reality, the number of deaths and imprisoned individuals is most likely significantly higher (Daily Sabah, 2019).

Rape and gender-based violence—as a war strategy—were not only used by Syrian regime forces, but also by other militant groups, including the Free Syrian Army (known as 'the opposition' or 'the rebels') and ISIS. For instance, women became a source of *profit* for ISIS members. In 2016, the United Nations Human Rights Council revealed that women and girls living under ISIS were being forced into sex slavery. They were physically abused on a regular basis, raped, and then resold. "If any of them tried to escape, she would end up being slaughtered or shot dead" (Chapman, 2016). In Syria, women who fell as victims of rape and sexual violence are most likely deemed as dishonorable by their families and communities.

Furthermore, although honor killing in Syria existed before the conflict, the number of incidents increased drastically during the conflict. An article published by *The Guardian* told the story of a fighter in the Free Syrian Army, who murdered his sister on camera amid adultery rumors (Carrie & Alomar, 2018). In areas controlled by the Free Syrian Army, human rights violations such as honor killing are not considered illegal. Many women who were victims of war rape have been accused of bringing dishonor to their families; others are stigmatized by their communities (Batha, 2013). As a consequence, many Syrian women were victims of honor killing, or deemed ineligible for marriage (Tuysuz, 2011).

All these incidents and circumstances increase the likelihood for Syrian women to experience trauma, "ostracism, shame, broken relationships, and health issues" (Porter, 2012). These common experiences among the female victims of gender-based violence are seldomly addressed in the Arab television news. Meanwhile, their agency is framed in the dominant media discourses as something that is entirely lost (Alhayek, 2015). Thus, this chapter attempts to determine whether news reports on the concept of violence reproduced a similar pattern of representation with regards to the notion of agency among the female victims of gender-based violence. Throughout the analysis, I focus on how the Arab television news framed the incidents of violence that have occurred in different locations such as bakeries, homes, checkpoints. Examples of these incidents of violence are public shaming, rape, torture, and detainment.

4.2   Research Data

To compile a record of the most frequent news reports on incidents of gender-based violence experienced by Syrian women during the recent conflict, I referred to the YouTube channels of three Arab television stations: *Al Aan, Al Jazeera*, and *Al Arabiya*. When using the search engine in the YouTube channels, I typed the following keywords: *Syrian women, Syrian conflict, violence, rape, torture, gender-based violence, sexual harassment, detention, imprisonment, shame, stigma, suffering, checkpoint,* and *prison.* Seven news reports were collected in total; 2 news reports were published by *Al Aan,* 3 news reports by *Al Jazeera,* and 2 new reports by *Al Arabiya.* They were published between January 9, 2012 and March 7, 2018. The table below provides the name, duration, and broadcasting date of the news reports.

Table 5. News reports in the context of violence

Report	Television Station	Title of the News Report	Duration	Date Published	Chapter Section
1	Al Jazeera	There are More than 13 Thousand Female Detainees in Syrian Regime Prisons	2:03	January 26, 2017	4.3.1
2	Al Aan	Testimonies of Women Who were Raped and Tortured by Syrian Regime Forces	3:19	April 28, 2013	4.3.1
3	Al Arabiya	The Story of a Girl Who Was Raped During her Imprisonment in Syria	2:30	January 3, 2013	4.3.2
4	Al Jazeera	Rape Victims are Detained in Syria	2:24	January 9, 2012	4.3.2
5	Al Aan	A Former Female Prisoner Talks About How She was Tortured in Prison	3:55	February 20, 2014	4.3.2
6	Al Jazeera	Thousands of Female Detainees are Raped in Syrian Regime Prisons	3:10	August 29, 2017	4.3.2
7	Al Arabiya	Former Female Detainees Discuss How They Were Tortured in Syrian regime Prisons	2:41	March 7, 2018	4.3.2

In most of the news reports, female victims of gender-based violence are interviewed anonymously by the reporter. Notions such as shame and stigma are associated with the representations. Thus, in order to explore how the Arab television news represented the detainment, imprisonment, and public shaming of Syrian women, I deconstruct the Arab television media discourse on gender-based violence during the Syrian conflict. To explore these media representations, I address the following questions:

1. How were the incidents of gender-based violence, that took place in different physical spaces such as checkpoints, bakeries, and homes, represented in the news reports?
2. How did the television reporting represent the notion of agency among the female victims who had been detained, imprisoned, and public shamed?

4.3   Analysis

4.3.1   Imprisonment, Sexual Assault, and Controlled Mobility

The news story from *Al Jazeera* published on January 26, 2017 reported on the large number of female prisoners in Syrian prisons. The reporter said:

> "*International human rights organizations have claimed that the regime's prisons are considered among the worst prisons in the world. Another report from a different organization asserted than more than 18,000 male and female prisons have died inside the prisons in Syria – the ones controlled by the regime – between the years 2011 and 2015. This means that 300 deaths occur every month.*"

Afterwards, the report quoted Muhammad Alloush, a member of the Syrian opposition. Alloush said:

> "*There are more than 13,000 female prisoners in the regime's prisons. The prisons are unique in nature because the regime does not differentiate between male and female prisoners. They apply the same torture methods to both men and women.*"

An image of a group of Syrian women supporting the Syrian opposition is displayed. Referring to the image, the reporter claimed that these groups of women confirm the truth behind the human rights violations in the prisons. The reporter explained how female prisoners are tortured more violently than male prisoners. He said:

> "*Female prisoners experience more brutal measures than male prisoners. This is due to the psychological torture that they are exposed to. Female prisoners are beaten*

up, raped, and assaulted in front of their partner or family members. Other female prisoners are forced to watch their relatives being abused and assaulted."

The news report mostly focused on the gendered aspect of the violence committed. It did not highlight the *strategic nature* of the violence used by the Assad regime as a way to pressure the opposition. Instead, the viewer's attention was diverted to how men and women are often equally tortured and violated, and how women frequently receive even worse treatment than their male counterparts.

The second news report focused on the detention and sexual violation that took place at checkpoints, homes, and bakeries. On April 28, 2013, the *Al Aan* reporter started the news story with the following statement:

"The Syrian authorities have applied brutal methods of torture to women, men, and sometimes children. This led many families to flee the country and cross the border."

The reporter interviewed former female prisoners who had left Syria and who now reside in Tripoli, Lebanon. The reporter asserted that these women were targeted by the Syrian regime because they are politically aligned with a Syrian opposition group. He explained how the Syrian regime captured these women at checkpoints and detained them for their political affiliation. One woman was interviewed. Without hiding her facial features, she spoke to the camera. She said:

"I was on the street, the street got bombed, so I yelled Allahu Akbar. And then the man on the street yelled back 'Allahu Akbar at you!', so I responded 'Allahu Akbar at you and at Assad!'. After two days, I was stopped at a checkpoint and detained. They investigated me, cussed me, and physically abused me. They tied my hands, threw me on the floor, and started kicking me. They cussed my whole family, my mother, my siblings. And they wouldn't stop beating me up."

The reporter commented:

"Some of the Syrian women interviewed in this news report refused to show their faces. They are scared the regime will target their relatives in Syria. But they wanted to speak up on television and tell their stories and what they have witnessed."

Another Syrian woman was interviewed. She told her story on camera while covering her face. She said:

"When I was detained at the checkpoint, I was beaten up, cussed and forced to watch men being stripped of their clothes as they were tortured by the Syrian Arab Army."

The reporter claimed that many women in Syria were forced to watch their relatives being killed at checkpoints. This is considered a form of public humiliation. He continued by saying that most of these women are usually taken to detention centers and are sexually violated in prison.

In this setting, the checkpoint is a unique physical space where power relations are revealed and the laws of the regime become visible. The checkpoint conceals and justifies the presence of laws that ought to be followed. Violent physical force is frequently used to enforce these laws (Mansbach, 2009). In the context of the Syrian conflict, sexual violence performed at checkpoints becomes a policing method used to enforce the laws of the Syrian regime. Syrian civilians passing through the checkpoint are reduced to one-dimensional subjects; they are moving subjects. If the sociopolitical background or identity of the moving subject is perceived as a threat to state security, the subject is seen as a "transgressor" (Kotef & Amir, 2011). Unique to this context, the only gaze permitted at the checkpoint is that of the army men. Hence, the makeshift checkpoint can be perceived as a *pre*-panoptic space,[1] in which the external gaze from the surveillance tower is somehow absent. As for the permanent checkpoints equipped with surveillance cameras, the space is akin to a panopticon. In this setting, both the army men and the transgressors are observed subjects.

During the Syrian conflict, the Syrian army operated makeshift and permanent checkpoints on a daily basis. If the dweller walking through the checkpoint is not perceived as a threat to the state, no direct physical force is exerted. However, this does not indicate that obedience and order were not created and maintained in this very moment. The regime's control over the civilian (the dweller) is achieved; in this case, however, it is achieved in invisible forms (Foucault, 1984). Kotef and Amir (2011) described the power relations that take place at checkpoints. They asserted that:

> "By making power transparent, making law visible and accessible, violence seems to disappear while, in actuality, it changes form, conceals itself and, thereby, becomes more permanent and sustainable: it becomes less erratic and more structural; it no longer brutally erupts in episodic incidents, but is, rather, a perpetuated structure of exploitation, expulsion, and oppression" (p. 73).

---

1   The Panopticon refers to direct State surveillance (Foucault 1975).

In other words, when violence does not occur through violent physical incidents of torture and assault, a more constant and structured form of violence
is established and maintained. This violence is shielded by the law and by the
right of the state to examine the identity of its residents. At the checkpoint,
criteria such as the following may be applied: Who fits the status quo? Who
poses a threat to the status quo? Who should be detained and who is free to
go? This process is termed 'a local signifying practice', where the army men
at the checkpoint have to solve the mystery of the resident's political (social
and religious) affiliation. This usually requires the inspection of the resident's
identification papers, which provide information on a person's place of residence, place of birth, family name, etc.

Another central role of the checkpoint is to control or hinder a person's
movement. When movement is deterred, so are mobility and daily routines.
In this case, checkpoints can make people feel less safe in their districts and
homes. Such a situation appeared in the Arab television news when *Al Aan*
reported on the government raids of the civilian homes. The raids included
the rape and detention of women in their own homes – in their own private
spheres. Here, the violence inflicted on women in residential areas may have
caused an increase in (internal) displacement or a restriction in their movement

The final segment of the news story described an incident of physical violence that occurred at a local bakery in Aleppo. A displaced Syrian woman,
who does not reveal her identity on camera, told the story of Huda, a female
baker who was attacked by members of the regime in her own bakery. In the
news report, the displaced Syrian women described the incident as follows:

> "Huda baked bread for a living. She baked bread for the opposition (the people of
> the Free Syrian Army) in Aleppo. She was beaten in her own bakery. The men of the
> Assad Syrian army ripped Huda's clothes off and exposed her breasts to the public.
> If the women in the neighborhood had not interfered as they begged for the sexual
> assault to stop, the men from the regime would have done worse things to Huda
> – publicly. In any case, it is too late, she had already been cussed, beaten up, and
> molested."

In the news reports, there was a clear connection between the sexual assault of
Huda and her act of providing bread to the Syrian opposition. Bread, as a sta-
ple food, plays an essential role during uprisings and conflicts. For instance, in
Egypt and Tunisia, the accessibility and price of basic food items contributed
to the uproar that prompted the uprisings. Similarly, in pre-conflict Syria,

a drought hit the agriculture sector in 2007, leading to a decrease in wheat production, which then increased "food prices by nearly a third in 2008 alone" (Beals 2016, p. 5). Granted, bread and wheat are part of the subsidized food provided by the Syrian regime. They are part of the social welfare services, other services include "free healthcare, education, and utilities" (Martínez & Eng, 2017, p. 135). Martínez and Eng (2017) asserted that:

> "Since the onset of violence in late 2011, the Syrian government has tried to maintain the bread subsidy in areas it controls by ensuring that bakeries are open, well stocked with flour, and consistently distributing the foodstuff. Interestingly, various opposition groups have sought to gain civilian support by mimicking elements of the government's welfare programs. Like the Assad regime, they interact and negotiate with local populations in exchange for their loyalty or compliance" (p. 135).

Thus, in times of war, the impact of subsidized bread is closely linked to the ability to maintain power and control over territories and its residents. In this context, by providing these social services, the Free Syrian Army is able to 'perform the State'. On the other hand, by bombing bakeries, the Syrian regime attempts to destabilize the Free Syrian Army's control over residential areas. Martínez and Eng (2017) claimed that:

> "In targeting bakeries, the Assad regime limits the ability of opposition parties to execute emblematic state performances. This prevents relations between incipient rebel governing bodies and civilians from being formalized or stabilized. At the same time, the Assad regime's provision of basic foodstuffs in territories it controls alleviates economic stress, averts popular unrest, and boosts morale among weary civilians, while subtly reminding them of the benefits of state power and administration" (p. 138).

From this point of view, I recognize two war tactics adopted by the Syrian regime. The first tactic could be described as *"dimuqratiyyat alkhubz"* (bread democracy). A term initiated by Sadiki (1997), *"dimuqratiyyat alkhubz"* describes a political contract or transaction between the state and the impoverished. This transaction grants the hungry the physical function of becoming unhungry, while the regime is able to transform suppression and yielding into a social and political reconciliation (Zureik, 2012). In Syria's *bread democracy*—a euphemism for dictatorship—the notion of demanding freedom and political life is out of the question. The second tactic is the regime's strategy to attack bakeries in areas controlled by the opposition. The attack signaled a message to the civilians: the regime "is the only viable source of such necessities" (Khaddour, 2015).

Therefore, when a bakery becomes the target of state violence, the physical assault on the baker cannot be perceived as arbitrary in nature. Perhaps that was the underlying message behind *Al Aan*'s news story about the bakery attack. Nevertheless, the social, political, and economic context of the bakery remains decontextualized in the news report. It is important to note that by physically attacking Huda in her own space — a space where she acts as her own breadwinner — Huda's agentive attempts are also directly attacked. The bakery is not only Huda's (private and public) space of work and income, but also a crucial and significant space for the public's survival. Bread is a fundamental need of life and a basic human nourishment for the working class. When the regime attacks Huda for providing bread to the opposition, the regime is not only punishing Huda, but also the working-class individuals need this bread to put food on the table. The attack on the bakery becomes a practice of expulsion of those who rely on the government's bread subsidies to survive. It symbolizes the act of selecting those who deserve basic human nourishment and those who do not.

The report concluded with the following statement:

"These women have sought a new home in a new country. By fleeing, these women have the chance to find a new and safe home that somehow helps them regain their feelings of hope, humanity, and safety."

The news report ended by stating that some of the Syrian women who fell victim to gender-based violence have sought a new life in Tripoli, Lebanon.

In the upcoming section, I explore how the Arab television news represented the Syrian women who fell victims to regime violence and gender-based violence, specifically those who crossed the border and are now living in exile. In the analysis, I ask the following question: Does the émigré status of Syrian women end the stigmatization they have faced as victims of regime violence and gender-based violence?

4.3.2   From Being Shamed to Being Silenced

In the news reports surveyed in this section, the female victims were depicted in relationship to the patriarchal norms that stigmatized them as victims of gender-based violence, on the one hand, and as subjects of shame and family dishonor on the other hand. The notion of silence was mentioned regularly in the news narratives. The representations of Syrian women demonstrated how: (a) The victims chose to hide their identity as they narrated their experiences of gender-based violence; (b) the victims *self-censored* their speech as they narrated their experiences in prisons; and (c) the victims chose to forget the past, chose silence as a 'coping mechanism' to endure the pain. I explore these three main representations in the news reports below.

The notion of silence appears in one of the news reports by *Al Arabiya* published on January 3, 2013. The news story focused on the coping mechanisms practiced by female victims of gender-based violence. The reporter in the news story said:

> "There have been many news reports on Syrian women and girls who have been tortured and raped inside of Syria. To cope with those experiences, the Syrian woman is using silence as a weapon. Here, in Amman, the capital of Jordan, we found hope."

The news story interviewed one of the victims without revealing her identity. The former female prisoner spoke on camera as she hid her face. She said:

> "I was detained on the 20th of October 2012. The police took me from my own home. They took me to the investigation room. This is when my journey started. I was tortured and a lot more."

Afterwards, the reporter continued narrating her story. He said:

> "Amal (a pseudonym for the victim) was raped more than once. The victim spent 40 days in transportation, the regime transported her from one detainment center to another. She was exposed to torture and rape. She hides her face from a society that does not have mercy on her for being a victim of gender-based violence. Amal said that she lived and died more than three times. She never found any source to ease the pain until she met Umm Zaher; a woman from the Sham region, who embraced Amal and is supporting many former Syrian female prisoners in Amman."

Umm Zaher, who established an organization to support former female Syrian prisoners, spoke about her project. She said:

> "I named the organization Amal because I want to create hope for the women of Syria.[2] I want to encourage women to open up to society and to speak about their experiences in the regime's prisons."

---

2   *Amal* means hope in Arabic.

The father of the former female prisoner, Amal, was interviewed. The reporter said that the father wants to keep his identity anonymous in order to protect his daughter from being *shamed*. Without showing his face, he spoke on camera, while crying. He said:

> *"I am the father. God has given me this responsibility to protect my daughter. I need to protect my daughter. I am trying not to cry, but my daughter's experience was very difficult. When she experiences those tragic things, my daughter's pride and dignity were taken away from her."*

The reporter ends the news story by saying:

> *"But Amal's willpower will never be taken away from her."*

In this news report, the repressive social norms of shaming the female victim were not challenged, but rather reinforced by the father of Amal, Amal herself, and the news reporter. Amal and her father's decision to remain silent resulted in reinforcing those oppressive societal norms. Amal's "choice" to remain silent about most of her prison experience was perceived as a form of strength.

Similarly, a news story by *Al Jazeera* (January 9, 2012) reported on another former female prisoner. The reporter said:

> *"She is known as the martyr. She has no name and no identity. She chose to hide who she is. Staying anonymous is part of her healing process. Hiding her identity gives the victim determination and confidence in order to overcome the tragedy she is living through and she has experienced."*

The reporter claimed that the anonymous female victim engages with an online platform created by Syrian refugee doctors. The reporter explained how the victims of torture and rape could benefit from this platform by anonymously reporting on their experiences online. The platform's database revealed that there are more than 1,500 rape incidents that have occurred since the outbreak of the conflict. The reporter interviewed one of the female victims; she had been to the victim of systematic rape and torture when she was caught at a checkpoint in Homs, Syria. She was detained afterwards. As she spoke on camera, her face remained hidden. She said:

> *"There are orders the Syrian Arab Army have to follow. If they are ordered to detain someone, torture and rape them, then they have to do it. This is a military order, those serving the military have no right to refuse any orders."*

A relative of the victim was also interviewed, also covering her face on camera. She discussed how the victims should receive help after they leave prison. She said:

> "She should be given financial support to find a safe accommodation. This is an important step for her security and psychological wellbeing. No one should pressure her into talking about her experience. She should be placed in an environment that makes her feel safe, and she should understand that many other women and men went through a similar experience as hers."

Afterwards, the reporter emphasized how society and the family place a great deal of pressure on victims of torture and rape. They still consider such incidents a social taboo.

Afterwards, a Syrian female activist is interviewed, she said:

> "Many women find it extremely difficult to communicate normally with friends and family. It is hard for them to integrate again in society. There are women who needed more than a month to start speaking again and to open up about their experiences in prison."

At the end of the report, the reporter emphasized how women and children who have experienced rape and torture symbolize the greatest form of sacrifice in Syrian society.

At first glance, the news reports on violence may appear as a counter-discourse towards the acts of violation and violence in regime's prisons. However, the incidents of torture and rape receive partial justification. The former female prisoner claimed that the men who committed these violations must abide by the military orders of Bashar Al-Assad's regime. This statement legitimizes the repressive and violent measures committed by rapists, supposedly in the name of a military order issued by the Syrian regime.

Another news story from *Al Jazeera*, published on August 29, 2017, also addressed the issue of public shaming in the context of rape and torture in the regime's prisons. The story revealed that the Syrian regime uses mobile phone footage during the torture, rape, and assault of Syrian women. These videos are used as a way to blackmail and public humiliate the victims. The news reporter stated:

> "Many female victims of rape and torture are (threatened to be) publicly shamed, ever since the regime started using video footage of the victims being tortured and raped in the regime's prisons."

Th reporter highlighted the story of Shahadah Zahira, a female prisoner, who was gang raped by five men from the Syrian regime army. Her rape was filmed using a mobile phone camera. Later on, the news report showed a video of a Syrian woman covering the lower part of her face as she addressed the public shaming of women who had experienced rape and torture in prisons. She addressed the men and women who argued these women were a source of dishonor to the family and in society. She said:

"You, the people who have claimed that the girl who gets detained is a girl who has hurt your honor. God only knows what this girl has gone through. What that girl experienced is a fate given to her by God. This is a life experience that God has chosen for her. It is a destiny. This is God's way of testing the girl's strength."

In her speech, she addressed how women and girls are perceived as threats to the family honor and how they are shamed for being victims of gender-based violence and publicly shamed. The speech had a significant message; yet, the news reporter did not provide any commentary on the video. Instead, he shifted the focus to the traumas experienced by former female prisoners.

Another news report in this section was published by *Al Aan* on February 20, 2014. It contained an interview with Warda Salman, a female victim of sexual violence. She spoke openly on camera, showing all her entire face. She spoke about the violations she faced while she had been held for 18 months in the regime's prisons. The reporter said:

"Warda was exposed to all kinds of torture. She was also exposed to other types of violations. She refuses to talk about them. She is currently working as a human rights activist. She wants to help her female acquaintances that are currently imprisoned in Syria under the regime."

The report also revealed how the Syrian regime forced Warda to appear on camera and plot against all activists and members of the opposition.

The news report gave a detailed description of the torture she received, but the news reporter did not use the terms "sexual violation" or "sexual assault" to describe it. Nonetheless, it becomes clear to the viewer that Warda had been sexually violated after she mentioned that she had been exposed to "other types" of violence during her imprisonment. Warda described her experience. She said:

"Because of all the torture and pressure inflicted on me, I was forced to admit things that never really happened to me. I was forced to lie. I was forced to admit those lies.

> *I was forced to say the names of many activists from the Opposition. These activists are not terrorists, but I was forced to claim them as terrorists. Of course, this was all a result of the torture and pressure they put me through."*

Afterwards, she mentioned that she would not be able to speak about this particular experience on camera. At this point, she self-censored herself, which is another form of silencing. Perhaps censoring parts of her story stemmed from her impotence to break a social taboo or to speak openly about her experience with sexual assault.

Similar to the previous news stories surveyed above, the news report concluded that many women remain silent about such experiences and refused to talk about them in public. Although Warda revealed her identity on screen, her identity was *hitherto* exposed publicly by Syrian regime; i.e., when she had been forced to record a video while in prison.

The last news report in this section is from *Al Arabiya*, published on Mar 7, 2018. The news story exposed in more detail the torture methods employed by the Syrian regime against female prisoners. The reporter interviewed three Syrian women who were previously detained in the regime's prisons. The identity of the interviewees remained anonymous and their faces were blurred out from the television screen. The reporter started the report by saying:

> *"These women were tortured and raped after they were illegally detained in the prisons."*

The first speaker described the methods of torture she was exposed to by the Syrian Arab Army while in prison. She said:

> *"The men of the Assad regime never took a break. They tortured us day and night. There were no 'specific hours' for the torture. We could not differentiate between day and night. The investigation room had an iron bed. The prisoners were forced to lie on the iron bed. They would tie your hand and force you to sit down. You couldn't move your body. I was only 24 years old when they threw me into this investigation room. They threw water on me and then electrocuted me, that was their method of torture. I was later on thrown into a room full of women. 43 female detainees in a room without a window. It had no ventilation. You could almost die from the smell of sickness. There were insects and worms everywhere."*

The speaker exposed how systematic violence is tied to routine or long hours of torture on a daily basis, revealing how the violence used by the regime became a weapon of war.

Public shaming is also another form of violence used as a war weapon. Tadroz (2016) argues that:

> *"Sexual violence is intended not only to shame the individual but the community at large. Public shaming has a collective impact because it destroys not only the victim but also the rest of the community who are often forced to watch" (p. 104).*

This notion appeared in a speech by one of the interviewees in the news report. A former female prisoner told how she had been dragged out of her home and had her naked body exposed to the public. She referred to her experience of sexual assault by using the word 'thing,' not wishing to use the real name of the act in public or on camera. She said:

> *"There was a female student in the 9th grade, she had been raped by six men. I was also exposed to this 'thing.' There is no female prisoner who wasn't exposed to this thing. My son was also investigated by the regime. They would grab my child, shake his body, and ask him: 'Where is your mother? What does your mother do?' My child couldn't speak anymore because he was terrified. My daughter was two and a half old when they separated her from me. They forced me out of my house, I wasn't wearing my headscarf; I wasn't wearing my Abaya either, nothing. I had nothing on me!"*

The third speaker told another story that occurred in a detention center:

> *"There was also a woman who was only six months pregnant. Due to the harsh torture methods inflicted on her, she gave birth in the middle of the investigation. Her child died. They shot the baby in front of her. This woman became crazy. She remains mentally ill until today. Her parents always lock her up in a room, they don't let her go out in public."*

This part of the story insinuated that the so-called 'mentally-ill' female victims will most likely be barred from public life. Excluding traumatized former prisoners from public life and from their right to re-integrate in public circles after they are released from their detainment, this fact exemplifies how society values the concept of honor more than the victims' wellbeing. Once again, the news report demonstrated how family honor is secured in the name of 'protecting the victim.'

4.4   Conclusion

This chapter illustrated how the news reports surveyed above, in the context of violence, were solely directed at the violence inflicted by Bashar Al Assad regime. The dominant discourse in the news reports was materialized in two main ways: by attacking the acts of violence committed by the Syrian regime and by highlighting and representing the victims of these acts. These two reporting approaches sometimes overlapped; at other times the reporting did not emphasize one aspect over the other. At first glance, the news reports on violence may have appeared as a counter-discourse, one critical of the violence committed by the Syrian regime. However, the chapter revealed that this counter-discourse has an undermining nature when critiquing the Assad regime's violent war strategies.

The news reports largely focused on portraying Syrian women who had been exposed to torture, detention, and sexual assault. While the news stories frequently reported on the phenomenon of sexual violence committed by the Syrian Arab Army, news report analysis showed that there are two factors that undermine the violence highlighted in the television news. The first factor is that the news reports did not investigate or highlight the strategic nature of this violence and the nature of the spaces in which these violent acts have taken place. The second factor is that most of the news stories tended to focus on the gendered aspect of the acts of violence. I regard this as a limitation in the reporting.

Furthermore, the chapter demonstrated that the experiences of rape, public shaming, and sexual assault were perpetuated as a public spectacle in the Arab television news. This strongly contributed to the humiliation of Syrian women. We cannot perceive these acts as merely violent or patriarchal but, more importantly, as political.

The general output of the reporting implied that female victims of rape and sexual assault 'chose' to remain silent about their past or remained silent because they feared being dishonored by their communities. None of the news reports mentioned the threats of honor killing facing Syrian women, carried out a form of punishment inflicted by the communities or families. Instead, the news reports only shed light on how silence became a weapon among these groups of women.

Another issue that has been overlooked in the television reporting is the issue of suicide among the victims. In some cases, suicide becomes another way of regaining dignity among women who had been raped during their imprisonment (WITW, 2016), especially among groups of women who were publicly shamed by their communities and by the Syrian regime. During those difficult times, suicide may become a desperate attempt to regain dignity among the victims.

In the news reports, the former female prisoners and the victims of gender-based violence were represented in relation to how they escaped to a neighboring country or how they were dismissed by their own community. These narratives portrayed those incidents as a form of *failure*. Granted, the displaced Syrian women's experiences of loss, dishonor, rejection, and exile presented in the television news reflect on "how people are living with shame and defining and transforming who they are" (Georgis, 2013, p. 238). Having been or having chosen to be expelled from the country, are these groups of women able to offer alternative ways of thinking about the dominant social structures they inhabit?

In her book *Feeling Backward*, Heather Love (2009) argues that valuing and reclaiming the "depressing" past can be a productive act to counter this same stigma – especially if the subject incorporates society's stigmatization on themself. This notion is stemmed from Michel Foucault's philosophy in *The History of Sexuality*, which discusses the "reverse" in discourse or the ways the subaltern may take advantage of the reversibility of power. "While discourse produces power," it "also undermines and exposes it; for those alive to the fragility of power, there are many opportunities to turn situations of domination to their advantage" (Love, 2009, p. 2). Reclaiming the past through painful stories on stigma is a type of 'reverse' discourse displaced Syrian women may have adopted after beginning a new life in exile. While they remain visible and fragile to power, their recognition to their vulnerability, their reclamation of the past, and their expression of loss and rejection can be an alternative form of power.

While the 'masculinist' model of acquiring agency is implied and practiced when one attempts to overcome one's state of vulnerability, Butler (2016) contends this notion by asserting that agency is employed when vulnerability is mobilized, rather than overcome. Throughout the news reports analysis, we saw images of Syrian women crossing checkpoints and exposing themselves to harm. We also saw Syrian women working in bakeries under siege to feed civilians, acknowledging the possibility of a government raid on the bakery. We saw a Syrian woman making a public appearance through a video that was circulated across public mediums, speaking directly to the men and the communities that shamed Syrian women for being publicly shamed and for being victims of sexual violence. These acts have increased the Syrian woman's visibility, making her even more vulnerable to the power that previously stigmatized her and continues to do so.

In the next chapter, I survey the news reports in the context of vulnerability.

5. Rethinking the Relationship between Child Marriage and Failed Infrastructure during the Syrian Conflict

5.1 Introduction

Lebanon hosts the largest number of refugees per capita in the world; a small country with a population of about 4 million in addition to1.5 million Syrian displaced persons. The presence of a large number of refugees is perceived as an unjustifiable burden due to the Lebanese government's failure to provide the most basic services to its citizens. The Lebanese population has suffered for years from contaminated water, constant electrical blackouts, air pollution, an amplified garbage crisis, high unemployment, a lack of healthcare services, a lack of public transportation, a lack of funding and resources for education, a poor infrastructure, and corruption. The fragile infrastructure was barely able to serve the Lebanese population, and now faces an even greater burden in its efforts a larger number of people amid a deteriorating infrastructure (Sanyal, 2018). In 2019, the Lebanese cabinet announced that the country was on the verge of economic collapse because of its currency and debt crisis (Fanack, 2019) and this continues to be the case.

All these factors have led to a growing antagonism between the country's host and displaced communities. Aside from the fact that there is a "disproportionate attention being paid by NGOs to refugees over the host population, who [is] equally vulnerable" (Sanyal, 2018, p. 71), the Lebanese government labels the presence of Syrian refugees a security issue. The major media outlets owned by political elites continue to blame the displaced Syrian communities for the deteriorating socio-economic conditions in the country, and for disturbing the country's sectarian balance that underpins Lebanon's power-sharing system (The Economist, 2019). The narratives behind the lack of development and the threat to the delicate sectarian balance pre-dates the Syrian conflict and the arrival of Syrian refugees in Lebanon. This pattern of scapegoating 'foreign elements' initially occurred after the arrival of the Palestinian refugees to Lebanon in 1948, the year the State of Israel was created, and many Palestinians were forced to flee their homes. Subsequently, the Palestinians "were unfairly blamed for Lebanon's 15-year-long civil war, from 1975to 1990, [and were] treated as demographic threats" (Jaoude & Ayyoub, 2018).

Parallel to propagating this racist rhetoric, which fuels tensions between the two communities, the Lebanese government continues to apply different policing strategies to control the mobility of the displaced population, similar to the strategy applied to the Palestinian communities in the past. As it is not possible to deport the Syrian refugees, the state applies "ad-hoc measures to create unwelcome spaces" (Sanyal, 2018). For instance, a recent report by Human Rights Watch (2019) revealed how the Lebanese Armed Forces uses forcible measures against the displaced Syrian population as a way to pressure them to leave the country. The report showed that:

> "The Lebanese Armed Forces demolished about 20 Syrian refugee shelters on July 1, 2019, contending they did not comply with long-existing, but largely unenforced housing codes, Human Rights Watch said. The armed forces also have been forcing refugees living in semi-permanent shelters on agricultural land to dismantle their own shelters' concrete walls and roofs and replace them with less protective materials, or face army demolition of their homes. The forced shelter dismantlement under an order by the Higher Defense Council significantly reduces the adequacy of refugee housing to withstand harsh weather conditions, particularly in the Arsal region, where winters are severe."

Furthermore, another major issue the displaced communities face is the renewal of residency permits. The Lebanese General security requires each displaced person to annually pay 200 U.S dollars as a residency validation fee (Human Rights Watch, 2019). This fee increases the financial burden on families, leaving many displaced Syrians with an illegal status in the country and placing them at risk of detention should they be caught by the police.

While the displaced and host communities compete for job opportunities, scarce resources, and living space (Sanyal, 2018), the increased restrictions placed on the Syrian communities, the harassment they experience as a result of the government's policing strategies, as well as the production of chronic forms of waiting remain unjustifiable.

In Jordan, similar restrictions have been imposed on Syrian refugees as a way preventing their permanent settlement (Dorai & Piraud-Fournet, 2018). Jordan hosts the second highest share of Syrian refugees per capita after Lebanon (Reliefweb, 2019). In the recent years, the Zaatari refugee camp on the Jordanian-Syrian border has grown into a city with its own informal economy and its many different neighborhoods. Nevertheless, the standard of living remains very low, as families continue to live in tents, where very little space is available to accommodate all family members. Additionally, the birth rates in informal refugee settlements increase every year, both in Lebanon and Jordan. Syrian women and girls have limited access to sexual health and healthcare in general. They face a high risk of sexual harassment and many end up in unwanted (early) marriages as a result of harsh patriarchal norms and the families' financial hardship.

In fact, child marriage during the Syrian crisis has significantly increased since the outbreak of the war (El Arab & Sagbakken, 2018). So far, most academic and journalistic articles have approached the topic of child marriage during the Syrian conflict by recognizing it as a negative coping mechanism or as a protection measure. For instance, a study on Syrian refugee girls in Lebanon showed the various factors that contribute to forced and early marriages, including "poverty, a lack of educational opportunities, and gender-based-violence" (Bartels, 2018). Alsaba and Kapilashrami (2016) argue that the displaced Syrian women's and girls' experience of gender-based-violence are highly tied to the region's political economy. Another study by Asaf (2017) draws attention to the way mainstream news articles approach their narratives of the war with a focus on the victimization and vulnerabilities of the Syrian women. The author limits her approach by examining only the effects of governmental policies on Syrian women's vulnerabilities and does not analyze other factors that constitute their state of vulnerability.

While the studies above provide great insight into the plight of Syrian women and girls living in refugee camps, none of them has based its analysis on how the state of vulnerability is tied to a failed infrastructure. Hence, this chapter posits a lack of deeper engagement with critical theory in studying the gendered media discourses around on Syrian women and girls living in vulnerable conditions. Aiming to fill this gap, the chapter compares news reports from three leading Arab television stations and follows a critical discourse analysis in order to engage with the subjects as mediation between the concept of vulnerability and failed infrastructure.

5.2   Research Data

To discover the most frequent news headlines in the Arab television reporting that portrayed the extent of the vulnerability among the displaced Syrian
communities, specifically focused on women and girls during the Syrian conflict, I referred to the YouTube channels of three Arab television stations: *Al
Aan*, *Al Jazeera*, and *Al Arabiya*. I obtained a sample of the news reports by using the search engine of the television stations' YouTube channels. I typed in
keywords such as: Syrian women, Syrian girls, Syrian conflict, vulnerability,
child marriage, early marriage, poverty, domestic abuse, suffering, humanitarian crisis, impoverishment, infrastructure, gender-based violence, sexual
harassment, and refugee camps. The two main themes that regularly occurred
in the search process were: the increase in child marriage cases in the Lebanon
and Jordan's informal settlements, and the deterioration of refugee makeshift
shelters in Lebanon's Beqaa valley during snowstorms.

Eight news reports were collected in total. Three news reports from Dubai-
based *Al Aan*, two news reports from Qatari-owned *Al Jazeera*, and three news
reports from Saudi Arabia-owned *Al Arabiya*. The news reports were published
between January 4, 2014 and August 8, 2017. They revolved around specific
groups of Syrian women and girls: Syrian child brides living in the Zaatari
refugee camp on the Jordanian-Syrian border, in the overcrowded informal
settlements near Beirut and the Beqaa valley, which include uncontrolled and
unguided urban sites of exclusion and marginalization, as well as displaced
Syrian women and girls living in storerooms, empty garages, and one-room
apartments with their families across Lebanon. The table below provides a
detailed description of each news report analyzed.

Table 6. News reports in the context of vulnerability

Re-port	Tele-vision Station	Title of the News Report	Dura-tion	Date Published	Chap-ter Section
1	Al Aan	Marriage of Syrian Minors in Jordan	4:35	August 8, 2017	5.3.1
2	Al Arabiya	Early Marriage Causes Psychological Problems in Syrian Refugee Girls	2:28	May 29, 2014	5.3.1
3	Al Jazeera	Syrian Refugee Girl Gets Married to Pay the Rent	2:26	January 14, 2014	5.3.1
4	Al Arabiya	Child Marriage Has Doubled Among Syrian Refugees in Jordan	2:31	July 24, 2014	5.3.1
5	Al Arabiya	Marriage of 750 Syrian Girls in Jordan	2:19	September 2, 2016	5.3.1
6	Al Jazeera	Syrian Refugee Women Are Being Exploited in Lebanon	2:26	April 23. 2016	5.3.1
7	Al Aan	A Tragic Scene of a Syrian Mother that Cannot Find Food to Feed her Children	0.47	January 9, 2014	5.3.2
8	Al Aan	Displaced Syrian women in Lebanon Complain About the Absence of the Family's Breadwinner During of the Strong Snowstorm in Lebanon	2:50	January 13, 2015	5.3.2

To explore these news reports, I address the following questions:

1. How did the Arab television reporting represent child marriage cases in relationship to states of impoverishment that shape the daily experiences of the displaced Syrian communities living in informal refugee settlements?
2. Did Arab television reporting perceive child marriage as a standalone issue that remains decontextualized from the general widespread socioeconomic injustice?

Because this chapter invites us to rethink the relationship between child marriage and failed infrastructure during the recent Syrian conflict, Judith Butler's conceptualization is taken as a starting point for my analysis. With consideration to each television station's sociopolitical views, I analyze how Arab television reporting discursively generates and naturalizes images of vulnerability among Syrian women girls. Although the phenomenon of child marriage and the deterioration of shelter during the snowstorm are analyzed in separate parts, the chapter argues that these two *supposedly* separate dimensions of vulnerability during the Syrian conflict are indeed interconnected.

5.3   Analysis

In several of the news stories examined, those concerning the vulnerability of the displaced female Syrians incorporated the opinion of the expert. By attempting to appear objective, the news report supposedly used the expert's opinion to provide a "rational" coverage on the topic. In the context of this research, the experts use their status in order to make their argument credible. The expert is conceived as a third party: not a displaced Syrian woman/girl, nor a person that has a direct influence on the vulnerability of female Syrians during their daily life. Throughout the news reports, the experts allegedly gave unbiased insights into the vulnerability of different Syrian women and girls. I examine those insights in the news report analysis below.

5.3.1   Child Marriage

On August 8, 2017, a news report by *Al Aan* television featured an interview with an administrator from the Jordanian Jurists Association, the lawyer Nour Al Immam. In the interview, they discussed the issue of child marriage among Syrian refugees in Jordan. Al Immam, the expert in this news report, began the interview by stating that —according to the Jurist Association —18 was the legal minimum age of marriage for girls and boys in Jordan, a law which had existed prior to the outbreak of Syrian conflict. However, the law was modified after the arrival of Syrian refugees into the country. She asserted:

> "A waiver can be granted for underage marriages, but this waiver is only authorized under the following conditions: (1) the male spouse should not be older than the wife in not more than 15 years; (2) the female spouse should agree to this marriage;

(3) the female spouse is not allowed to abandon her education; (4) the male spouse must provide an initial mahr[1] payment before the marriage takes place."

The expert then continued to describe the laws of child marriage, by appealing to the idea that they were made for "the Syrian girls' benefit." She emphasized how the *mahr* should supposedly lessen the girl's vulnerability. Afterwards, she explained how the law guarantees the *mahr* payment, and how this mandatory payment provided by the groom to the bride is a pre-marital condition that can protect or provide support to child brides. As a response, the reporter emphasized how the child brides are living in dire conditions, as if trying to justify the family's decision to marry off their underage daughters. Although the reporter labelled these dire economic conditions as a problem which need to addressed, no mention was made to the deficiency of health care, education, food, and shelter at the Zaatari refugee camp.

Both the expert and the reporter agreed that the subjugation of women and girls is due to child marriage. Nonetheless, they perceived it as a phenomenon solely stemmed from the circumstances of war. They did not identify the states of vulnerability and impoverishment as symptoms of an unjust economic model, thus leaving the issue of class inequality unmentioned.

On May 29, 2014, a news story from *Al Arabiya* also focused on the issue of child marriage and its physiological impact on child brides. The report started with an opening statement affirming that the state of refuge is what forced Umm[2] Wael, a widowed mother, to marry off her 14-year-old daughter, who now suffers from serious physical and psychological problems. During the news report, the reporter briefly interviewed a social worker at a local NGO in the district of Akkar, Lebanon. The NGO worker said:

"Child marriage among Syrian refugees in Lebanon is partially an educational problem, especially among those coming from rural areas; and the other part of the problem is related to the material and economical needs of these refugees. In fact, child marriage did not exist in Sham (the region of Syria located east of the Mediterranean Sea) before the Syrian conflict, but it was very common in the Syrian provinces of Idlib and Dar'a."

---

1   *Mahr* means dowry in Arabic. It is ancient custom in Islamic societies that obliges the male spouse—prior to the marriage ceremony—to provide property, money, or any sort of gift to the bride.

2   *Umm* is the Arabic word for "Mother of".

Here, the NGO administrator does not mention how Lebanon has no constitutional law forbidding child marriages. Although Lebanese civil society has submitted a draft law in early 2017 that aims to ban marriage for anyone under 18, the Lebanese parliament has yet to deliberate about changing the law yet (Abirafeh & Nassif, 2018). The NGO worker made it seem as if the Syrian refugees coming from the rural areas in Syria have brought the phenomenon of child marriage with them to Lebanon. Granted, "outside of the refugee communities, nearly 6 percent of women in Lebanon between 20 to 24 years old were married before the age of 18" (Abirafeh & Nassif, 2018).

A news report by *Al Jazeera* published on January 14, 2014, reported on Hanifa, a 14-year-old girl that "agreed" to marry a 44-year-old Lebanese landlord. Hanifa's family could no longer pay the $250 monthly rent for their one-room apartment; in response, the landlord demanded Hanifa become his second wife. Hanifa and her mother were both interviewed in this news report:

> Hanifa: *"I am not obliged to marry a 44-year-old man just to survive, but I have to do it so that my family can survive. I feel that my whole life has been destroyed, because I do not want to marry him. But if I do, my family can stay in this house."*

> The News Reporter: *"This young girl says she feels exploited, but it is a sacrifice she and her family say she must make."*

> The Mother of Hanifa: *"Every mother wants to see her daughter secure and married to the man she loves. No mother wants to hurt her child, but we have no choice. If we move out of this one-room apartment, we will then need to live in a tent. My husband, who suffers from heart problems, as well my asthmatic son, wouldn't be able to survive in the cold, and my 12-year-old son, who has a job helping a mechanic, can barely make enough money to provide food for us."*

Although this news report interviewed the child bride and her mother, most of the other news reports analyzed in this chapter included no such interviews. As a result, the precariousness of Hanifa and her family remained decontextualized. The Lebanese landlord, who used his marriage proposal to a 14-year-old girl as commodity exchange between him and his tenants (Hanifa's family), was not presented as an active participant in this child marriage case. On the other hand, the mother of Hanifa was depicted as a parent who allowed the daughter to become a tradable good in times of economic hardship. In other words, she was willing to sacrifice her own daughter and "harm her," in order to keep other members of the family safe from cold and disease. No mention was made to how the Lebanese landlord—the person who holds the family's destiny in the palm of his hands—is one of the main protagonists in this oppressive phenomenon. The news report only used the word "demanded" to describe how the 44-year-old landlord chose the 14-year-old girl to become his wife. Here, the innocence of Hanifa was contrasted with the behavior of her mother and her family, who allowed such a sacrifice to take place.

The news reporter ended the report by attempting to contextualize Hanifa's story in the issue of Syrian refugees in Lebanon. The news reporter said:

"Hanifa's story is an example of how desperate many Syrian refugees have now become. The majority cannot survive without help, and humanitarian organizations cannot reach all those who need assistance. Lebanon hosts the largest number of refugees from Syria. Over one million have come here. But not all have been registered with the United Nations, which means they are not eligible for aid. Aid agencies are calling the Syrian refugee crisis a humanitarian tragedy. For Hanifa, it has been one tragedy after another. She manages to smile when she remembers the man with whom she was supposed to spend her life. But her 22-year-old cousin died fighting in Syria last year. She now feels helpless."

Although the reporter attempted to contextualize the plight of Syrian refugees in Lebanon, significant social, economic and political factors were not addressed. For instance, the absence of a law that protects girls in Lebanon from child marriage was not mentioned. The ad-hoc measures the Lebanese State applies to refugee-inhabited shelters (in order to keep these shelters with a 'temporary' status, thereby creating unwelcome living space) was also entirely ignored. The bureaucratic laws that oblige every displaced Syrian refugee to pay a large annual fee to maintain their legal status in the country to avoid imprisonment was also disregarded.

Instead, we only learn that Hanifa and her family are obliged to pay an exorbitant rent fort their one-room apartment. In the news report, the apartment appears to be in an unfinished building. The news report also failed to mention how Hanifa's marriage to the landlord will be advantageous for her, as it will grant her a 'legal' status in the country, freeing her of the obligation to pay the aforementioned annual fees. The reporter also emphasized that, because of the many Syrian refugees, the humanitarian aid agencies are not able to help everyone in the displaced community. This situation was described as a humanitarian tragedy and as a tragedy of social exclusion and misfortune. This is what Didier Fassin (2012) described as 'a drift towards sentimentalism.' The reporter used the language of compassion to the describe the social reality of the displaced community. The reporter's speech appeals to the viewer's emotions while also naturalizing the suffering of the displaced community, which he presents as a burden on the humanitarian agencies and on Lebanon.

On July 24, 2014, another news report by *Al Arabiya* reported on a thirteen-year-old girl in Jordan who was forced into an early marriage. The reporter mentioned that the child bride is now suffering from health problems due to her early pregnancy. In the news report, the child bride is interviewed for a few seconds. The unnamed child bride said:

"I never wanted this marriage, I am still young, and I wanted to continue my education. But my father didn't let me continue my education."

Afterwards, the husband of the bride is interviewed. The husband said:

"The doctor said that she might lose the baby due to her fragile body. Her medicine is so expensive to buy. She is not capable of carrying on with the pregnancy. Hopefully, she will lose the baby. We cannot afford to raise a baby."

The notion of "one less mouth to feed" occurs as rhetoric. In this circumstance, the married couple is hoping for a miscarriage because they are financially unable to raise a baby. The reporter then ends by stating that, before the outbreak of the conflict, early marriages existed in Syria.

Another news report on September 2, 2016 from *Al Arabiya* reported on 750 cases of child marriage in Jordan, asserting that many other child marriage cases are left unreported. The news reporter appears as an expert and claims that child brides try to escape the unsuitable living conditions in the refugee camps by marrying older men. Lastly, on Apr 23. 2016, a news report by *Al Jazeera* (*Arabic*) briefly declares that child marriage is becoming a protection measure among Syrian families in response to sexual harassment Syrian girls face in informal settlements across Lebanon.

Most of the experts interviewed in the news reports agreed that Syrian girls are forced into (early) marriage as a way to escape the drastic living conditions and by becoming "one less mouth to feed" in the family. Granted, poverty-stricken families living in informal settlements are the biggest demographic among the displaced Syrian populations that resort to child marriage as a coping mechanism (Halldorsson, 2017). A study conducted by UNICEF (2017) on early marriage among displaced Syrians disclosed the following:

"Among the so-called negative coping mechanisms are child marriages and child labor. Some [children] are forced to work for their family, while others are forced into early marriage for their own protection and to save money. [Early marriage] can also be a protection measure, considering the vulnerability and risk of sexual harassment girls can face in informal settlements".

The expert's justification of child marriage as a protection measure recalls Timothy Mitchell's (2002) critique of colonial expertise. The experts' speech incorporated a fixated understanding on the complexity and nature of a certain environment; the environment in this case study is the refugee camp, the slum, or any urban settlement the displaced Syrian people inhabit as shelter. Mitchell (2002) referred to these spaces as "projects," arguing that these projects have no autonomous scientific status, however "the projects themselves formed the science" (p. 37) — the science refers to the expert's knowledge.

Accordingly, Mitchell (2002) argues that human agency is acknowledged only in relationship to this "science." Mitchell's notion of human agency speaks to the words of, for example, the expert from *Al Aan*. Al Immam argued for the obligatory presence of *maher* during child marriages, as a way to protect child brides and/or lessen their state of vulnerability. Here, a technocratic and human centric perspective was applied. The expert used her scientific expertise as a lawyer to praise the efficiency of the child marriage laws implemented by Jordanian Jurists Association. She reaffirmed that the laws have a positive impact on the human power structures in child marriages. The expert did not acknowledge the subjectivity of the child brides in her "science." Furthermore, she did not acknowledge the external and internal factors that directly influence the child brides' wellbeing. She spoke on behalf of the child brides through an *objective* scientific method based on a previously conceived belief: the "correct" way child marriage should be implemented and the "suitable" socio-economic structures that should exist within this reality.

Moreover, the expert from *Al Arabiya* spoke about the early marriages among girls who come from families that have lost their breadwinner in to the context of "anxiety." In his speech, the expert mentioned an early marriage *only* becomes problematic when it is used as a tactic to overcome states of exile, insecurity, and economic hardship. In another news report by *Al Arabiya*, the expert highlighted which living conditions in the refugee settlements are considered "unsuitable" for young, unmarried girls. This indicates that the expert understands what a refugee settlement should be like or at least what makes conditions in the settlements "suitable" for an unmarried Syrian girl/woman. Nevertheless, no description was given to *in what way* the living conditions were unsuitable, and more importantly, *why* they were. The only unsuitable condition that was stated was in the reporting by *Al Jazeera*, when the news reporter mentioned the high risk of sexual harassment present in the informal settlements. However, even this reference was only directly tied to the justification of child marriages as a protection measure.

In general, the state of destitution among the displaced Syrians was never depicted as a form of injustice or economic inequality, but merely as a *tragedy* or as justification to the breadwinner's "failure" or "inability" to provide basic socio-economic necessities to the family. In other words, most of the news reports focused on the unsuitable living conditions, which are directly tied to the concept of failed infrastructure. However, none of them tackled these conditions as a serious problem that needs to be solved.

5.3.2   Failed Infrastructure

This part examines the Arab television reporting on the annual snowstorms in Lebanon. The television stations reported on the decay of the refugee settlements due to harsh weather conditions of one such storm. Mitchell (2002) argues that sometimes naturally occurring environmental events may support the construction of a widely recognized concept: human expertise and nature are separable elements. Drawing on Mitchell's ideas, I argue that *nature* (e.g., the high winds, blizzards, flooding, and freezing temperatures, snowstorms) was not responsible for the deterioration of shelters in this refugee settlement in Lebanon. I regard these snowstorms as unfortunate events that contribute to the demise of the failed infrastructure in these ad hoc settlements, and I relate it to Judith Butler's (2016) understanding of the state of vulnerability.

In the context of this case study, the naturally occurring event here is the "destructive" snowstorm. The television stations reported on it as the only cause for the collapse of the tents and makeshift shelters in the refugee camps. Moreover, the television reports showed how many displaced women and children had lost their lives or were afflicted by serious respiratory diseases caused by famine and the cold and bitter temperatures. Therefore, in this section, *changes* will refer to the collapse of shelters, as well as the spread of death and sickness, whereas *human expertise* will refer to the governmental laws on the legal status of displaced persons.

On January 9, 2014, *Al Aan* streamed a news report with the following headline: "A tragic scene of a Syrian mother who cannot find food to feed her children." The news report showed the Syrian woman standing in front of a disused garage that she and her three children used as their home in Lebanon. The reports mentioned that the mother paid $200 for rent per month. The mother, while weeping, spoke into the camera. She said:

"We don't have any food! And if we don't pay the $200 rent, the landlord will kick us out and lock our belongings inside. We ran away from war, violence, and bombs, and we came here [Lebanon] to become homeless. We are dying from hunger, from the expensive living conditions, and poverty."

The reporter tried to arouse pity among the viewers, but did not comment on what this tragic scene really portrays by showing images of destitution without any societal contextualization. In most of the news reports, the family's destitution was portrayed as an individual problem, not as a societal one. Similar to other news reports, it dealt with the state of destitution as a circumstance of war. Moreover, the reporting was not class conscious but, rather, class illiterate by portraying poverty as a personal state.

On January 13, 2015, *Al Aan* reported on a snowstorm in Lebanon. The headline read "Displaced Syrian women in Lebanon complain about the absence of the family's breadwinner during the strong snowstorm in Lebanon."

The news report directly tied the woman's suffering to the absence of the family's breadwinner and the harsh weather conditions. The reporter said:

"The snowstorm that hit Lebanon brought very difficult weather conditions, which have added yet another burden on these women. These women do not have a source of income because the breadwinner of the family went missing. In the Beqaa Valley, the tents have been destroyed from the storm. Many Syrian families are living in tents, and their situation became worse during the storm. Hunger became more severe. Help only comes from people who want to do good deeds."

The news reporter then interviewed the mother. She said:

"My oldest son has missing fingers; they are chopped off. My husband is detained. I don't have one human being in my life that can get me one Lebanese Lira so I can survive with my family."

Afterwards, the reporter interviewed a displaced Syrian woman who lives close to the family's tent, and the woman described the family's situation further. The displaced Syrian woman said:

"The tent fell onto their heads because of the snowstorm. The tent was not supported properly in the first place!"

The displaced Syrian woman makes an important remark that the reporter does not stress or even mention, which is that the tent was *initially* poorly built. The infrastructure of these settlements was built to fail or built as a temporary solution. This phenomenon of erecting poorly built shelters to accommodate displaced people is not new in Lebanon. Doraï (2010) examined the urbanization of the Palestinian settlements in Lebanon "as temporary spaces that are always subject to destruction or unilateral state intervention" (p. 7). This notion is tied to the fact that both the displaced Syrian and Palestinian populations in Lebanon were never entitled to a refugee status by the Lebanese authorities.

The Ministry of Social Affairs in Lebanon has and still considers Palestinians and Syrians in refuge as mere "visitors" in the country. The government uses the word *naziheen* (the Arabic word for displaced) to describe the legal status of the Palestinian and Syrian people (Cornish, 2018). In this context, the term "displaced" demonstrates the "transient"" quality theses visitors have in the eyes of the Lebanese authorities, who believe they are destined to leave the country and go back to their homeland once the conflict is over.

This leads us to question the clear distinction made by the UNHCR and UNRWA between "refugees in camps" and "refugees outside camps." Not all displaced Syrian families are situated in camps funded by the UNHCR. Many are settled in preexisting, informal urban and rural settlements. Not only do Palestinians live in them, but also migrant workers and their families, as well as Lebanese Shia families, who were pushed out of their towns in South Lebanon because of the Israeli-occupied southern border zone. These host communities have also built informal neighborhoods next to the settlements inhabited by the "visitors" or "migrants" (Doraï, 2010, p. 18). These realities blur the distinction between the camp and the rest of the informal urban or rural neighborhoods. While the news reports did not differentiate between women who are "camp dwellers," and women who are "urban refugees," no mention was made to how the infrastructure of the camp settlements is maintained or *not maintained*. Doraï (2010) asserts that a clear resemblance appears between a camp that survives on supposedly humanitarian assistance and the poor urban and rural areas around Lebanon that were *once a camp* and have become permanent labyrinthine slums.

For instance, a recent article by the Financial Times (2018) describes the infrastructure of Shatila camp as one of many overcrowded camp settlements in Lebanon, in which displaced Syrians have become the latest to seek shelter. Initially made for displaced Palestinians who fled to Lebanon nearly 70 years ago, Shatila was built by the displaced persons themselves during conflict. Like many of the other "camps turned slums," the Lebanese government does not exercise any power in these spaces. Consequently, basic sewage, electricity, and water system were never installed, and it is not uncommon to have leaking roofs and tangled electric wires everywhere, increasing the risk off electrocution. As there is no planning or enforcement of building regulations, the residents tend to build upwards, transforming their tents into one, two, or even up to six-storey buildings. Most of "the concrete [used for building] is made using briny [sea] water, causing the structures to corrode from the inside" (Cornish, 2018).

Moreover, while many of the residents do not exercise their legal right to get a job, many tend to work illegally. This increases their chances of being detained by the Lebanese police; hence, many take under-paid or illegal jobs inside or close to the slums in order to limit their daily commute, by working in or close to the slums, or very near the borders. This makes Shatila and other labyrinthine slums in Lebanon resemble a heterotopia (Foucault, 1984); a space that is inaccessible to the Lebanese general security forces and police and with an independently run economy, i.e., a black market, infrastructure system that was built unofficially and run by the inhabitants themselves. Lefebvre (1970) described it as a space "excluded from the political city and those who inhabit these spaces are also excluded from politics and denied a voice" (p. 17). Heterotopia is also described as a space of otherness, where the concept of time ceases to exist until a more permanent solution is found (Ramadan, 2012) — in that case the permanent solution is to go back to Syria or Palestine or to become resettled elsewhere. In a heterotopia, the temporary "visitors," who have been waiting for a long time, eventually become permanent dwellers that rely heavily on charity and aid agencies to maintain their homes. For instance, in Shatila and other slums around Lebanon, the charity organizations provide up to 1,500 U.S. dollars in aid for every household. They either pay the family to conduct the infrastructural improvements themselves or provide them with a budget to buy material goods such as doors, windows, and pipes, in order to repair the leaking rooftops, and plumb the pipes (Cornish, 2018).

Therefore, the deterioration of settlements after the snowstorm was the result of problems caused by earlier "projects," or, more specifically, the Lebanese government's project to deprive displaced populations from a permanent status in the country. This significantly affected many aspects of the refugees' lives, such as health, opportunity, infrastructure, and basic human rights. According to Mitchell (2002), social problems, including child marriage, poor living conditions, the spread of disease and sickness, and the deterioration of shelters, were deemed by government institutions to be problems of *public health* and *economic inclusion*, or what the humanitarian organizations label as "humanitarian crisis." Mitchell's (2002) writes:

> "These projects began to arrange the world as one in which science was opposed to nature and technical expertise claimed to overcome the obstacles to social improvement" (p. 51).

Indeed, programs implemented by the UNHCR and other NGOs made us perceive a world that appears as such: the snowstorm versus infrastructure, bodies versus cold and sickness, and vulnerable displaced persons versus displaced persons that oppress the vulnerable ones (e.g., child brides versus desperate mothers, or child brides versus oppressive fathers).

I detect a sense of betrayal when the news reports fail to place impoverishment in a social context. What constitutes poverty, and why has the notion of "one less mouth to feed" prevailed among numerous Syrian families, leading to the increase and dissemination of many problems such as child marriage? Why are the socio-economic necessities (elements of basic human rights) so difficult to obtain, and why are the drastic living conditions so pervasive among the displaced communities and among the certain host communities living alongside the displaced communities?

Perhaps the media images of poverty and the role of exploitation among the disadvantaged displaced Syrian community renders forms of systematic violence as the "normal" state of affairs. Žižek (2008) writes:

"When the media bombard us with those 'humanitarian crises,' which seem constantly to pop up all over the world, one should always bear in mind that a particular crisis only explodes into media visibility as the result of a complex struggle" (p.2).

Conceivably, this might reflect on how the consequences of the snowstorm on the refugee shelters are 'socially mediated,' because shelters were forcibly built to be semi-permanent and often dismantled by the Lebanese authorities in a forcible manner. In this context, it was "as if the natural [event] was repeating itself as a social catastrophe" (Žižek, 2008, p. 81). The vortex of the snowstorm disrupted the vortex of a social reality that has long been shaped by forms of systematic violence. In the context of the Syrian conflict, the systematic violence appears through the exploitation of the impoverished and the forcible measures and policing strategies applied by the Lebanese Armed Forces.

5.4   Conclusion

This chapter demonstrated that the rise of child marriage cases and the deterioration of shelters were inseparable aspects that have contributed to the vulnerability of the displaced Syrian communities. Judith Butler (2015) writes:

> "I've suggested that we rethink the relationship between the human body and infrastructure so that we might call into question … a way of thinking about the human body as a certain kind of dependency on infrastructure, understood complexity as environment, social relations, and networks of support and sustenance that cross the human and animal, and technical divides" (p. 105).

It is important to understand where the deficiency of the urbanized camps' infrastructure is rooted. Without contextualizing the social, economic, and political composition of these spaces, the viewer is left to consume mere images of dispersed tragedies: oppressed child brides and desperate mothers living vulnerably in damaged tents. Their voices became merely depictions that were created and framed by the television reporting.

The news reports were more interested in interviewing experts; as they engaged very little with the child brides. Moreover, the notion of the desperate mother sacrificing her daughter to ease the family's financial hardship was portrayed from an elitist perspective. This particular representation recalls Gayatri Spivak's (2010) essay 'Can the Subaltern Speak?' in which the female subaltern embodies a battleground for the dispute between two ideological discourses. In the context of this research, the visibility of child brides became a battlefield between patriarchal norms and an elitist media discourse. While child marriage is represented as a barbaric practice of the poor, the reporting hampered the child brides' as well as the mothers' freedom to speak.

Blame for the spread of famine, sickness, and cold was placed solely on the snowstorm and the bad weather conditions. Similarly, early marriages were blamed on the poverty-stricken families. Viewers were left wondering if it was the snowstorm that left the mother and her five children living in a broken tent, starving and suffering from the cold; was it the family's own fault for not being able to feed every one of its members; was it simply a tragedy of life; and is it even worth discussing the plight of social injustice?

Perhaps, the news reports disseminated a reflection of neo-liberal ideals that are based on the harsh idea of personal responsibility. In today's hierarchal society, who is to blame for the state of impoverishment but the impoverished themselves? We cannot be objective in our assessment of the norms that create child brides and vulnerable mothers (because of absent breadwinners) without understanding the social, political, and economical factors that reinforce these norms in the first place.

In conclusion, most of the news reports seemed sympathetic but emotionally removed, aware but uninvolved in the state of impoverishment. Without recognizing what constitutes the families' states of destitution and vulnerability, the reporting somehow produced a problematic and flawed representation of them. Poverty is not merely a tragedy. When the reporting does not tackle the issue of poverty as a prevailing political phenomenon, which stems from inequality, this results in removing poverty from politics and producing harmful implications on the subjects. Poverty appears as a socio-economic requisite in today's disparate economic model in which society necessarily produces winners and losers. In other words, the blame is never placed on the system that values the concept of the "survival of the fittest" (House 2009); rather, the poor are blamed for not being able to make ends meet.

As a final note, whether or not the Arab television reporting perceived child marriage as a destructive or hurtful measure to ensure protection and gain secure shelter, it is important to bear in mind how "the failure of infrastructure brings out the most valuable of neoliberal character traits, [which is] resilience" (Butler, 2015). In the upcoming chapter, I survey the news reports in the context of resilience.

6. Displaced Syrian Women at Work: Everyday Resilience and the Neoliberal Subject

6.1 Introduction

There is no doubt that the Syrian conflict has changed the women's role in the workforce. After years of violent conflict, many family male members have been killed and injured, others have joined the military, or gone missing. As a result, women are taking on more responsibilities and are the "breadwinners in almost one in three Syrian households" (Hilton, 2019). In fact, many Syrian women are starting to take jobs that were predominantly reserved for men. The number of female-led Syrian households has drastically increased both inside and outside of Syria. While many Syrian women have become more financially independent, this does not necessarily imply that they have acquired equal opportunity (Hilton, 2019), nor that they live in healthy and fair conditions.

In pre-conflict Syria, Syrian women were marginalized in the workforce. Although the civil and commercial codes adopted in Syria in 1949 gave women the right to have full control over their own assets and property, as well as manage their own businesses, there remain contradictory laws that permit men in Syria to forbid women from these entitlements. For instance, there is a penal code that allows the male spouse to prohibit his wife from working outside the household. This penal code heightens the social barriers imposed on women, confining them to their domestic spheres and their household and childcare duties and limiting their participation in many job sectors or their chances to seek work outside home in a broader sense. Nonetheless, there are many job sectors that are dominated by women in Syria. For example, women prform90 percent of the jobs in agriculture, but rarely receive ownership of land and machines. The education and health care sectors also have a large number of female participants, but this does not necessarily imply that there is equal pay in these sectors. Syrian men generally earn higher salaries than women (Hilton, 2019), while female coded jobs are rarely valued.

After the outbreak of the conflict, 80 percent of the Syrian population started living below the poverty line. The low employment rate left 78 percent of the young Syrian population jobless. As a result, the work opportunities for Syrian women became restricted and expanded at the same time. With the widespread of gender-based violence and the patriarchal social norms, the Syrian women's mobility became restricted. This caused a drop in their economic participation. However, a study done by the Global Gender Gap (2015) revealed that Syrian women's work did not entirely disappear, as many displaced Syrian women started taking up informal jobs that did not require a long commute. Nonetheless, the number of working women from the displaced Syrian communities remains very low. The female-led households in these communities earn less than the male-led households (Khalaf, Asad, & Tawil, 2016). For instance, in Lebanon, "Syrian women earn on average roughly half of what their male counterparts do and only a quarter of the Lebanese minimum wage" (Hilton, 2019). Hence, many Syrian families in Lebanon are not able to secure their most fundamental human needs. This has led many Syrian children to leave school and enter the child labor force, whilst many Syrian women have become targets of sexual harassment perpetrated by landlords and aid workers (Hilton, 2019).

Furthermore, the Syrian displaced communities continue to face challenges policy implications. An article by *The Tahrir Institute for Middle East Policy* (2017) revealed that:

> "Syrian refugees have experienced significant barriers to working in host countries such as Jordan, Lebanon, and Turkey due to legislations that restricts their right to work. To gain a one-year work permit in Jordan, refugees must be sponsored by an employer, and there are quotas for Syrian workers that prevent them from crowding out Jordanian laborers [...] Turkey uses similar employer-sponsored work permits, but they can only be issued after six months of residence, leaving refugees vulnerable in those first pivotal months and, as of April 2017, only four percent of refugee work permits had been issued to Syrian women."

A more recent report from *Humans Right Watch* (2019) asserted that:

> "[In Lebanon] only 1,733 Syrians have valid work permits out of the nearly one million Syrians registered with the Office of the UN High Commissioner for

Refugees. Even the number of refugees is now unknown, since the government has not allowed UNHCR to register new arrivals from Syria since 2015. Few of the refugees [...] had valid legal residency, and some had not registered with UNHCR. The high cost of getting a Lebanese sponsor for legal residency [is] a barrier to renewing their legal residency, along with General Security's annual $200 renewal fee, which is still often required even though the government has officially waived the fee."

Therefore, many Syrian women continue to face challenges because of gender inequality, patriarchal norms, and employment discrimination based on national origin and sex. The financial burdens they face to qualify as "legal" residents in the host countries leaves them more vulnerable than ever.

After contextualizing the history and current state of Syrian women in the workforce, I explore how Arab television news represented displaced Syrian women at work during the Syrian conflict. Before I start the analysis, I provide a brief description of how I obtained the news report samples for this chapter.

6.2   Research Data

I surveyed nine news stories that depict internally and externally displaced Syrian women in (post)war adjustment settings. I obtained the samples of the news reports by using the search engine of the television stations' YouTube channels. I typed in the following keywords: *Syrian women, Syrian conflict, resilience, work, cash-for-work, humanitarian aid, vocational programs, survival techniques, coping mechanisms, protection,* and *refugee camps.* During the early stages of the sample collection, I found 22 stories that included the notion of resilience: one report by *SANA*, six reports by *Al Aan*, ten reports by *Al Jazeera*, and five reports by *Al Arabiya.* Twenty of the 22 news reports showed externally displaced Syrian women participating in vocational and cash-for-work programs. Seven of the news reports displayed the participants cooking, nine of the news reports showed the participants sewing and knitting, two of the news reports displayed the participants making soap, one of the news reports presented a Syrian woman working in the hairdressing profession, and another news report showed Syrian refugee women participating in a greenhouse project.

Throughout the analysis process, I decided to re-sample the 22 news reports that I had previously collected. Nine news reports out of the 22 were selected non-randomly by using purposive sampling: one news report by *SANA*, five news reports by *Al Aan*, one news report by *Al Jazeera*, and two by *Al Arabiya*. The chosen news reports included speech acts by the participants (displaced Syrian women), the organizers of the programs (the humanitarian workers), and other social workers. Among the original number of reports, I found only one news report published by *SANA*, an Arab television station that is controlled by the Syrian regime. This news story is examined in *Section 6.5.1* and depicts an internally displaced Syrian woman working as a tailor in Syria. *Section 6.5.2* focuses on the news reports published by *Al Aan*, *Al Jazeera*, and *Al Arabiya*, which are Arab television stations with a political agenda critical of the Syrian regime.

In the selected news reports, the Arab television news mainly depicted externally displaced Syrian women working in Lebanon, Iraq, Jordan, and Turkey. These groups of women were shown participating in vocational and cash-for-work programs funded by the UN and other NGOs. Another group of displaced Syrian women are depicted participating in other types of blue-collar jobs such as sewing, plumbing, and housecleaning. The table below lists the news reports in more detail.

In the television reporting, the notion of resilience appears as part of the representations. Therefore, my analysis in this chapter focuses on the symbolic function of resilience among different groups of Syrian women, who, I argue, have been rendered as *good resilient subjects* by the Arab television news. The good resilient subject is a term I borrow from Sara Bracke (2016). It describes how resilience in neoliberal societies is perceived a desired good or a prize the subalterns seeks in their daily lives in order to recover from crises. By examining how the Arab television news depicted displaced Syrian women practicing daily forms of resilience, I explore whether the dominant discourse has reinforced this particular understanding of the notion. The questions I explore in this chapter are:

1. What is the symbolic function of resilience in the Arab television news, and what does it tell us about the representations of displaced Syrian women throughout Syrian conflict?
2. Are there any patterns of speech practiced by the displaced Syrian women that challenge the dominant media narratives?

Table 7. The news reports in the context of resilience

Re-port	Tele-vision Station	Title of the News Report	Dura-tion	Date Published	Chapter Section
1	SANA	Zeinab,a Syrian Woman who mastered the art of life	2:57	April 7, 2018	6.5.1
2	Al Jazeera	Syrian Refugee Women Participate in an Agri-cultural Project in Su-laimaniya	2:10	Decem-ber 22, 2015	6.5.2
3	Al Arabiya	The Craft of Sewing Comforts Syrian Refugee Women in Zaatari Camp	2:55	December 25, 2013	6.5.2
4	Al Aan	Syrian Refugee Women in Jordan Create Handmade Products to Support Their Families	4:37	July 8, 2014	6.5.2
5	Al Aan	Syrian Women Make and Sell Wool Clothes to Earn a Living in Turkey	3:55	May 2, 2014	6.5.2
6	Al Aan	Syrian Women Work in a Sewing Workshop in Deir Ezzor	2:53	November 13, 2013	6.5.2
7	Al Arabiya	A Syrian Refugee Lost her Husband in the War and is Now Supporting her Fam-ily	2:39	June 12, 2016	6.5.2
8	Al Aan	Syrian Refugee Women Defy Society and Work as Plumbers in Jordan	2:50	May 1, 2017	6.5.2
9	Al Aan	Syrian Women During Times of Asylum	15:24	June 9, 2015	6.5.1 & 6.5.2

6.3   Analysis

6.3.1   Talking to Good Resilient Subjects: Displaced Syrian Women Erasing the Past or Painting it through their Work

On April 7, 2018, *SANA (The Syrian Arab News Agency)* reported on Zeinab, a Syrian woman who lived through the war and siege in Eastern Ghouta. The news reporter described Zeinab:

> *"Zeinab is a war victim who refuses to surrender to the prevailing circumstances. A woman who has protected her family and prevented her family members from engaging with terrorist groups. These terrorist groups have forced Zeinab and her family to live under siege for almost 7 years."*

The news reporter did not mention the violent measures and attacks the Syrian regime has committed in Syria and no differentiation was made between ISIS members and the members of the opposition or the rebel groups. Instead, he painted these fighting groups with a single brush – insinuating that whoever opposes the Syrian regime's authority was perceived as a terrorist.

Zeinab was interviewed by the news reporter. She said:

> *"We never left the apartment; we always tried to avoid any contact with them. We lived inside a tunnel; it was all muddy. We had nothing, no food. Today we came out of the tunnel. It is as if we came out of our grave. It was as if we were living in a cave for such a long time! All we wanted was to get out! When we came out, we saw the Syrian army by our side, I could not describe this moment. Most of us started crying."*

Zeinab's speech indicates that the arrival of the Syrian army came as a shocking, yet liberating moment that somehow took away all the suffering she and her family had experienced. Her speech implied that the men of the Syrian Arab Army were the saviors of the people, who fought the terrorists that have started the war in their homeland. This indicates that Zeinab perceives the Syrian Arab Army as the warriors who saved the people from all the suffering the terrorists had inflicted on them. The news report only disclosed speech acts that depict the Syrian Arab Army as the liberator of the Syrian people and from the brutality and violence of the so-called 'terrorists.' The news reporter did not interview displaced women in areas held under the Syrian Opposition. These groups of women most likely perceived the Syrian Arab Army as the oppressor rather than the liberator.

The reporter continued to describe Zeinab's resilience throughout the war:

"Zeinab arrived 20 days ago to the temporary settlements in Herjallah, in Darayyah, Riwaaq. It was a great surprise that she has become an owner of a small business. This helped her excel in her career as a tailor. This makes her a role model to others, because of how quickly she adapted to the new living circumstances."

Zeinab said:

"I want to secure a living so I can live differently than the way I lived during the war. Sometimes I do services for free. My life is not just about securing food and drinks. My life is to also be able to work for my husband and children. Hamdellah, everything is available, and being offered. But at the end of the day, as human beings, we want to have our fingerprint, which means we want to have a purpose in life. The children are the ones who suffered the most. The children have been deprived of their right to an education. A girl must get an education. An education is the strongest weapon a girl can possess. [The terrorists] have ruined our lives. Everything could be lost, but as long as the person comes out of the situation safely, this is what matters the most."

While showing the image of a man with a missing leg, the news reporter said:

"No matter how difficult the circumstances are, the most important thing is how the person can come up with innovative ways to keep on living, to continue leading her life and developing it further. This is the current status of the Syrian woman in Syria."

The news report ends with a very intriguing statement by Zeinab, who said:

"I do not want to remember anything about the war. I want to forget everything, as if I have an eraser, and I want to erase all the bad memories of it."

It is important to point out that the news story only interviewed one person to reflect on the daily forms of resilience among Syrian women in postwar Syria. Zeinab was used as an example for how a good Syrian citizen/woman should strive to adjust to the new living circumstances. The reporter described her as a role model, connotating that whoever does not push to forget the past by putting the bad memories of the war behind them and or who does not endeavor to adjust as quickly as possible, is simply not doing things correctly. But how can war survivors rebuild what the war has taken away from them or heal the mental, emotional, and physical wounds they suffer without bringing up what actually happened, what they have been through, or what they were forced to do in order to survive? Perhaps, Zeinab's longing to erase the past demonstrates her desire to live a normal life. In other words, her desire to erase the painful memories of the past can be seen as wishful thinking. She wishes to move past the dire circumstances of the temporary settlements in Herjallah and the traumatic circumstances she experienced when she was under siege in Eastern Ghouta.

The news report from *SANA* ends with a glimpse of a man with a missing leg. The man is not interviewed in the news story, and, ironically, one significant part of Zeinab speech includes the following statement: '*Everything can be lost, but as long as the person comes out of the situation safely, this is what matters the most.*' Clearly, this man is one of many who survived the war. He is still alive, flesh and bones; yet the viewer does not see what shapes this man's daily life. How did his life change after he lost part of his body? From what emotional distress and trauma does he suffer, and how does this affect him and his loved ones, if any are left?

On a similar note, I was not able to find any news reports that spoke about the injured civilians during the war. It is as if *SANA*, the state-owned television station, is pushing Syrian society to go into a state of amnesia. It is asking the people of Syria to praise and applaud the Syrian Arab Army for getting rid of all the 'terrorists,' with the motive to censor any discussions about the aftermath and the human causalities of the war. [1] Lastly, it is important to point out how the news report conveniently chose Zeinab, a female tailor who appears to be healthy.

A news report by Al Aan published on June 7, 2015 interviewed Fida Al-Waer, a displaced Syria woman who started painting images of the Syrian war while in exile in Lebanon. She explained in the interview how she resorted to painting as a coping mechanism. Most of her paintings depict the struggles she and her family underwent during the war, her personal experience throughout the war in Syria, and finding exile in Tripoli, Lebanon, together with her mother and sisters.

In the interview, Fida said:

"*I decided to resort to painting because I love painting, and it is also a way for me to express myself and remember my two brothers, who both were killed by the Syrian*

---

1   The severely (physically as well as psychologically) injured Syrians, and their struggles or abilities to adjust to postwar adjustment settings

regime, and became martyrs. I also want to present a different picture of the cir-
cumstances of the asylum we are living in. In my paintings, I paint different people
and about the events that I experienced during the Syrian uprising. For instance, the
image of the Syrian woman working on farms. I believe when the displaced Syrian
woman works on the fields in Lebanon, she acquires a source of security for her, her
family, especially since many husbands went missing or have a hard time finding a
source of income while in exile."

She continued by talking about her own journey of refuge: how she became internally displaced in Syria, how her home in Homs was burned by the Syrian regime forces, and how her family members were burned alive and killed in front of her eyes by the Syrian Arab Army. She explained how the main subject she illustrates in her art is the Syrian woman:

"I believe that women are made to create men. Women are able to face any struggles
in life. Even if she lost everything, she could start again from zero and rebuild her
life again and again. As long as she believes in herself and her dreams, a woman can
do anything."

Fida then described the main themes she depicts in her paintings. She said:

"My paintings usually depict the great war crimes that are committed in Syria and
outside of Syria against the Syrian people. My main subjects are Syrian women and
children, and the martyrs.[2] The working Syrian women, the Syrian women in exile,
and the children who became orphans, who became homeless, and who lost their
chances to pursue an education. Most of my art is non-fiction, it depicts the plight
of the Syrian people."

Afterwards, she explained why she dislikes the term 'refugee.' She said:

"I hate the word refugee. We are only refugees to our God and not to society. The
word exile or refuge is being exploited by many people in order to give Syrian women
a bad reputation. Others use this word to sympathize with the Syrian people. But
I dislike this word. When the Syrian woman left her home and her country, many
tried to take advantage her. The Syrian woman has suffered a lot, and she is still suf-
fering. The Syrian woman is in pain. Many Syrian women continue to suffer psycho-
logically. This pain comes from all the incidents and events they witnessed through-
out the war and all the experiences they lived through. Nevertheless, I believe the

---

2   In this context, Martyrs refer to anyone who died fighting against the Syrian regime
     during the war.

Syrian woman is majestic and strong, and she will continue to be strong no matter what. However, we cannot deny how many people tried to exploit the vulnerable Syrian woman. And at some point, the Syrian woman was standing alone, and no one was supporting her."

In contrast to Zeinab, Fida wants to illustrate and paint the past instead of erase it. Evidently, the content chosen for this news report was highly dependent on the media ownership of the television station. *Al Aan*, a pan-Arab television station known for its content on women's empowerment–including programs that highlight aspects of Arab women's lives–gave Fida visibility and enabled her show Arab audiences her own way of depicting war memories through painting; painting was a way for Fida to glance back at the painful past.

It is also important to acknowledge how Fida's speech resembles the story of the defeated opposition in Syria; how they fell as victims of the regime brutality. The story of the defeated opposition was widely adopted by *Al Aan* throughout its reporting on the Syrian conflict. Therefore, if we try to compare the representations of Zeinab and Fida, one may see their visibility as opposite sides of the same coin – their visibilities were framed in accordance with the partisan inclinations of the television stations that interviewed them. For instance, when Zeinab, a tailer living in regime-controlled areas, articulated her longing to forget the past, her speech became part of an ambiguous public sphere "where the truth that is trumpeted cannot be publicly questioned but only mimicked or tolerated" (Wedeen 1999; Haugbolle 2008, p. 263), it becomes clear how Zeinab's articulated desire also intrinsically aligns with regime's dominant narrative.

On the other hand, Fida, a Syrian woman in exile who is clearly politically aligned with the Syrian opposition, attempts to use her paintings "to appropriate the violence, to which [the opposition] was subjected, and to turn it against their oppressors and, in so doing, to challenge the state narrative" (Haugbolle, 2008, p. 262). Her speech is clearly aligned with *Al Aan*'s sociopolitical views on the Syrian conflict. While *SANA* remains a local television station that strictly serves as a mouthpiece to the Syrian regime, *Al Aan* here appears as a pan-Arab television station that produces content "to exemplify a new politics of truth-telling, which has emerged across the Middle East in conjunction with the expansion of national and transnational public spheres since the 1990s" (Makdisi & Silverstein, 2006; from Haugbolle, 2008, p. 262). Both *SANA* and *Al Aan*, two stations with opposing political views, similarly tried to represent Zeinab and Fida respectively as *the good resilient subject*. For instance, *SANA* showed how Zeinab tried to make her daily life as normal as possible by longing to erase the past. Meanwhile, *Al Aan* exposed how Fida copes in exile by painting and retelling the opposition's story through her art.

In the upcoming section, I expand the discussion on *the good resilient subject* by analyzing news reports that represented displaced Syrian women taking part of vocational and cash-for-work programs,[3] and other displaced Syrian women who started their own initiatives to secure an income or are working in the informal labor market in Syria's neighboring countries.

6.3.2 Training the Good Resilient Subject: A Survey of News Reports on Displaced Syrian Women Participating in Vocational and Cash-for-Work Programs and other blue-collar Jobs

Nearly half of Syria's population has been displaced externally during the recent conflict. Many displaced Syrian communities in Syria's neighboring countries are living in informal settlements, known as refugee camps or in other urban settings. Many displaced families do not have a reliable source of income to provide food and shelter or other basic needs (UNHCR, 2018). In Jordan, Turkey, Iraq, and Lebanon, many local and international NGOs have set up programs that help displaced Syrians build a "skill, which allows them to generate income by providing a service or by creating a product" (Abou-Raad, 2018). These programs are usually called vocational programs, cash-for-work programs, skill-building programs, or income-generating programs. Most of these programs usually target women and are tailored to create opportunities for their economic and personal development.

In the context of Syria, the normative gender division of labor includes occupations such as sewing, knitting, cooking, soapmaking, etc. The Arab television news reported regularly on displaced Syrian women working in these occupations. Most of these occupations are promoted by the vocational and cash-for-work programs funded and organized by UNHCR and other NGOs. Only one news report reported on an agricultural project funded by the UN-

---

3   These are programs organized and funded by humanitarian organizations for the purpose of providing financial support to externally displaced Syrian women during the conflict.

HCR that is tailored to displaced Syrian women in Iraq. I survey the news reports below.

On December 22, 2015, *Al Jazeera* published a news report on 30 or more Syrian refugee women who participated in a greenhouse project created by the UNHCR in the Sulaimaniyah Camp, part of the Kurdistan Region of Iraq. The news report began with an opening statement:

> "Just like they take care of their children and nurture them, Umm Abed does the same with her seedlings. Um Abed is Syrian-Kurdish refugee women, and she is a widow and a mother of four."

Umm Abed is interviewed. She said:

> "My husband has been dead for many years now. I have young children. We have no one to support us. This is the reason why I decided to participate in this project. At first, we grew cucumbers, and it was a success. I earned almost 1,000 U.S dollars. And now we are planting for the winter, and we are waiting for the results."

In the news report, an unnamed UNHCR social worker stated that the aim of the project was to enable Syrian women to become financially independent and empower them while living in exile. During the interview, the social worker said:

> "This program is made especially for widows, for women who have no income or provider, or for those who have special conditions such as an ill (unemployed) husband. This program is tailored for women in order to strengthen their integration in the host country, to help them engage with the community, and to be help them become more financially independent so they can support their families."

The news reporter ended the report with the following statement:

> "This program has great significance; it will help enhance the social and psychological conditions of these Syrian refugee women."

Agriculture is a (non)domestic occupation, where men and women work alongside each other in farming and raising livestock. In fact, 22% of Syria's economy was made up of the agriculture sector, and Syrian women actively participated in such work before the outbreak of the conflict (Mahamid, 2013). Therefore, if these groups of Syrian women were able to return to their previous occupation while in exile, this could eliminate or lessen the problem of *liminality* that many displaced persons face when they try to acquire jobs in the host countries.

I was only able to find one news report on displaced Syrian women in agricultural sector; the remaining seven news reports in this subsection portray displaced Syrian women participating in more traditional occupations such as sewing, knitting, etc.

On December 25, 2013, *Al Arabiyah* reported on a program organized by the UNHCR that aims at promoting gender equality among Syrian refugees in the Zaatari camp in Jordan. The opening statement in the news story declared the following:

> *"The program supports more than 700 Syrian female refugees in the Zaatari camp to overcome their state of exile. After these women have lost all their rights and properties in their home country, the program helps them support themselves financially through the craft of sewing."*

A woman is shown sewing a white dress while the reporter remarks:

> *"She is sewing the dress of freedom."*

The reporter hints that sewing might bring this woman some form of emancipation. Afterwards, the woman described her experience:

> *"This occupation gave me serenity and inner peace."*

On July 8, 2014, *Al Aan* published a news report that addressed the reason why there is an urgent need for displaced Syrian women in Jordan to seek work and generate income. The news report starts by criticizing the UNHCR aid programs that help displaced Syrian families living in dire conditions with their household expenses. The reporter claimed that the UNHCR does not provide enough financial support to refugees; therefore, many displaced Syrian women need to find a different source of income. Rima Flayhani, a female Syrian writer and activist is interviewed as an expert on the subject. Flayhani said:

> *"During this war, the men of the family went missing; therefore, women are now pushed to work. Of course, we are in favor of seeing women in the workforce; I am not saying it is a bad thing to see women seek jobs outside their homes. However, the job the Syrian women seeks should be an efficient type of work, that will bring her enough income to support her family. The workforce here in Jordan is not very open or available for Syrian refugees. Most of the Syrian women who work here are underpaid."*

The reporter interrupted Flayhani to ask the following:

> "Can we solve the plight of displaced Syrian women by creating small projects, such as family-based projects that will help Syrian women to support themselves, without relying on any other sources of aid?"

Flayhani responded:

> "The UNHCR and other NGOs do not provide such programs; however, they provide basic courses for women to learn skills such as sewing, knitting, soap-making etc. We need such programs that support the small family projects which women create after they take the classes with the UNHCR. The first important step is to create governmental laws that grant displaced Syrian women the right to lead such projects, as well as receive aid for financing the projects."

The narrative exposed how certain governmental laws in Jordan prohibit refugees and displaced communities from independently leading their own projects for economic and personal development. Flayhani asserted that a step needs to be taken in order to achieve the possibility of family-based projects.

On May 2, 2014, another news report from *Al Aan* was published with the following headline: *Displaced Syrian women are now forced to find work, due to the high living expenses in Turkey*. The news reporter said:

> "In the small town of Rihaniyah, on the Turkish-Syrian border, a number of displaced Syrian women spend their time knitting as a way to secure income for their families. Although they spend a lot of time working, they are not able to forget the times of war they have experienced in their home country, Syria."

The reporter alluded to the fact that many women are finding it difficult to put the painful past behind them. The news report showed a group of Syrian women sewing together, and the reporter commented:

> "In the factory where they work, they produce a lot of different clothing items made from wool. Ninety displaced Syrian women work in this factory. They earn around 50 or 60 U.S dollars per month. It is a very small amount of money, but it is covers small expenses such as the electricity bill or buys them bread and other basic groceries for the household and satisfies their hunger."

Marwa Al Sayed, the manager of the women's knitting workshop, was also interviewed. Al Sayed said:

"The amount of money they receive monthly is not a big amount; it is as valuable as one or two of the food-supply boxes they receive from the NGOs. But the advantage of this work is that the Syrian woman is working in her own household, and she is keeping her dignity, and at the same time she is helping her family."

The manager of the women's knitting workshop stressed on the concept of dignity, particularly the dignity of Syrian women. Dignity, particularly the dignity of a displaced women, is a frequently cited by humanitarian workers and initiatives. "Aid programs and policies rarely identify exactly what [dignity] is, or how they are trying to support" (Grandi, Mansour & Holloway, 2018, p.1). However, on a general note, maintaining the dignity of displaced communities is usually invoked through providing food and required non-food items. As for the dignity of women and girls, this issue is usually tied to protecting them from incidents of sexual and gender-based violence (Makki, 2014).

On November 13, 2013, another news story by *Al Aan* reported on a workspace used to teach sewing and other similar skills in the eastern Syrian town, Deir Ez-Zor, which is under the Free Syrian Army control. The story showed Syrian women attending sewing and hairdressing classes. The news reporter said:

"These women hope to take those skills and turn them into a source of income. The classes are funded and organized by a local NGO, called Hayat… In Syria everyone fights their battle, the way it is applicable or suitable for them."

Similarly, on June 12, 2016, *Al Arabiya* showed Umm Ahmad, a single Syrian mother fighting her own battle. A displaced Syrian mother, who lost her husband at the beginning of the war, Umm Ahmad fled with her 3 children to Hatay, Turkey. While she was being interviewed, she spoke about how her husband was burnt to death in one of the Syrian regime prisons. Afterwards, she described her daily life as a displaced single mother in Turkey and how the war led her daughter to abandon her education and work alongside her mother in order to make a living. The reporter mentioned that most of the displaced Syrians children and young adults have lost their right to an education during the war. Umm Ahmad was interviewed. She said:

"At first, my daughter cried a lot because she left school. But then she convinced herself it is okay because she wanted to help me with the expenses. And she came and she started working with me here. This is where I knit and sew for living. She

used to be one of the most successful students in class, and now she came here, and she is serving tea and coffee to the customers."

Fatin, the daughter of Umm Ahmad was also interviewed. Fatin said:

"I wish I could go back to school, but we are forced to work in order to pay for the expenses in our new home here in Turkey. I need to help my mother pay the rent, buy food, etc. I used to be at the top of my class, but I had to leave school in order to help my mother with the expenses."

The news reporter ended the story by mentioning how Umm Ahmad and her children feel orphaned and lonely in Hatay, Turkey, especially after they lost their father and husband. The news reporter said:

"This is why Umm Ahmad insists on staying in Hatay. She and her family will be the first people to return to Syria once the war is over."

The news reporter indicated that going back to Syria was the only solution for Umm Ahmad and her family. Another important aspect that appears in the news report is how her daughter, Fatin, was deprived of her right for an education.

Granted, continuing one's education in Turkey as a displaced Syrian is especially difficult because of the language barrier and the financial expenses displaced Syrians have to keep their children in school. Education in Turkey is provided in the Turkish language; in other neighboring countries, such as Lebanon and Jordan, the official language is Arabic, the official language of Syria. Nonetheless, even in countries where Arabic is the official language, 75% of Syrian children do not attend school (Succar, 2014). A study by a local NGO in Lebanon, *Jusoor*, claimed that "if the Syrian refugee population were a country, that country would have the lowest school enrollment rate in the world" (Succar, 2014).

On a similar note, NGO-based projects have founded schools– such as *Kayany* Schools in Lebanon– for Syrian refugee children. However, many children and young girls do not attend school because of harsh patriarchal norms as well as financial struggles. Some are pushed into child marriage (as discussed in Chapter 5), and others are pushed into blue-collar jobs (Succar, 2014). These jobs are usually gender normative types of work, which are considered socially 'appropriate' for women, such as serving tea and coffee, cleaning homes, hairdressing, embroidery, knitting, sewing, cooking, soap-making, etc.

A news report published by *Al Aan* on May 1, 2017 exposed how Syrian women in Jordan have taken up a less traditional gender normative occupation such as plumbing. The headline read "Syrian Refugee Women in Jordan Defy Society and Work as Plumbers." The news reporter said:

> "Plumbing is no longer an occupation only for makes. Syrian refugee women are starting to enter this occupation. They have established an entire women's center where plumbing services are provided to households by Syrian refugee women. This has broken a long-standing social taboo in a conservative society."

The news report showed the woman behind this project. The news reporter said:

> "This is the woman who broke all the social taboos and has established a craftsman center specializing in plumbing. This is considered the first career center for women who want to pursue plumbing as an occupation. Plumbing is the only source of income these women have, especially that they are female refugees who have fled the war in Syria, and as a result they found themselves [in Jordan] without any income or provider."

Safaa Sukariyah, the Syrian woman behind the creation of the Women's Plumbing Center is interviewed. Sukariyah said:

> "All the responsibilities fell on my head. It has been five years since we fled the war. We are still facing the same difficulties. I have many responsibilities. I am responsible for my children. I also have responsibilities to take care of my husband. These are not easy responsibilities. I do not consider this occupation as something Ayyb.[4] I really love this occupation, it comes natural to me, and I have an emotional connection to it."

The news reporter continued describing the female plumber, while the camera showed Sukariyah working. The reporter said:

> "These soft hands have created a firm relationship with these harsh tools. A very contradictory relationship between the two. This has created a skillful type of work. Previously, the ones who used to disassemble and assemble the pipes were only men, and now these women have taken up those jobs."

---

4   *Ayyb* / عيب is an Arabic word that refers to something viewed as a social taboo in Arab Muslim societies.

It is clear how the reporter's speech tried to emphasize the femininity of the female plumber. He used the adjective 'soft' to describe their hands, while emphasizing how plumbing is a strictly 'masculine' occupation in the Arab world.

Afterwards, the news reporter interviewed a man named Kassem Al Mansouri, who is one of the Safaa Sukariyah's customers. Al Mansouri said:

> "In any wise society, the man should believe that a woman is a life partner. These women are challenging social taboos (Thakafat Al Ayyb). This occupation was traditionally and strictly reserved for men. These women challenged themselves, they challenged society, and turned this occupation to a source of income, and they proved their existence and eligibility. They are indeed very special."

The news reporter ended the story by saying:

> "The revolution in Syria has forced them to flee and leave their home. They are now leading another revolution; they are challenging the image of a traditional Syrian woman. They are now setting a new example with a different image, the image of a Syrian woman who is a partner and a participant in building a better society and new cultures."

The news report portrayed groups of displaced Syrian women as if they were defying traditional general norms by taking matters into their own hands. However, the reporting lacked context. Since 2014, Jordan has faced a grave water shortage crisis. Duromg the period covered here, most households in Jordan suffered from pipe leakages. Thus, plumbers were in high demand in the country. To target the problem, the Jordanian Hashemite Fund for Human Development (JOHUD), the Jordan's Ministry of Water and Irrigation, the Germany Agency for International Cooperation (GIZ), and the German Federal Ministry for Economic Cooperation and Development (BMZ) cooperated to develop the *Water Wise Women* program in 2014. As part of the program, more than 600 Syrian women were trained to enter this profession, one that was traditionally preserved for men (Al Hayari, 2017).

For instance, an article from *apolitico.co* on the *Water Wise Woman* program mentions that a main reason program focused on training female plumbers was because of traditional cultural norms. In traditional Arab society, a male plumber can enter a household only when a male family member is present. This may delay the repair of leaks, as female-led households might find it challenging to find a male family member to be present (Al Hayari, 2017). Therefore, the need for female plumbers in female-led households also stemmed from the societal norm of not allowing a male stranger into a household without a male family member present. This specific norm is sometimes related to security. There is a common societal understanding in Arab Muslim cultures that a male stranger entering a household might pose a threat to widows, single women, girls, and single in general if a male figure is not present. In other instances, this practice of not allowing a male stranger into one's home is related to concepts of honor and shaming. In the Arab world, these two concepts traditionally forbid women from having contact with male strangers in private spaces. Therefore, it is safe to assume that the female plumbers usually were from female-led households, rather than male-led households. The project description of the *Water Wise Women* project reads: "After training, the women are then able to fix leaks in their own homes as well as in [those of] their female neighbors' houses" (Al Hayari, 2017).

Therefore, the need for more female plumbers to work in w female-led households may infer that even though there are women entering the plumbing sector, gender segregation in the work place still takes place. Many displaced Syrian women may prefer women-only working environments because of issues related to sexual harassment, taboos, and norms. Therefore, I disagree with the news reporter regarding his claim that the group of female plumbers are defying society and breaking social taboos. I do, however, believe that their initiative to enter predominantly male occupation in order to become the family's breadwinner is a form of everyday resilience. Moreover, their perseverance to prevail and find a source of income by learning a new skill in a foreign country may perhaps also be perceived as a way to resistance socioeconomic oppression and inequality.

The news report's speech somehow idealized their plumbing work and labelled it as challenge to social norms and taboos. Granted, the issue of sexual harassment remains an issue displaced Syrian women face in the workforce. Entering the plumbing sector surely does not solve this problem; rather, it avoids it, especially when the female plumbers are only working in female-led households.

The issue of sexual harassment among Syrian refugee women in the informal labor market was addressed in the new report surveyed in *Section 6.5.1*, in which the painter Fida was interviewed. In the same news report (published by *Al Aan* on June 7, 2015), Ni'maa Al-Ahmad, a Syrian mother in Lebanon living in the countryside outside the Syrian city of Hama was interviewed. Ni'maa sought refuge in Lebanon with her children after her husband was killed by the Syrian regime. The news reporter stated that the regime threw his body in front of his home's doorstep, as a kind of revenge. Ni'maa now cleans homes for living in order to support her children. She spoke about her experience as a single mother in Lebanon. Ni'maa said:

> "I am not ashamed that I clean homes for living. I am not shy to admit that I clean people's homes. I do not see 'Ayyb[5] in working as a housecleaner, because I am working and exhausting myself for the sake of my children, and not for some stranger. I prefer to have little money for my children instead of begging people for help. I work all day every day, and I only come back home late at night, but at least I come back home with money that I earned with honor and dignity, and I use it to feed my children. And one day, when my children are all grown up, they will be proud of their mother and that she worked hard and earned her living as a housecleaner. I will never be ashamed about it."

Ni'maa continued to address a sexual harassment incident she experienced at work, claiming that sometimes her employers take advantage of the fact that she is a single mother with a refugee status, thereby abusing her state of vulnerability. Ni'maa said:

> "I will work day and night, and it does not matter how much money I earn. I have been exposed to it many times.[6] And when I do not give them what they want, they yell at me, and sometimes beat me up. I have escaped the house many times while cleaning. I jump from the balcony or the window or run away. One time, they grabbed my things and my documents, and wanted to confiscate them because I did not give them what they wanted. And afterwards, they accused me of theft. But thank God, I never thought of doing anything Haram.[7] I even went to the police and reported the incident. And the police backed me up Hamdillah.[8] And I was able to get my documents back without letting him touch one hair on my body."

She also mentioned that she was not ashamed to appear on TV to tell her story, asserting that she was proud to be able to withstand the difficult conditions she lived in while in exile in Lebanon.

There are two significant aspects that appear in this news report: the recognition of Nimaa's state of vulnerability and her performative resistance. Firstly, as opposed to the groups of displaced Syrian women depicted taking

---

5   'Ayyb, is an Arabic word that refers to an act that is considered a social taboo.

6   It, in this context, refers to sexual harassment.

7   Haram is an Arabic term for 'forbidden'.

8   Hamdillah, is the Arabic term for 'Thank you, God'.

part of vocational and cash-for-work programs, Ni'maa's visibility was not framed in a humanitarian discourse. The absence of the humanitarian discourse in the reporting made her vulnerability more evident. Secondly, Ni'maa practiced *performative resistance* (Butler, 1997) through her speech. She spoke openly about how vulnerable she was a single mother living in exile alongside her children. Moreover, Ni'maa called out the issue of sexual harassment by speaking about her very own personal experience with it. Although she uses the word *it* to refer to the sexual harassment or "Al Taharrush Al Jinsi التحرش الجنسي" in Arabic, it is still clear to what she was referring. In the book *Excitable Speech*, Butler (1997) explains how "the subject can protest her situation and "talk back" to socially constructed authorities." This appears to be the case with Ni'maa: When society interpellated her and situated her in a subordinate position, she attempted to talk back and resist her employer's attempt to abuse her. Thus, the act of calling out sexual harassment is a form of resistance, particularly when Ni'maa expresses her refusal to being abused and being called into a subordinate position.

6.4   The Notion of Resilience in a Humanitarian Discourse

In this section, I continue to reflect on the news reports surveyed above. I contextualize the findings from the news stories that adopted a humanitarian discourse; namely the news reports on the vocational and cash-for-work programs.

The news reports analyzed in this chapter described the skills taught and promoted by the UNHCR and other NGOs in the vocational and cash-for-work programs and how they are used as tools that empower women and girls in exile. The findings showed that most of these programs offered gender normative types of occupations that teach the participants quick solutions for securing an income. Throughout the reporting, only one displaced Syrian woman was able to articulate her state of vulnerability in her own words: Ni'maa, the single mother who cleans houses to make ends meet. The rest of the news reports either reinforced the Syrian regimes' sociopolitical agenda, or the Syrian opposition's political narrative[9].The displaced Syrian women's state of vulnerability was highlighted under the umbrella of humanitarian

---

9   For example, Zeinab, the internally displaced Syrian woman, wanted to erase the past and get one with her daily life. Fida, the externally displaced Syrian women in Tripo-

discourse, as the news reports aimed at promoting the desirable outcomes of the programs and the benefits the participants receive.

The television reporting also proposed that programs help the participants become more self-reliant, as a temporary solution to make ends meet while living in exile. In this context, these 'temporary solutions' exemplify a form of self-resilience as a way "to develop strategies in order to adjust to difficulties" or to find "a way to 'get on' with daily life without acquiescing to the political, economic or social situation that you are in" (Bourbeau and Ryan, 2017, p. 9). This makes those vocational and cash-for-work programs resilience-building programs as well. In this setting, the idea of training displaced Syrian women to acquire and practice everyday resilience becomes quite arresting, because resilience is something people naturally do to survive. Resilience is a trait that the impoverished already acquired when they realized that resilience was the only way to survive. Thus, when the humanitarian aid programs claim to teach the impoverished the practice of resilience, aren't these aid programs borrowing the traits of the poor, as they provide a 'platform' to train and materialize the hitherto inherited skill among the participants?

Bracke (2016) explains how resilience is becoming 'a desired good' in today's neoliberal economies. She writes:

> "I understand this power to operate in complex manners, not merely as programs imposed on unsuspecting individuals, although that is surely one of the ways in which the impact of resilience in our world is felt, but also as a desired good, or the prize that many of us have come to set our eyes on as we seek to navigate the constraints and possibilities of our daily lives. The way in which resilience permeates popular culture is truly striking, finding a notable expression in the popularization of psychological theories that revolve around the notion of the "resilient self :" *Build Your Resilience: Teach Yourself How to Survive and Thrive in any Situation; Resilience: Bounce Back from Whatever Life Throws at You, or The Power of Resilience: Achieving Balance, Confidence, and Personal Strength in Your Life* are just a few titles of literally thousands of recent books that offer visions on becoming resilient as well as exercises and techniques to do so" (p. 53).

Granted, this prize or desired good is being resonated beyond popular culture and has become the main goal for most of the humanitarian projects target-

---

li, Lebanon, spoke about her experiences during the conflict and conveyed the Syrian Opposition's dominant narrative in her art.

ing displaced Syrian women. These programs individualize solutions to displaced persons' problem that have social and political origins. These projects are usually called 'resilience-building programs in response to crisis.' For instance, one of the many integrated UNDP projects in the Middle East region is called *Building Resilience*. The slogan for the project is "Empowered Lives, Resilient Nations" (UNDP, 2019). This project is a regional refugee and resilience plan for Syria, Lebanon, Iraq Turkey, Jordan, and Egypt, and it aims to robustly invest in the resilience of people, communities, and institutional systems affected by crisis. Another example of a resilience-building program is PRESERVE, a project aimed to "develop localized solutions to a lack of participation of women in local economic governance" (UN Career, 2019). The ultimate outcome of this project is to enhance resilience among displaced and conflict-affected women in Syria (UN Career, 2019).

What I find problematic here is not the direct product the UN and other humanitarian projects try to offer–they are offering a job opportunity– but the function they perform in a societal system governed by neoliberal ideals. As previously mentioned, the indirect product these programs are tailored to promote is self-resilience. I do not perceive self-resilience as something negative per se, especially given the fact that, in precarious times, resilience becomes the most direct source of strength to cope with stress and hardship. The issue I wish to raise, rather, is how self-resilience is perceived as the only long-lasting solution to the plight of the displaced Syrian women or the subaltern subject in general. In the context of this case study, the subaltern is the displaced Syrian communities that have lost all their belongings and their sense of belonging and are currently living in poverty. In other contexts, the subaltern subject is today's overworked employee who juggles "several insecure and part-time jobs" and has to "overcome life's hurdles, such as facing retirement without a pension and bounce back from whatever life throws at them, whether it is cuts to benefits, wage freezes, or global economic meltdown" (Bracke 2016, p.61); the neoliberal subject here is an entrepreneurial self.

Within this frame of reference, the question of security becomes an obvious one, as security is a significant part of the problem, particularly when discussing the plight of the displaced Syrian women. Is their plight not related to economic security rather than economic aid? Is it not a question of protection from gender-based violence or safety from harsh weather conditions (as discussed in Chapter 5)? And when we try to observe the humanitarian response to such so-called 'emergencies' or 'disasters,' do the humanitarian organizations and media reportages on the crises (often) not slap us with the term resilience?

Bracke (2016) stated that self-resilience alludes to a specific bio-political power at work, where the act of resilience "produces a new regime of subjectivity, that is to say, new resilient subjects" (p. 63). When adding the word 'self' to the term resilience, the term starts acquiring a meaning beyond the dictionary definition of "rebounding; recoiling; returning to the original position" (The Oxford English Dictionary 2019). The term self-resilience becomes part of wider neoliberal discourse, in which the good subjects are represented. The good subjects, according to Neocleous (2007), are individuals who constantly respond to any situation in resilient ways. Their ability to bounce back, hence, becomes the norm, and their attempt to exercise their agency becomes highly tied to their everyday forms of resilience. In this context, self-resilience starts branding the displaced Syrian women's survival, "making it an object of fascination for" the television viewers (Mourad, 2020). Bracke (2016) writes:

> "In a neoliberal political economy, resilience has become part of the moral code: the good subjects of neoliberal times are the ones who are able to act, to exercise their agency, in resilient ways. Good subjects [...] will survive and thrive in any situation, they will achieve balance" (p. 61).

Perhaps Bracke's words echo the manner SANA's news report represented Zeinab as the good resilient subject, the role model every Syrian citizen and every Syrian woman should look to when striving to adjust to any new (difficult) circumstances. It is a role model for all resilient subjects that pushes them to forget the past, puts the bad memories of the war behind them, and to adjust as quickly as possible. A broader example is how neoliberal ideals are reestablished through the training of the self: "a training to withstand whatever crisis capital undergoes and whatever political measures the state carries out to save it" (Bracke, 2016, p. 61).

When these so-called cash-for-work and vocational programs train their participants on 'how to be self-resilient,' is resilience here not being turned away from vulnerability? Don't these projects somehow represent the process of transforming resilience to a property of the neoliberal system, one that relies on the subject's resilience to remain 'operable'? In this setting, resilience becomes the only source of security inhabited by the subjects, as it starts operating as "a new security apparatus" (Bracke, 2016). Sara Mourad (2020) writes:

"Resilience is a marketing stunt for a political and economic system that runs on crises, that manufactures crises in order to sustain itself. Resilience celebrates survival at the expense of justice. It is the rhetorical and symbolic symptom of the normalization of injustice."

6.5   Conclusion

Most of the news reports surveyed in this chapter included a humanitarian discourse that promoted the advantages of the vocational and cash-for-work programs, such as giving displaced Syrian women the opportunity to work and secure an income. At the same time, these news reports idealized the participation of the displaced Syrian women in these humanitarian programs, without highlighting the factors that shape their state of vulnerability.

Although the humanitarian programs may enable many displaced Syrian women to become the family's breadwinner, it is important to point out that none of the news reports mentioned how some of these programs require the female participants to provide–because of traditional patriarchal norms–their husbands' approval to participate (Abou-Raad, 2018). Moreover, the reality on the ground seems to show that nothing is being done to support the husbands who remain unemployed at home. Syrian refugee men may feel left out because there are very few, if any, programs tailored to them and their need to find a job. In the meantime, Syrian women participating in the programs are learning about their rights and are provided with vocational trainings to generate an income. This might change the family structures of the displaced Syrian communities. The roles of women may be transformed from solely a housewife to a housewife who generates income to her family. This has advantages and disadvantages: women participants are gaining the ability to financially support their families; at the same time, however, the husbands may feel helpless or unable to contribute. Thus, this may lead to tension between husband and wife, as a double burden is being placed on the women (Abou Raad, 2018).

Undoubtedly, the programs provide a platform for Syrian women to generate an income from their place of residence. In this setting, the problem of sexual harassment at workspaces can simply be avoided. However, this turns a blind eye to the problem of harassment many Syrian women face on a daily basis. Moreover, many displaced Syrian women, who do not have access to these programs, may revert or have reverted to other occupations to secure an income. Many are working alongside people from the host communities and are taking up other jobs that require long commutes. As a result, many of them do leave their refugee social circle on a daily basis. While we could argue that this lifestyle could make the female workers more vulnerable and less protected, the pressing questions here are: How does this source of vulnerability function: can it be productively mobilized; or can it do more harm than good, and how?

As a final note, the news reports individualized the societal problems the displaced Syrian women face in their daily lives, thereby ignoring how these problems are both political and global in origin. This resulted in decontextualizing them and making the transcultural nature of the plight of displaced Syrian women invisible in the television news.

In the upcoming chapter, I survey the news reports related to the concept of resistance.

7. 'Mothers of the Nation':
The Ambivalent Role of Motherhood in Assad's Syria and the Non-liberatory Subject

7.1 Introduction

In the second half of the 20th century, Syria went through a phase of state development that included fairly secular features; however, the personal status law in Syria remained based on the Shari'a law. This dual system of both secular and religious courts left Syrian women vulnerable to discrimination. Although there is an existing personal status law that permits women to take control over "issues related to marriage, divorce, custody, and other family matters," the patriarchal values and the laws tied to the Shari'a law continue to have a huge impact. For instance, marital rape and domestic violence are not recognized by the law, and marriage contracts must be filed between the father of the bride and the groom (Charles and Denman, 2012). If a divorce must take place, the man can simply order this divorce by going to court and requesting it verbally three times in a row. However, for a woman to request a divorce, she first needs her husband's approval and must prove to the juridical court that she has a valid right for a divorce; for example, she must have proof that she was abused or neglected by her spouse. Moreover, a husband in Syria can forbid his wife from working outside the home and is entitled to forbid her from travelling outside of Syria (Freedom House, 2010). But because the personal status law is arbitrary, most of these prohibitions can be toppled if women in Syria were more informed about their legal rights. For instance, a study done by Freedom House (2010) revealed that:

> "Many [Syrian] women, particularly those living in rural areas, do not fully understand their legal rights and cede what rights they do have in response to social or family pressure. This is particularly evident with respect to prop-

erty rights. The unequal inheritance rights mandated by Shari'a-based laws are commonly justified by the requirement that men provide for the women in their family, but women often turn over the entirety of their inheritance to their brothers to keep it in the family. Such practices greatly exacerbate women's financial dependence on men."

Therefore, although women can normally be active in Syrian society, there are arbitrary laws and patriarchal norms that drastically limit their participation in many political, social, and cultural features of their daily life.

After the war began in 2011, Syrian women faced greater and newer obstacles. Many became victims of war rape, a tactic used by both the Syrian regime and the opposition forces to pressure the opponent. Other women suffered from honor killings in areas held by extremist and terrorist groups, such as Daesh (ISIS) and Al Nusra Front. In the television coverage of the war, Syrian women were predominately represented as victims of violence; however, there were other images that showed women taking part in activities of armed and unarmed resistance.

For instance, the Assad regime formed an army unit that included only female soldiers. Political analysts have asserted that the regime's decision to recruit female fighters in the so-called armed resistance comes from Bashar Al-Assad's motivation to portray his forces as a 'progressive and secular alternative' in the face of the forceful Islamists in Syria (Leduc, 2015). Granted, this creation of female battalions is not a new project in Assad's Syria. Hafez Al-Assad, the father of Bashar Al-Assad who governed Syria from 1972 until 2000, also created a female army unit as part of the regime's propaganda to represent itself as secular and modern (Macdonald, 2016). For propaganda purposes, the Syrian regime has long stressed the important roles women play in Syria, which include those of the female fighters in the Syrian Arab Army. These images are not merely *empty* representations for the sole purpose of appealing to the West. Syria has a long history of women's empowerment.

In the 20th century, Syria's first women's organization, known as the *Light of Damascus* (or *Noor al-Fahya in Arabic*) was formed by mostly educated upper-class women. Nazik Al Abid was the main founder. Aside from her activism in women's rights, Al Abid boldly criticized the long presence of the Ottomans in Syria and condemned French colonialism in the region (Arenfeldt, & Golley, 2012). She was granted an honorable rank in the Syrian Arab Army after she heroically fought in the Battle of Maysaloun; she later established the *Syrian Arab Red Crescent* in 1942 (Zachs, 2013).

When the Ba'ath Arab socialist party took power in Syria in 1963, equality between men and women was one of the main political reforms in the Syrian constitution. As part of the reformations, GUSW, or General Union of Syrian Women, a women's rights organization, became affiliated with the ruling party and part of the government structure. This gave GUSW a great advantage, as other similar organizations were no longer allowed to operate outside the control and political structure of the Syrian regime (Arenfeldt & Golley, 2012).

GUSW held several events during the recent conflict in Syria. Their events on International Women's Day were widely reported by television stations owned or controlled by the Syrian regime. The television news reported these events by focusing on a diverse group of Syrian women: women activists, women on the battlefield, women supporting the Syrian Arab Army, etc. The reporting also emphasized notions of resistance, solidarity, and sacrifice, associating these with the role of motherhood.

These representations have widely existed in dominant narratives of nation states. In the book *Woman-Nation-State*, Anthias and Yuval-Davis (1989) asserted that the link between women and the state is multifaceted. Different government institutions, such as schools and trade unions, as well as communication structures, such the mass media, can formulate dominant state narratives that idealize the participation of women in the nation-building processes. Many of those roles have aspects of motherhood. Anthias and Yuval-Davis (1989) explained:

"On the one hand, [women] are acted upon as members of collectivities, institutions, or groupings, and as participants in the social forces that give the state its political projects in any particular social and historical context. On the other hand, they are a special focus of state concerns as a social category with a specific role (particularly human reproduction). It is important to note, however, that these roles cannot be understood in relation to the state reproducing itself or that any absolute control by the state would be achievable, given women's incorporation at a number of other social levels within civil society and in the economy" (p. 6).

Syrian women who appeared in the news reports were portrayed participating in different roles to serve the nation, such as: the duty to bear children; the duty to transmit and maintain culture and national identity; and the duty to participate in the armed and unarmed resistance. These responsibilities bare a strong resemblance to what Anthias and Yuval-Davis (1989) have described as "the major ways women participate in the national processes." Their study showed how national narratives portray women,

> "...as biological reproducers of members of the nation, as participating centrally in the state ideology reproduction and the transmitters of its culture, as participating in national, economic, political and military struggles" (p. 7).

Table 8. A comparison: the different roles of women towards the nation

Roles of Women in Nation-Building by Anthias and Yuval-Davis	My Findings in the News Reports Analysis on Syrian Women in Assad's Syria
"As biological reproducers of members of the nation"	The duty to bear children
"Participating centrally in the state ideology reproduction and the transmitters of its culture"	The duty to transmit and maintain culture and national identity,
"Participating in national, economic, political, and military struggles"	The duty to participate in the armed and unarmed resistance during the conflict

In this chapter, I examine news reports from television stations owned or controlled by the Syrian regime. The news reports represented different groups of Syrian women in relation to the notion of resistance, both armed and unarmed. In the analysis, I show how these representations are related to what Anthias and Yuval-Davis (1989) termed 'the national processes,' by looking at how motherhood was the main duty ascribed to Syrian women participating in the so-called armed and unarmed resistance.

7.2   Research Data

My analysis takes eight news reports from four main television stations, SAMA (three news reports), SANA (three 3 news reports), RT Arabic (one news report), and Syria Al Ikhbariyya (one news report). RT Arabic sympathizes with the Syrian regime, SANA, SAMA, and Syria Al Ikhbariyya are controlled by the Syrian regime. The sample selection was conducted in two main steps. Firstly, I went on the YouTube channel of each television station and used the search engine, entering the following keywords: Syrian women, Syrian conflict, armed resistance, unarmed resistance, rebellion, fight, battle, struggle, military, sacrifice, weapons, defense, and opposition. These keywords were purposely selected to collect news reports related to the context of resistance. The resulting news reports were few in number; only fourteen videos met the criteria. The second step was to select the most relevant news reports. I watched each news story three times. The relevance of the content was measured in terms of context (the Syrian conflict), and date of publication (the news story should be published between 2013 and 2018). Afterwards, eight news reports of the fourteen were selected for the case study sample. The news reports were published between April 2, 2013 and September 27, 2018. The table below lists details about each news report:

Table 9. The news reports in the context of resistance

Report	Television Station	Title of the News Report	Duration	Date Published	Chapter Section
1	Syria Al Ikhbariyya	The Braids of Fire: From the Front, They Came Directly with their Military Clothes	25:33	March 21.2018	7.3.1
2	SAMA	International Women's Day Syrian Women Give Back to Society	1:23	March 8, 2018	7.3.2
3	SANA	On International Women's Day, Syrian Women Embody the Act of Sacrifice and Heroism	1:43	March 8, 2018	7.3.2
4	SAMA	Under the Slogan "Women are a Homeland in a Homeland … the Syrian Women Have a Meeting."	2:09	September 27 2018	8.3.2
5	SANA	A Lecture on Resistance with the Women Forum and the Dialogue of Civilizations	2:19	March 13 2017	8.3.2

Report	Television Station	Title of the News Report	Duration	Date Published	Chapter Section
6	SANA	Syrian Women: Success stories and Strong Will during Difficult Times	3:37	March 3, 2017	8.3.2
7	SAMA	Syrian Mothers in the Villages of Hama are Preparing Food for the Heroes of the Syrian Arab Army	1:22	April 2, 2013	8.3.3
8	RT Arabic	A Collective Wedding Celebrates 30 Syrian Arab Army Soldiers	2:04	March 12, 2017	8.3.3

In these news reports, different Syrian women were depicted in diverse contexts and situations: women serving in the military, women serving food to male soldiers, women marrying soldiers, and women taking part of social and cultural events on women's rights organized by the GUSW. Although these groups of women came from different demographical and socio-economic backgrounds, the notion of 'mother of the nation' appeared in all the representations– regardless of whether the women were actual mothers. I explore these depictions in the analysis section of this chapter.

7.3   Analysis

7.3.1   From Manly Fighters to Ornamented Flowers

This subsection focuses on the Syrian women's participation in the armed resistance in Assad's Syria.

I start this section by focusing on a 25-minute news report published by *Syria Al Ikhbariyya*[1] on March 21, 2018. The news story covered a Mother's Day

---

1   Syrian News Channel is an Arab satellite television station based in Damascus, supportive of the Syrian regime.

ceremony organized by the Ba'ath Party; the political party that has been leading the Syrian government since 1963. Asma Al Assad, the first lady of Syria,
appeared in the news report and gave a speech honoring the girls and women
of Syria, specifically the young female fighters in the Syrian Arab Army and
their mothers.

Asma started her speech by thanking the young female fighters. She said:

> "We are proud, and we appreciate and acknowledge all the things you have done,
> and you are doing alongside with your families. This is what everyone should see,
> that Syria was being defended by everyone, everyone without any exception, in-
> cluding its young women. The young women that hid their long hair, and put their
> dreams on hold, and left their parents, and wore the military attire instead of the
> wedding dress, and carried the guns instead of their educational books, and they
> went to defend the soil of their homeland."

As she described the female fighters, her speech hinted at the idea of 'having
to let go of one's femininity' by hiding one's long hair, by choosing to volun-
teer in the military rather than pursuing a marriage, and by leaving school
in order to defend the homeland. She continues by reminding her audience
of the significant history of 'the Syrian woman.' Asma pointed out how the
Syrian woman was always ahead of other Arab women in her historical accomplishments. She addressed Syrian women in a singular form and said:

> "The woman in Syria has been for a hundred years and she probably was the pioneer
> among all the women from the other Arab countries. She was the leader in many
> disciplines. She was the first female doctor, the first female pharmacist, the first fe-
> male journalist, the first female ambassador, the first female judge. From the times
> of Zanubiya to Nazik Al Abid, until today."

Afterwards, she incorporated the notion of 'us versus them,' by hinting at the
opposition's female fighters. Asma said:

> "When I say sacrifice and defense, of course I mean it through taking action, not
> through 'talking, or the 'media' or 'advertising' or 'propaganda,' as the others have
> already done. They dressed them up and sent them under the slogan of 'defending
> the nation,' and they made them recite a few words, and they snapped a few staged
> photos of them. And then they pushed for the country's segregation. During this
> time, you, and the other female and male fighters were sacrificing everything to
> keep this country unified."

In her speech, Asma tried to portray the female fighters in the Syrian Arab Army as 'authentic' by drawing a comparison to the other female fighters from the opposition, claiming that they are merely pawns used by rebels to segregate Syria. Later on, she condemned gender discrimination, insinuating that the Syrian State endorses unity and equality among the two genders. Asma said:

> "Syria, to you, means unity. And for Syria, Syria means that you and all the fighters are one entity. When you went on the battlefield to defend Syria with your own bodies, you faced death, and saw death face-to-face, but in these instances, you eliminated the difference between a man and woman. When the bullet passes by you on the battlefield, it does not differentiate between a female or a male, or a girl and a boy, or a female fighter and a male fighter. In death there is no gender differentiation, therefore in life there should not be any gender discrimination. This is what you have shown the world, you let all the world see you as human beings. A strong human being, a capable human being with great determination, with a solid will that no one can break."

The news reporter then tried to reaffirm the 'presence' of the non-existent gender differentiation and discrimination in Assad's Syria, by interviewing the mothers of the female fighters. One mother said:

> "I remember I raised her the same way I raised her brothers. I don't differentiate between them."

Another interviewed mother said:

> "In Syria, a girl is the sister of the man. Just like we have male heroes, we have female heroes as well."

These statements allude to Ba'ath's narratives on gender equality and national unity. In the context of this news report, the resistance and solidary of the Syrian female fighters, were demonstrated as a unifying symbol of a nation that condemns gender differences. Yuval-Davis (1997) wrote: "Women are often constructed as the cultural symbols of the collectivity, of its boundaries, as carriers of the collectivity's honor and as its intergenerational reproducers of culture" (p. 67). Granted, Ba'ath always tried to mobilize women politically, not as Syrian women, but rather as Syrian citizens; "citizens with the same rights and duties as their male compatriots" (Sparre, 2008, p. 8).

In the news report, the representations of 'same rights and duties' for both male and female fighters appear, as one female fighter was shown speaking on the phone to her father, while she sat in a sniper's room.

In the news report, the father told the daughter over the phone:

"Please take care of yourself, may God protect you."

The daughter answered:

"Don't worry father, you have given birth to men, not girls."

He responded:

"I know I have given birth to men, not girls."

In this conversation, aspects of masculinity became associated with the image of the female fighter. These representations did not express a neutrality in gender. Although the first part of the news report attempted to frame the female fighters as 'equal counterparts in the Arab Syrian Army. In the second part, the representations embodied the female fighters as 'men' because they are active in military.

Afterwards, notions of femininity were introduced in the news report, as Asma Al Assad complimented the physical beauty of the female fighters. She said:

"I know you have lost many battles in this war, but I am very certain that you have never lost, and that you will never lose how beautiful you are as girls. You are very beautiful. You ornamented the Sham with your beauty, you ornamented all the governorates of Syria!"

This part of her speech came as a reaffirmation, as a way to comfort the female fighters, telling them that their resistance and solidarity on the battlefield did not and will never threaten their femininity. This indicates that aspects of their physical female appearance remain important. Afterwards, she addressed the mothers of the female fighters. She said:

"There are mothers here who had their sons murdered or injured, while their daughter was on the front. I know that there are mothers here who have not only one daughter on the front, but two daughters, two daughters!"

She continued by describing what motherhood really means to Syria, extending the definition to not just the notion of creating a family, but also to the notion of sacrifice, specifically sacrifice for the homeland. She said:

> *"Motherhood is greatness. Motherhood is not just about conceiving children. The greatness of motherhood is about sacrifice. The mother should sacrifice her soul for the homeland."*

Afterwards, Asma Al Assad congratulated the female heroes on their accomplishment, their faithfulness and most importantly on not just acting as if they are the 'mothers of Syria,' but for *also becoming* 'mothers of Syria' through their sacrificed and the time they spent on the battlefield. She emphasized the female fighters' femininity by comparing them to flowers. This came as a contradiction to her previous statement that insinuated that a 'good' and 'true' Syrian family raises its children without any gender discrimination. She ended her speech by saying:

> *"There is no female hero, there is no male hero without sacrifice, without courage, without greatness, without a complete family. A female hero and a courageous one. A complete family, that raised its daughters like its sons. And made everyone great like a human being, without any discrimination. On the basis of the same principles and values, and according to high qualities from patriotism to the love of the land. and for this reason, it would have been impossible not to have you here, at this ceremony on Mother's Day. It is impossible for you not to exist, because your mothers have raised you that way. And it would have been impossible to congratulate your mothers without your presence, the daughters' presence. Because this flower from this holy soil, and this holy soil is the one that raised and made the flowers grow bigger, and their brothers from the Syrian Arab Army. And these flowers, although when needed they become thorns, but they are at the same time mothers. They are the mothers of today, not just because they are defending Syria (we all know Syria is our Greatest Mother), but they are defending Syria also because Syria is like their little son or daughter that needs their care and their sacrifice in blood. You are the mothers, morally at the moment. And of course, in the future, inshallah, you will be real mothers. Because every look in your eyes has so much strength, and this will never eliminate the essence of companionship and tranquility and calmness, in which the woman provides in life."*

These representations of the female fighters were somehow contradicting. The fighters were initially depicted as strong human beings on the battlefield, regardless of their gender. Afterwards, they were addressed as 'men' on the battlefield. Later on, metaphors were used to objectify the female fighters as flowers that have ornamented Syria or as flowers with thorns. The last depiction incorporated ideas about the female fighters' destiny, which was directly tied to their femaleness; they were destined to act as the 'mothers of the nation'. This was reaffirmed when one of the mothers in the new report said:

> *"I tell my daughter Happy Mother's Day, instead of expecting my daughter to greet me for Mother's Day."*

The images of the female fighters were linked to the idea of "remaining feminine, and not to give the impression of being overly masculine" (Schuring, 2014). The importance to maintain one's femininity and to fulfill one's role as 'mothers of nation' while also participating in a generally masculine occupation was articulated in the reporting. However, we cannot deny that the images challenged the common orientalist assumption that women in the Arab world are fundamentally oppressed and 'need saving' (Mohanty, 2003); the female fighters were depicted as the new heroines of the Syrian State. By encouraging women to join Syrian Arab Army, Ba'ath emulates the Kurdish female fighters in the PYD and the policy of gender neutrality and equality on the battlefield. However, it is important to point out how the news report does not reveal the socioeconomic status of the female fighters, and perhaps conceals the fact that only girls from poor families are likely to become fighters. We also notice that most of the female fighters are young and unmarried. Hence, this discloses how the young female fighters may remain subjected to patriarchal interpretations of traditional Syrian society. Although they might be carrying guns, the male figures in their life remain present and dominant, as shown with one of the fighters who spoke to her father on the phone. Furthermore, only young and unmarried women are allowed to join the military in Syria, in this way the Syrian regime is able guarantee the female fighter's honor and sexual purity. Building on that, I would argue that these groups of women are not entirely toppling patriarchal norms, but perhaps only escaping them temporarily on the battlefield. Meanwhile, their representations also remained framed by stereotypical gender binaries such as 'ornamented flowers,' and 'mothers of Syria.'

7.3.2   Motherhood as a National Duty

This subsection analyzes the news reports on the Syrian woman's unarmed resistance. The reporting mainly focused on the Ba'ath party's policy for equality and gender neutrality. The General Union of Syrian Women (GUSW) is the only licensed governmental women's rights organization in Syria. This is because, under the Syrian government, it is illegal to permit any human rights organizations that are not controlled by the state itself. Since Ba'ath runs the Syrian government, GUSW is only allowed to work according to the rules and policies of the political party. It focuses on women issues, as well as projects on 'illiteracy, early childhood education, and natal health' (Alous, 2017). I found three news reports by *SANA* and two news reports by *SAMA* published between 2017 and 2018. The news stories reported on the events held on international women's day and other events on women empowerment that took place under the organization of the GUSW and Ba'ath. The Syrian woman's role in society was always the core topic of the dialogues and discussions that took place during the events.

SAMA published a news report on international Women's Day, on March 8, 2018. The reporter conducted Vox Pop interviews with Syrian women attending the event organized by GUSW.[2]*.* They were asked about the role of Syrian women in Syrian society. The reporter started by saying:

> *"During International Women's Day, the Syrian woman is 'the greatest source of giving back to society' as she is aware of huge amount of work she accomplishes daily, she is inspired by the generation of her grandmothers, who are the root of her history."*

The women interviewed were asked to give their opinions on women's rights in Syria. Most of the answers highlighted the significant role Syrian women play in society, such as the caregiver, the hard worker, the teacher, and the mother. The interviewees saw that as an integral part of women's rights in Syria. The first response was concerned with how the Syrian mother raises her children:

> *"The Syrian woman is building our society, she is raising heroes, she is raising the young men. The Syrian woman has a strong role in our society."*

The second response was:

> *"The Syrian woman has a role in raising the children, to direct them to what is wrong and what is right. She should take them away from what is wrong, and direct them toward the right path."*

These statements insinuate that the Syrian mother is the person who will guarantee that the future generations will not go 'down the wrong path,' or

---

2   SAMA TV is a Syrian television station that has been broadcasting from Damascus since 2012; it is politically supportive of the Syrian regime.

join the opposition groups. The third response addressed how the Syrian woman is expected to be a perfectionist, whether at home or in the work place:

> "If she is married, she should raise her children in a lawful way. If she is a working woman, then she should conduct her job in a perfect way."

The fourth response also spoke about perfectionism, and the Syrian woman's duties to love the nation and the president:

> "In terms of working women, the Syrian woman should be dedicated to her job, she should love her motherland, she should love the leader of our motherland. She should accomplish and be perfect in everything she does in life."

On March 8, 2018, *SANA reported on an event that hosted a number of leading Syrian women from the Ministry of Administrative Development.*[3] It was another honorary ceremony under the title of *Women's Leadership, Work and Development* that took place on International Women's Day in Damascus. The female Minister of Administrative Development, Dr. Salam Safaf, was interviewed.[4] He said:

> "The Syrian woman is culture, the woman is history, the woman is power, power for work, power for development. The Syrian woman was present in all the fields. She was present in the construction field, in the creative field, medicine, cultural, military, even the resistance. She was present in any field that has all the capabilities, capacities and the potential in our society. She was never dismissed or excluded."

A female member of the Syrian People's Council, Janet Kazan was also interviewed. She said:

> "All the resistance, and all the challenges we face by us, the Syrian women challenged the whole world in this war that came to our land. It is not only the mother of the Martyr that took part of this challenge, but we also have many women who participated in this battle, by giving up their comfort and their state of mind. Other women had a living martyr at home, whether it is the husband or son."

---

3   A television station owned by the Syrian state (Syrian Arab News Agency 2019).

4   Minister in Arabic was written in its masculine form, not in its feminine form, although the interviewee was a woman.

Moreover, Shahira Fallouj, the Director of the General Authority for Schools for Sons and Daughters of the Martyrs, spoke.[5] She said:

> "Honestly, we are proud that us women are Syrian. During this ceremony, I would like to say to the mothers of the martyrs that they are heroes. She is not only a hero in Syrian history, but also a worldwide hero."

On September 27, 2018, SANA reported on a meeting organized by the Directorate of Culture in Jaramana, in the Damascus Governorate. The meeting introduced the first open dialogue on the role of Syrian women in society. Its slogan for the event was 'The Syrian woman is a home in a Homeland.' The reporter said:

> "One is wrong to assume that the woman is the weakest element during a conflict. The Syrian woman has proven that she is the strongest factor for resistance and solidarity, especially in the shadow of the conflict and the circumstances we are passing through. She is the person that taught the world the true meaning of patience and the act giving for the sake of the homeland, its sovereignty, and its dignity. She has a record of sacrificing acts and positions she has taken for our communities. These important positions she has taken are nothing new to the Syrian woman. The Syrian woman had a strong role in building society, and she has still this responsibility until today."

The reporter then interviewed Colonel Hala Bilal from the Office for the Care of the Wounded in the Internal Security Forces.[6]. She said:

> "The Syrian woman is a home in a homeland, because we women are a home, and the woman is a root or the base for the homeland. She is the one that creates the household, and the household is a family, and the family is based on children, and the children are the saviors and the protectors that kept Syria safe."

The reporter continued by saying:

> "When the role of the Syrian woman was rising and gaining more significance, especially for her will to participate in politics, she was given all the care and attention, her career was supported, and her bid was valued. We

---

5   The word director in Arabic, was written in its masculine form, not in its feminine form, although the interviewee was a woman.

6   The word colonel in Arabicwas written in its masculine form, not in its feminine form, although the interviewee was a woman.

made her a key partner in making history. During that time, dialogue sessions should have been established in order to shed the light on the Syrian woman's role as a mother, a caregiver, and a fighter *and a resister*."

Another commenter was Layla Saab, the Director of Culture in Rural Damascus.[7]. She said:

"The Syrian woman has proven that she is a legend for resistance, and a legend for reconstruction. And regardless of all the challenges she faced, and all the pain she went through, she is still insisting on survival and resistance."

Afterwards, the reporter ended the report with the following statement:

"A Syrian woman has a big and significant role. She is the one that creates society, and she plays a major role in sustaining a good and healthy society and educating this society. And she is behind every victory recorded in history. She is no longer half of the society; she is the basis of it."

A similar news report published on March 13, 2017 by *SANA* reported on a forum that included a lecture on women resistance and in dialogue with Syrian civilization. In Mazza Damascus, organized by Youth Union in Syria. 'The Woman for Resistance' was the title of the event. The reporter started with the following statement:

"The Syrian woman is the one that got prepared and helped to prepare, the one that planted and harvested, resisted and triumphed, participated and shared. From home education to educational upbringing, reaching social life, she is the one with the biggest role."

Vera Yammeen, a member of the Ba'ath Party, said:

"Syria was always a country that provided a platform and space for people with competencies. And for this reason, as long as the Syrian woman is active in this country, the Syrian woman that symbolizes upbringing and education, the woman that symbolizes national identity, that symbolizes this land. Therefore, is it not a surprise that today, the Syrian woman is very active in social life. If the woman were not active, we would not have a stable and balanced society. And the social stability is what leads to the satisfactory outcomes, especially that, today, we began debating, in one way or another, about the solutions needed and the adjustments needed

---

7   The word director in Arabic was written in its masculine form, not in its feminine form, although the interviewee was a woman.

> *to set us on the right track. Therefore, for this reason, when I talk about the woman, I do not talk about her as a separate body or element, but rather, the complete opposite. I see her as a basic part of a well-balanced social structure, because there is no balance, not in the social life, and not in the political life, and not in the national life, not without a balance between man and woman, together. And this is what the Syrian women has proven and was devoted for. When Syria acts as a caring mother, then the Syrian woman becomes a reflection of this culture."*

SANA published a news report on March 3, 2017 with the title *"Syrian women: Success stories and Strong Will in Difficult Times."* This was the only news report that covered issues related to the low number of female representatives in Syria' People Council, sexual harassment in Syria, and the lack of laws that protect women. The news reporter started with the following statement:

> *"After she has proved her active presence alongside the man, in all aspects of life, and she showed great resistance and courage during the war that has been waged against her nation, she was the mother, the worker, and the fighter, the Syrian woman deserves a parliament that acknowledges her struggles and aspirations, in a safe space, where laws and legislations are enacted to protect her rights."*

This statement suggests that Syrian women should have a more active presence in Syria's People Council and there should be a higher number of female ministers. An unnamed woman was interviewed. She gave her opinion on the low female representation in the People's Council. She said:

> *"I believe that the number of women in Syria's people council should increase. One of the reasons for that is how the percentage of Syrian women in the Syrian population became higher than the number of men after the war. Therefore, the number female representatives in Syria's people council should reflect on the female population in Syria. It is impossible for male representatives, regardless of their consciousness and empathy, to be able to engage in women's issues as much as a female representative could. Therefore, the women's presence in the People's Council will have a positive impact on women's rights and accomplishments in Syria."*

Another unnamed woman addressed the need for Syrian women to practice their voting rights and be active in the voting process. She said:

> *"I would like to see the Syrian women take part of the voting process in the People's Council in Syria. However, I hope and ask each woman participating in this voting process, to be faithful and follow the ideas she hopes to implement in the People' Council. She should not forget who and what she is fighting for."*

A different interviewee also addressed the need to change Syria's laws and policies to benefit of Syrian women. She said:

> "The minimum number of female representatives in the people's council should be at least 40%. If she is my representative, and a representative to the council, that means her dreams are like my dreams. But what are my dreams? I am currently in need of safety. I need to feel safe emotionally, physically, and economically. She should help me accomplish this."

The same news story from *SANA* also addressed the issue of sexual harassment in Syria and the non-existent laws that grant women protection. One unnamed woman was interviewed; she spoke indirectly about the sexual violations that were committed during the conflict. She said:

> "I ask from our government to thoroughly examine the economic situation in our country, and the social life as well. In our society, especially during the difficult times in war, certain events happened. There should be a more thorough study on the laws in the country, especially to the benefit of the Syrian woman. As you know, the Syrian woman became a victim in certain situations, situations in which the terrorists were involved. There have been incidents of rape and torture. Therefore, we need to study the laws that will protect her in the future. The most important thing is to make sure that Syrian woman is protected by the law in our society. It is also important to enlighten the Syrian woman about those laws."

Most of the news reports surveyed in this section represented the idea of the *tanwir* or the enlightening process that the Syrian regime has long been promoting in its ideological narratives (della Ratta, 2012). There was a dominant narrative being pushed regarding the national role Syrian women should play during the conflict. The Syrian women interviewed in the news reports did not wear a headscarf. This may indicate that the Syrian regime is attempting to appear modern and secular in its media images. The Syrian women interviewed also had high-ranking governmental positions such as directors, colonels, ministers. It is important to point out that, in the reporting, their titles were in the masculine form. In Arabic, the words director, colonel, minister, etc. are declined according to the subject's gender. The female speakers were given a 'masculine' title instead of a 'feminine' one. In her research on educated women in Syria, Sparre (2008) wrote:

> "Unlike the ideology of 'neo-patriarchalism,' which emphasized women's roles as mothers and wives, the state feminism ideology of the Ba'th Party portrayed women as muwazzafin (public employees)."

Muwazzafin is the plural for the word employee, but for a group of men, not women. The feminine form of this word is *muwazzafaat*. Hence, the Syrian constitution's declaration of forbidding discrimination on the basis of gender may perhaps explain why the women interviewed in the news reports had their title addressed in a masculine form.

Moreover, another aspect that attracted my attention was that none of the reports portrayed or interviewed any Syrian women from a working-class background. The news stories only spoke on behalf of the subjects. The news reporters and the interviewees spoke about *one* Syrian woman, painting her in a single image, as if she were one entity, had one face, and came from the same demographical background. Hence, we do not really see *who* or *what* or *how* different groups of Syrian women have accomplished their acclaimed forms of resistance or how they have embraced solidarity, triumphed, and fought using their female roles alongside men in Syria. We only saw women with high-ranking government positions appealing to the Syrian women to rise, resist, and be empowered.

Granted, the reality in Syria shows that there are also very few women in high-ranking positions in the country. Research done by UNIFEM (2007) claimed that:

> "Syrian women hold high ranking positions in all government and civil institutions, vocational unions, popular organizations and the doctors/ pharmacists/ lawyers/ artists/ teachers/ workers/ artisans/ farmers\unions but in unsatisfactory numbers."

In her speech, Asma Al Assad glorified the Syrian woman's history and her accomplishments. For example, she mentioned how the Syrian woman was the first Arab women to become a leader in many disciplines; the first female doctor, the first female pharmacist, the first female journalist, the first female ambassador, the first female judge. At the same time, she disregarded the low number of Syrian women in high-ranking positions.

Furthermore, 'the Syrian woman' was always associated with the following labels and roles: the basis of the homeland, the legend, the international hero, the person that creates a good and healthy society, and the person who rebuilds what the war has taken away. These representations are flattering and empowering, but they remain an exaggeration of the reality. While the Syria constitution of 1973 declares all citizens equal under the law and forbids gender-based discrimination, having an official discourse is one thing and the reality on the ground another. While there is no doubt that these events are a very valuable source of empowerment to many Syrian women, the notion of 'mothers of the nation' did prevail in most of the representations. This has led to idealizing the role of the Syrian woman rather than discussing what still needs to do to improve the laws that protect her and further her empowerment.

Women in Syria have not yet acquired equal rights with regard to the personal status law and the penal and naturalization laws. For instance, as previously mentioned, when a Syrian man and Syrian woman establish a family, the woman is not granted the power of divorce or custody of the children; and there is no law that protects women from domestic violence. Many Syrian women are victims of domestic violence and are often subject to molestation and even rape or murdered on the pretext of preserving the family's "honor." These practices are tolerated because there are no laws that protect women from such misdeeds (Alous, 2017). Hence, all these social practices and arbitrary laws place women in an inferior position to men.

In the news reports surveyed above, only one unnamed Syrian woman reflected on these realities. Addressed the incidents of rape and torture, which occurred throughout the conflict, she called for the need to review the laws that will protect Syrian women in the future. She fell short, however, of calling for a change in laws. In general, the speech acts in the news reports did not call for notable changes in laws or policy reforms to the benefit of Syrian women. The news reports tended to focus predominately, if not entirely, on the idealization of 'the role of the Syrian woman.'

7.3.3   Reflecting on other News Stories

This part surveys the two remaining news stories. The groups of women in the reports are elderly Syrian women who support the Syrian Arab Army and young Syrian women in a public marriage ceremony.

On April 2, 2013, *SAMA* published a news report on a group of Syrian mothers who had been interviewed. The title of news story was 'Syrian mothers in the villages of Hama are preparing food for the Syrian Arab Army Heroes.' The report started with an old woman speaking on camera. She said:

"Whatever we do, it won't be enough. May God bless them and give them victory."

The reporter then continued by describing the women preparing food for the fighters in the Syrian Arab Army:

"In these two hands, she was not able to carry weapons. However, with her two hands and with a heart full of hope, she prepared food for the heroes fighting on the frontlines. Meanwhile. she pushes away all the evil forces and terrorism. The women of the town of Salhab, on the country side of West Hama, have sent packages of food and medicine as well as first aid kits to the Syrian Arab Army fighting on the country side of Hama and Idlib."

The news report ended with a woman saying:

"We are trying to provide whatever we are able to in order to support the courageous men on the frontlines who are fighting to save Syria from terrorism, these men will eventually save us as well — because we are Syria."

In this news report, senior Syrian women were shown risking their lives to help the fighters of the Syrian Arab Army. The reporter's speech implied that these groups of elderly women were too weak to carry weapons, but that they joined 'the resistance' by providing support from their domestic realms. This could be read as a form of unarmed resistance. Their acts of resistance were tied to their obligation to fulfil their national and civil duty.

The notion of fulfilling one's national and civil duty also appears in a news report published on March 12, 2017 by *RT Arabic*.[8] The title of the story was '*A Collective Wedding Celebrates 30 Syrian Arab Army Soldiers.*' Thirty Syrian men, dressed in their military attire, walked down the streets of Aleppo with their brides dressed in white. The rest of the news story showed the Syrian police patrolling the streets on their motorbikes. It also showed the families dancing, feasting, and rejoicing the brides and grooms, as if the collective wedding celebrations were a national festivity and triumph. The Syrian brides walked into the public square and were praised as they took steps towards their 'motherhood.' In this setting, the act of marriage is represented as a kind of political calling rather than simply a social or ritual union of man and wife.

These images mirror the "idea of the Syrian collective family" that "is established through endlessly repeated narratives of sacrifice and familial loy-

---

8   The Russian international television network is funded by the Russian government and is supportive of the Syrian regime (RT Arabic 2019).

alty" to the Syrian regime (Haugbolle, 2008, p.264). The television representations emphasized the role of the mother and caregiver in Assad's Syria. On the one hand, these representations can be read as a reflection of how the Syrian constitution prioritizes the women's right to maternity leave and child care (Sparre, 2008). These laws are a symbol of state development and modernization. On the other hand, since the Syrian regime has made 'reproduction' a public rather than a private issue (Sparre, 2008), one could argue that the government's program on state feminism is ambiguous in nature.

7.4   Motherhood in Relation to Agency

In the television reporting, the notion of motherhood was visible in the representations of various groups of Syrian women. The ideal Syrian mother was described, idealized, and romanticized in the news reports. The ideal Syrian mother was depicted as a woman who works hard, properly raises her children thereby setting them on the right path to love the motherland and its leader, and as the young woman who fights for the motherland because she is a mother herself. Almost all of the Syrian women interviewed in the reports held high-ranking government positions. In their speech, they associated the value of work to a form of service that ought to be fulfilled by the Syrian community. Moreover, they claimed that both men and women equally have to fulfill a moral duty towards the Syrian state. When describing this moral duty among Syrian women, the reporting associated it with notions such as 'the power for work and the power for development.' Furthermore, women in Syria were described as 'a home in a homeland,' while also emphasizing women's role in building a better and stronger generation, one faithful to the Assad regime.

Although the Syrian women from the GUSW and Ba'ath spoke strongly in support of empowering Syrian women, their monologues emphasized the importance of being a 'devoted believer' to the Assad and Ba'ath ideology. These speech acts did not truly advocate for the Syrian women's independence, as much as they tried to encourage women to 'follow' the right path and eventually fulfill their role by becoming 'mothers of the nation.' Notions such as independent thought and making moral decisions regarding one's own responsibility were not truly endorsed in the reporting. It was as if Syrian women were not encouraged to think for themselves and make moral decisions on their own. Perhaps these ideological narratives eliminate the chances or limit the spaces in which Syrian women are able to express their 'individuality.' This loss of individuality is reproduced when the television narratives constantly dedicate aspects of a Syrian woman's life to serving the community and the nation as a whole. In other words, the television representations may have contributed to discouraging the individuality of the Syrian women. The image of 'the Syrian woman' and 'mother' was overshadowed by women's moral and national duties being speculated in the news.

Throughout the news reports, almost all Syrian women were framed in relation to the notion of 'we are Syria,' or 'we are the homeland.' These implications produce a political discourse around the Syrian women's bodies in which "the body itself no longer remains in the private sphere of the individual, but [is] subordinated to the national interest" (Pine 2003). It is as if, when Syrian women go to work in their private and public life, everything they do fosters the betterment of the people, and helps build a stronger nation. Similarly, becoming a mother, a caregiver, and a fighter for the motherland– or the holy land as Asma Al Assad described it– becomes or is seen as a national duty.

These ideas on the loss of individuality reflect on ideas introduced by Shereen Abuelnaga, an Egyptian socialist, feminist, and gender theorist (Kohl Journal, 2019). Abuelnaga (2018) writes:

> "We women who live in Arab societies have been raised with the notion that our lives and bodies do not belong to us. And despite the disparities of our lived realities, philosophically, and materially, we are held to the same societal expectations when it comes to motherhood" (p. 198).

Thus, if a Syrian woman or girl fails to achieve her duties as 'a mother of the nation,' does she exist in the eyes of the state and her community? Abuelnaga (2018) asserted that the Arab women's role as a mother is a given, and it is her duty to fulfill it. More importantly, this particular role is decreed by social norms and not by the woman herself. Hence, we cannot perceive this role as a separate element disconnected from societal structures such as class, religion, and context. While Ba'ath claimed to promote the same equal rights and opportunities for men and women' Syrian women, unlike Syrian men, were expected to serve as mothers of the nation. This automatically reinforces the subjugation of Syrian women to gender binaries, thus reproducing patriarchal norms that govern their existence, body, and role in society.

Under the Syria regime, a woman's body has a role to fulfill in the public sphere and is no longer a private possession of the woman; rather, society expects her to achieve her obligatory role as wife, mother, daughter, caregiver, teacher, etc. These compulsory roles become the basis of initializing forms of systemic power. In other words, the power of the Syrian state is being performed through the Syrian woman's body.

In light of this, could spaces such as the GUSW become a space of productivity or function as a 'harem,' where sites of struggle and acts of transgression take place? In other words, could the spaces occupied by women, in a male-dominated political party such as Ba'ath, become places where Syrian women can promote and speak about their personal and 'trivial' struggles? Could defiance take place, as opposed to the expected forms of compliance such as the assigned feminine roles of the Syrian women, or even the masculine ones that have been assigned to the Syrian female fighters? Additionally, is the Syrian woman 'only allowed to exist through someone else' (Abuelnaga, 2018), e.g., as a child, a husband, a brother, or a whole nation. Lastly, is there no other passage but the rite of passage to the ultimate stage of a woman's life: motherhood?

In the context of Assad's Syria, the function of womanhood has become directly tied to the reproduction of future children and motherhood to the nexus of nationhood. Throughout the news reports, we saw how the female members of the Ba'ath party viewed the capacity of Syrian women as mothers and thus as the crucial link to the modernization process, and even an effective source of passing the Syrian state's ideology onto future generations.

By perceiving childbearing and baring children as a national obligation, is it fair to say that *all* Syrian women – especially those who have been displaced or who come from middle and lower middle-class families – perceive the role of motherhood as a pure *burden*? Within this framework, I wish to refer back Abuelnaga (2018), an Arab woman and a professor at the American University of Cairo, and quote her personal journey, particularly how she *resisted* society's expectation of her becoming a mother. She writes in her short memoir:

> "I am expected to raise them; bond with them; sacrifice for them; bear with all their absurdities; worry about their drowning; punish them; fulfill my dreams through them; impose my wishes on them; carry their picture in my handbag; cry and worry for them. If I am not a mother, then I am not complete. I, who did not make it to the rank of other, who plans her life without taking children into consideration, am not a mother, therefore I don't exist" (Abuelnaga, 2018, p. 198).

But what if a woman aspires to raise her children, bond with them, sacrifice for them, and bear with them and for them? Does marriage not sometimes have a significant source of power and control among certain groups of women, especially women living in economically distressed communities or women living in exile? In certain contexts, marriage is the first step towards the bastions of support, honor, and familial respectability.

Afshar (1989) discussed marriage as an instrumentation that transfers control to women via reproduction and the marriage market, where women become the main organizers of choosing prospective marriage partners for their children, as well as undergoing the process of 'assessing their wealth, health, and suitability.' Building on his case study on Iranian society, Afshar (1989) wrote:

> "...although men negotiate the actual marriage contract, women control the future of their children. Not surprisingly mothers see the process as desirable and empowering and a means of becoming something of a matriarch within the domestic sphere. As long as the traditional values are maintained, all mothers have the prospect of power and prestige. Once the married couple produces children, then grandmothers are accorded the prestige of the custodians of family health, welfare and morality. Traditional ceremonies run by women and for women initiate and protect each and every stage of child-rearing and enhance the authority of older women over the family as a whole" (p. 117).

These factors of married life and matriarchy are significant, especially for working class women. For many Syrian women, grandchildren are one of the main, if not the only available source of financial security at old age. Hence, entering grand-motherhood is cherished by many, and is perceived as an essential stage of life that provides them with familial control and authority. Therefore, we cannot limit our analysis and interpretation of motherhood, in the context of the Syrian conflict, as a solely patriotic duty or as a social obligation stemmed from patriarchy. While it is important to acknowledge, in a theoretical sense, that motherhood can be an institution that holds oppressive and patriarchal norms, we also cannot turn a blind eye to the maternal control many women acquire and aspire to acquire in their domestic spheres. Their role as mothers, aside from being a national obligation in Syria, may perhaps be publicly revered, especially among lower and lower-middle class communities in which women face difficulties gaining a secure livelihood.

In this context, the Syrian women's domestic obligations may become a source of power and control. Repressive as they are, the Syrian state's policies that encourage the domestication of women, and a society that grants men, for instance, the right to forbid their wives from holding a waged employment and working in the mixed labor market, makes the role of the mother valued and appreciated among Syrian women. This brings the discussion to the 'enacting' function power enables. In this context, power embodies the Syrian regime narratives on motherhood, along with the patriarchal norms in Syrian society. Judith Butler (1997) explained how power can have an ambivalent function, one in which the subject subjected by this same power may emerge in two ways: "as the effect of a prior power and as the condition of possibility for a radically conditioned form of agency" (p. 14). Butler perceived agency as something power diverges *unintendedly*. In other words, this oppressive power also allows the emergence of "the ambivalent scene of agency," which represents the reversal of that power (Butler 1997, p. 15). "No subject comes into being without power... the subject produced by power becomes heralded as the subject who *founds* power" (Butler, 1997, p. 16). Butler's explanation may exemplify how women in Syria sometimes embrace the role of motherhood, assigned to them by the state and by society, as a way of paving their way through life and acquiring security and dominance through their matriarchal roles.

This sheds light on the importance of acknowledging the *desires* of the subjects under feminist thinking. Saba Mahmoud (2006) has argued that liberatory goals set by feminist theory have long situated desire in the same position as freedom and liberation. At times, these emancipatory feminist visions contrast with the cultures, desires, and sensibilities of third world women, particularly women in Arab Muslim cultures. Mahmoud (2006) wrote:

> "It is quite clear that both positive and negative notions of freedom have been used productively to expand the horizon of what constitutes the domain of legitimate feminist practice and debate. For example, in the 1970s, in response to the call by white middle-class feminists to dismantle the institution of the nuclear family, which they believed to be a key source of women's oppression, Native and African American feminists argued that freedom, for them, consisted in being able to form families, since the long history of slavery, genocide, and racism had operated precisely by breaking up their communities and social networks" (p. 40).

Here, Mahmoud's words echo Nazik al-Abid's testimony against the French colonialism in Syria and her activism and resistance against the Ottoman occupation of Syria. Interestingly, the name of Nazik Al Abid appears in Asma Al Assad's speech, as she addressed the historical accomplishments of Syrian women in the workforce.[9] Thus, my argument would be to rethink the role of motherhood and what function it could have beyond its national, patriarchal, and stereotypical gender one.

On a similar note, the issue of sexual freedom becomes relevant to this discussion. The first section of this chapter argued that female fighters, who were able to escape patriarchy temporarily on the battlefield, are still not able to dictate their sexual freedoms. It is perhaps important to provide a rebuttal to my argument by acknowledging that not all Syrian women may support these particular *liberatory* feminist values, particularly not those related to sexual liberation. Many may perceive the rejection of marriage and raising a family as something shameful or unnatural. On the one hand, we may perceive this perspective as 'an ideology in practice;' on the other hand, we should also acknowledge that the process of enlightening certain groups of Syrian women on the repressive traditional norms of shame, modesty, and dignity is an emancipatory feminist vision that embraces hegemonic practices and hegemonic Western values. I am not saying that all Syrian women reject the idea of sexual freedom, nor that Western values should only be applied to women in Western cultures. Rather, I am attempting to establish an understanding on how this emancipatory (hegemonic) feminist vision may function as a form of *enlightenment* and is thus a vision that may comprehend these groups of women as "unenlightened".

This same vision can have a similar hegemonic function to that of the propagandic media narratives of the Syrian regime; namely Ba'ath's narratives on the 'mothers of the nation.' Evidently, these media narratives came from a source of authority; they also attempted to educate Syrian women about the role they ought to perform in society. I perceive Ba'ath's so-called modernization process as a form of hegemonic as well as a form of 'tanwir,' Arabic for *enlightenment.* Educating different groups of women about existing or non-existing provisions of family protection laws in Syria (as a way to learn about

---

9   Nazik Al Abid was the first woman to earn a rank in the Syrian Arab Army, as she fought for national independence and for the women's right to work and vote in Syria (Zachs, 2013).

one's rights and how to secure them), is a better approach than simply enlightening them.

If my feminist scholarship chose to understand the agency of these groups of Syrian women only through the acts of resisting the dominant male order or through the model of doing and undoing traditional social norms, does that not make my thoughts and my feminist writings part of the greater hegemonic feminist narrative that only articulates agency as a structure against the hegemonic male cultural norms of Arab Muslim societies? And if so, does it not make these two hegemonic practices opposite sides of the same coin? Both practices indulge in forms of enlightenment. The former pushes for the emancipation of Syrian women from the traditional social norms in Arab society, and latter pushes Syrian women to pursue those norms in keeping with societal expectations. In this line of argumentation, I find myself echoing Mahmoud's (2006) understanding on the importance of writing feminist thought without deploying one's own interests and agendas.

Lastly, it is important to point out two aspects ignored in the news reports. Firstly, the notion of fatherhood was not mentioned in any of the news reports. The synonyms used for motherhood and 'mothers of the nations' to describe notions about womanhood, the family; the state never incorporated the role of the father in the family and in building the future nation. Male figures in the family and society are dominant, especially in terms of setting the social norms, choosing whether the wife or the daughter should take up waged employment, and deciding whether the female members of the household are allowed to travel outside the country or not, etc. Throughout the news reports, we only saw one side of the narrative, one in which Syrian women were depicted through their role of raising brave men (and women). However, we never saw the role Syrian men play in their adulthood.

While the private role of the mother played in domestic sphere was framed as a national one, could Syrian women use their roles as mothers to make the personal *political*? Can this national duty become a space of contestation, where political agency is asserted within the framework of the family, society, and the state? Can the publicized private relations, bring personal topics related to womanhood into the public arena and politicize them, as opposed to keeping them in the trivial zone?

7.5   Conclusion

This chapter surveyed news reports that depicted different groups of Syrian women practicing forms of armed and unarmed resistance. Throughout the news report analysis, I found that the Arab television news associated these forms of resistance with the role of motherhood in Syria. Thus, the notion of 'mothers of the nation' has prevailed in the news, as Syrian women were represented as the 'resisting subject' during the war.

The notion of the 'mother of the nation' is a common and stereotypical representation of women in war and conflict. This notion illustrates how dominant state narratives designate main roles for women as part of their participation in the national process (Anthias and Yuval-Davis, 1989). These roles could be traced in the Arab television news through the three main duties assigned to Syrian women: (a) The duty of child bearing; (b) the duty of transferring and maintaining culture and national identity; and (c) the duty of participating in armed and unarmed resistance. These duties are depicted as part of the Syrian women's role in serving the nation – the Assad regime.

Furthermore, I did not limit the analysis of the news reports to the (stereotypical) representations of women in war. I moved the account further to discuss how the subjectivation of Syrian women appeared in the news and discussed this subjectivation in relationship to the notion of agency. By referring to Butler's (1997) theory of subjectivation and Saba Mahmoud's (2006) concept of agency and the non-*liberatory* subject, I contextualized the visibility of the subject and the conditions of subjugation prevalent in the news reports. I addressed the problematic aspect of "reading agency primarily in terms of resistance to the regulatory power of structure of normativity" (p. 48) and suggested revisiting the notion of agency beyond the dualistic framework of upholding and dismantling social norms. In the upcoming chapter, I interpret and discuss the finding from Chapters 4 through 7.

8. The Construction of Syrian Women in the Arab Television News

This chapter provides a deeper analysis of the main findings from the previous chapters. In *Section 8.1*, I explain how violence against women was normalized in Arab television reporting. In *Section 8.2*, I discuss the role of the expert in the television news by referring to two Latin terminologies on the act of witnessing; *testis* and *superstes*. I then explain how the humanitarian and personal testimonies in the television reporting were constructed with consideration to the aesthetic dimension of the camera. In *Section 8.3*, I juxtapose the notion of agency with the theoretical concept of performativity. I use Saba Mahmoud's ethnographic study on the women's piety movement in the mosques of Cairo as an analogy, and draw meanings from the power dynamics of shame, dignity, and fear that were constructed the television news. In this chapter, I distance myself from the television representations in order to provide a deeper understanding of how agency, in the context of the Syrian conflict, could be read beyond liberal and post-structuralist perspectives.

8.1 Normalizing Violence and Reaffirming Victimhood in the Television News

Meltem Ahiska (2016) addresses a significant problem: "Why does violence against women continue unimpeded despite the seemingly high awareness of it, and why is it normalized in society?" (p. 212). In a case study on violence against women in Turkey, Ahiska reflects on Butler's (2004) notions in *Precarious Life* to discuss the notion of victimhood in media representations. According to Butler (2004) there are two distinct forms of normative power:

"...one operates through producing a symbolic identification of the face with the inhuman, foreclosing our apprehension of the human in the scene; the other works through radical effacement, so that there never was a human, there never was a life, and no murder has, therefore, even taken place" (p. 147).

Butler's first distinct form of normative power refers to the violence against women that gets very little, if any, media attention.[1] Butler's second distinct form of normative power exemplifies how mainstream media cover death during conflict by only reporting *statistically* on the number of people killed. By framing the killing of someone as just another number, the viewer is usually presented with a faceless image of the victim. This hinders the possibility of sympathizing with the killed or injured individual, as the media narrative leaves no possibility for mourning.

Though the second distinct form of normative power could not be traced in the news reports, the research found that a third distinct form of normative power is established in the Arab television news. This form appears when "the faces of women are neither rendered as *inhuman* [...] nor completely effaced; in fact, they are highly mediatized in sentimental ways" (Ahiska, 2016, p. 213). The news reports surveyed in Chapter 4 constantly represented images of Syrian women who had been exposed to regime violence and gender-based violence. These representations emphasized, reproduced and confirmed the Syrian women's victimhood. Furthermore, the television reporting embraced sentimentalism as a way to appeal to the viewer's emotions. Subsequently the Syrian women's victimhood became associated with gender difference and their suffering became naturalized in the news. Ahiska (2016) explains how,

"the representations that evoke the victimhood of women cancel the multiple temporalities of vulnerability—that is, how women, as subjects, have lived, desired, and struggled differently through the experience of violence. When no desire for ...living differently is allowed for women in these representations, victimhood is petrified and fixed in time, and hence normalized" (p. 213).

---

1   For instance, in this research project, I found that the television news reports from *Al Jazeera*, *Al Arabiya* and *Al Aan* did not report on the groups of Syrian women that fell victim to honor killings during the Syrian conflict.

The news reports from the Arab television stations implied that, in times of conflict, Syrian women are destined to be victims of violence. These discursive constructions in the news not only reproduce and normalize violence against women in society; they also enable the media narrative to establish the representations of the instances of violence to a certain time period (during the Syrian conflict), without any context and reference to the past (pre-conflict Syria), nor the future (after the violence has taken place).

Furthermore, the findings demonstrated that representations of Syrian child brides, desperate mothers, and the economically struggling displaced Syrian families usually lacked contextualization to both the internal and external factors that shape and heighten their states of vulnerability and impoverishment. Another finding demonstrated that men, as actual and potential perpetrators in the child marriage cases, were rendered invisible in the news. The lack of contextualization and the absence of the men, as "sovereign norm setters," in the media narrative reduced the likelihood of generating a sense of "dissonance" among the viewers. Although the images of the child brides were personified in the news, the images of personification did not necessarily translate into humanization.

In the following section, I focus on a different set of findings, specifically the news reports that perpetuated a media narrative that was heavily influenced by a humanitarian discourse. As I survey the findings, I ask the following question: Does the personification of the television media images translate to humanization?

8.2   Humanitarian Reasoning and Personal Testimonies in the Television News

Georgiou (2012) asserted that news production, media content, and the consumption of the media message need to be examined in the context of gender as well as migration. These factors reflect on "pre-existing socio-political realities" and "contribute to framing meanings of the self, the *Other*, the society we live in" (Georgiou 2012, p. 791-792). She claimed that:

> "The institutional basis of the media informs the ways representations are framed, while regulation of the media and of everyday life shape the context and limits of their consumption [...]. Media power does not just trickle down from the producers through media representations to consumers. It is

a social process 'reproduced in the details of what social actors do and say' (Couldry 2000, p. 4) and is more complex than a lineal model of media transmission implies" (Georgiou 2012, 792).

A more recent study by Georgiou (2018) found that digital "media systematically spoke about refugees and migrants, but they rarely appeared themselves as narrators of their stories" (p. 45). Meyer, Sanger, and Michaels (2017) showed that mainstream television stations reporting on the Syrian conflict mainly referred to humanitarian workers, as they are able to provide immediate information as well as their own expertise on the situation.

The findings in this research project showed that the news reports, which included themes on everyday resilience among displaced Syrian women, interviewed humanitarian personnel working in the refugee camps. This indicates that the partisan entity of the television news station was not only influenced by the media ownership of the station, but also by the experts that were interviewed in the news reports. In this case, the humanitarian workers served as a reputable expert and significantly participated in the social process of framing the television representations of displaced Syrian women.

In these news reports, the humanitarian workers served as witnesses to the scenes depicted in the news, by providing their testimony on the subjects observed, that are the displaced Syrian communities. Didier Fassin (2012) asserted that in Latin, there are two terms used for the word "witness;" *testis* and *superstes*. The former is a "third-party" or an external witness who is qualified to provide a neutral observation "that forms the grounds for hearing and believing him, including in legal proceedings" (p.204). For instance, in Chapter 5 the lawyer Nour Al Immam appeared as a *testis*; she gave her legal testimony on the cases of child marriage in Jordan. As for the latter, Fassin (2012) asserted that *superstes* is the witness "who lived through the ordeal" and represents the "the victims of the event," and thus are the survivors (p. 204). The *superstes* in this case embody the displaced Syrian women who survived the war and are now striving to make ends meet. Fassin (2012) stated that the *superstes* "has become a figure of our time" (p. 205). Having experienced the war and having experienced living in exile, the *superstes* is able to tell their story and their experiences with "the highest guarantee of the objectivity of the testimony" (Fassin 2012, p. 205).

In the context of these two terms, the humanitarian workers in the news reports fall under neither of these two categories. Their role as witnesses, rather, lies somewhere between *testis* and *superstes*. The humanitarian workers were part of the events presented in the news reports. They engaged with the people in the refugee camps where the humanitarian work was taking place. Hence, their testimony on the plight of displaced Syrian women did not really come from a third-party position, namely the external position of the *testis*. They were not a *superstes* either, because the statements and testimonies they made were not about their own survival but, rather, about the survival of the people with whom they worked and interacted on a daily basis. Fassin (2012) explains the role of the humanitarian worker. He writes:

> "Through a sort of reversal of the traditional roles, they occupy the structural place of the *testis* but employ the reasoning of the *superstes*. In other words, they privilege experience over observation, but this experience is the experience of others" (Fassin 2012, p. 206).

Therefore, the humanitarian workers' testimony is based on what they have seen first-hand, while being on site with the *superstes*.

Having differentiated between the three parties, what can these notions and comparisons tell us about the humanitarian discourse present in the television news? Fassin (2012) asks: "What political work of subjectivation does humanitarian testimony produce?" (p. 202). In this framework, the term subjectivation refers to the way the subjects are described by the humanitarian worker in the news reports.

To reflect on Fassin's question, I first refer to Judith Butler's notions about *ambivalence* and *subjection*. In her book "*Psychic Life of Power*," Judith Butler (1997) draws from Louis Althusser's (1971) notion of interpellation to describe the site in which the subject emerges. 'The site' refers to the power relation between language or discourse. This appears in the dominant media narrative that *interpellates* the individual (e.g., the displaced Syrian women), hence bringing them into subjectivation. Butler (1997) asserts that the subject is hailed into existence by language or discourse bringing them to an ambivalent site in which the subjectivation takes place. In other words, the subject is formed in this ambivalent site, thus revealing "the very condition of [the subject's] existence and the trajectory of its desire." (Butler 1997, p.2). On this basis, Butler claims that the discursive production of the social subject "consists precisely in this fundamental dependency on a discourse that [the subjects] never chose but that, paradoxically, initiates and sustains [their] agency" (Butler 1997, p. 2).

Having explained the relationship between subject and discourse, how can we further interpret the humanitarian testimony in the television media narratives and the work it produces on the subject (e.g., displaced Syrian women)? Granted, the person providing the humanitarian testimony – who is neither a *testis* nor a *superstes* – serves as a witness and contributes to the production of the news story. This research project demonstrated that the humanitarian worker's testimonies described the displaced Syrian women as victims of war, who are in need humanitarian assistance in order to survive. The news reports also represented the vocational and cash-for-work programs as the only solution to the displaced Syrian women's plight [2]. Furthermore, resilience was constructed as a 'skill' that displaced Syrian women have gained through their participation in the vocational trainings and are now employing in their daily life in exile. Thus, in those representations, the act of resilience is nuanced. The nuance appears when the humanitarian discourse in the news disassociates the Syrian women's acts of resilience from their states of vulnerability. Furthermore, these representations reflected on the idea of how the state of crisis lived by these groups of Syrian women has become the norm. The television reporting showed that many displaced Syrian women found themselves depending on their own self-resilience in order to survive this state of crisis. Thus, their resilience became framed as their only source of security.

In her study on *resilience humanitarianism*, Dorothea Hilhorst (2018) found that:

> "The resilience paradigm is as much based on selective understandings, foregrounding particular properties of social realities, while ignoring others. Equally, it consists of a set of ill-tested assumptions that seem to reduce the multiplicity of social reality to a singular discourse" (p. 10).

In the context this research, the humanitarian testimony in the Arab television news provided a "highly selective views of reality." Because parts of the representations were based on the stories the humanitarian experts *chose* to tell, their selectiveness in the humanitarian workers' testimonies has led to decontextualization of the displaced Syrian women's states of vulnerability. Furthermore, the findings showed a number of news reports depicting displaced Syrian women talking about their own living conditions and experiences in exile. In other words, the *superstes* was interviewed as the witnesses to their own situation, providing their own testimony. By telling their own

---

2   A common approach used by *resilience humanitarianism* that trains people affected by disaster or crisis on 'how to be self-resilient'.

stories on screen, did the Syrian women's testimonies better contextualize their states of vulnerability?

Drawing on Louis Althusser's doctrine of interpellation, Butler (1997) asserts that the subject is hailed into existence and subjectivation through the act of interpellation, an act that occurs through the matrices of power and discourse. In this framework, Butler (1997) asks the following: "Why does this subject turn toward the voice of law, and what is the effect of such a turn in inaugurating a social subject?" (p. 5). I want to rephrase Butler's question and, instead of why, ask *how* the subject turn towards the voice of law? In other words what stories (or parts of a story) does the subject tell, not tell, or choose (or not choose) to talk about? Moreover, does "the subject lose [her]self by telling the story about [her]self" (Butler 1997, p.11)? Fassin (2012) asked a slightly different question: "What [part of the] truth are they trying to make [her] tell, or to tell through [her]?"[3] (p. 202).

Ni'maa Al-Ahmad, a Syrian mother from the countryside surrounding s Syrian city of Hama and who now lives in Lebanon, was interviewed in a news report published by *Al Aan* on June 7, 2015 (in Chapter 6, *Section 6.5.2*). In this interview, Ni'maa narrated her own story as a single mother, who sought refuge in Lebanon for herself and her children. In the interview, she explained how she resorted to cleaning homes to make ends meet. Throughout the news report analysis, I found that Ni'maa's visibility was not influenced by a humanitarian discourse. Her state of vulnerability was not overshadowed by a narrative that focused on the victimization of the subject – as a way to promote the NGO's humanitarian initiatives in place to help the displaced persons. Ni'maa's visibility resembled that of the groups of displaced Syrian women working alongside people from the host community and other jobs require long commutes. Hilhorst (2018) explained that the displaced peoples who live outside the refugee camps, become indistinguishable from other, including local, members of the urban poor. Hence, they are not directly approached by the humanitarian organizations, who cannot easily locate or distinguish them.

In her interview, Ni'maa described the socioeconomic aspects that shape her daily life as a single mother living in exile. Her role as a *superstes* allowed her to contextualize her state of vulnerability. For instance, she talked about how she was exposed to sexual harassment at the work place and about

---

3   In the context of this research, the pronoun "they" refers to the journalists that have interviewed displaced Syrian women, as a source of testimony for their news story.

her financial struggles to make ends meet. The representations underscored Ni'maa's suffering.

Fida also gave her personal testimony in the same news report. Unlike Ni'maa, Fida provided little 'evaluative content' on the events that shape her experience as a displaced Syrian. The news report did not directly ask her about the cause of her vulnerability, specifically as a displaced Syrian woman living in Tripoli, Lebanon. In other words, her personal testimony did include little information about the actual and current external (and internal) world she inhabits. Nonetheless, like Ni'maa's, Fida's suffering was at the center of her visibility.

Chouliaraki (2013) explains how news production uses "a ritual of dramatic action" involving "those who act at the scene of suffering and those who watch from a distance" (p. 149). In this setting, the *suffering* (as a form affect or emotion) communicated by the *superstes* (e.g., Fida) on screen, becomes the only source of authenticity in the news story. This reveals the aesthetic choice that was made during the news production. The passionate "I" in the personal testimonies becomes part of "specific combinations of language, image and sound that do not simply reflect on an external world but render this world a sensible and meaningful reality for those who engage with it" (Chouliaraki 2013, p. 152).

By looking at the 'constructed' nature of the personal testimony in the television news, we can question the forms of reflexivity that the subject experiences when encountered by the camera and approached by the interviewer. Butler (2005) writes: "Telling the truth about oneself comes at a price, and the price of that telling is the suspension of a critical relation to the truth regime in which one lives" (p. 74). When approached by an interviewer, I am asked to give a "narrative account of myself because I am spoken to, because someone insists that I address myself to whoever addresses me, and thus form myself as a reflexive being before the Other" (Ong-Van-Cung 2011, p. 149).

Thus, the questions I would like to raise here are: What is the *superstes* aware of when she is being interviewed? Is she aware that she is experiencing subjectivation, that she is being framed by the aesthetic dimension of the camera, that she is being interpellated by the gaze of the interviewer and vice versa? [4] What is she feeling – moment to moment – during the interview, and how do these moments affect, disturb, or influence the personal narrative she is telling? What happens when she reflects on her own emotions or senses?

---

4   Subjectivation is the process by which one becomes a subject of discourse.

Does her speech change? Does she change? Donovan O. Schaefer (2019) asks: "What happens when someone asks you how you're doing – do you change?"

I reflect more on these notions and insights in the following section by posing questions on agency, resistance, and power.

8.3   Questions on Agency and the Dynamics of Shame, Fear, and Dignity in the Arab Television News

Butler (1997) looks at subjectivation by posing a very insightful question. She asks: "If power works not merely to dominate or oppress existing subjects, but also forms subjects, what is this formation?" (Butler 1997, p. 18). This question proposes, from a Foucauldian perspective on power, that the body is both productive and subjective. The dominant media discourse in the television news is a form of power that hailed different groups of Syrian women into their role as 'mothers of the nation.' The subjects are subject to the process of subjectivation under this form of power. Foucault (1982) suggests that "power is a situation we are always invested in, even when we resist it" (from Schaefer 2019, p. 31). Thus, the (displaced) Syrian women can resist this very subjectivation, but she is most definitely invested in it.

Building on these notions of Foucauldian power, I draw parallels between this research's case study and Saba Mahmoud's (2005) ideas on the pious subject. I use this analogy to contest a common approach to the understanding of agency, which is the idea "that the only valid thing women can do with conservative power formations is resist them" (Schaefer 2019, p. 59), an approach initially embraced by liberal and post-structural feminist perspectives.

Based on her fieldwork in Cairo on the female mosque movement in the mid-1990's, Saba Mahmoud (2005) presented a case study on groups of women who were prompting an Islamic revival from their local mosques across the city. Her analysis on Islamist cultural politics provided insights on the notion of agency, as well as a critique to certain structures of western feminism that failed to recognize Muslim women's own formation of agency within conservative movements; e.g., the revival of Islam in the female mosque movement. What I found particularly valuable in Mahmoud's study was her approach to reading agency through the capacity of action. Her rejection of reading agency "as a synonym for resistance to relations of domination" (Mahmoud 2005, p. 18) pointed out certain shortcomings in the repertoire of Enlightenment liberalism, with which many liberal feminists align themselves, particularly in the context of Islam and Islamic practices such as the hijab. The limits of this approach arises when "the liberal feminist position could only affirm that women who revived conservative forms of Islam were mindlessly amplifying their own oppression" (Mahmoud 2005, from Schaefer 2019, p. 56).

Mahmoud (2005) asserted that the colonial political project is replicated in feminist thought when western values are perceived as universal, dismissing any perspective that falls outside of these values or does not conform to this project. In Chapter 7, I developed my analysis by referring to Mahmoud's ideas. I suggested reconsidering the role of motherhood, and proposed exploring what this role could achieve beyond its national, patriarchal, and stereotypical gender function. Looking at agency as a "capacity for action" rather than a "resistance to relations of domination," I took Mahmoud's case study as an analogy of my work. While Mahmoud (2006) built her ideas on "pious subjects of the women's mosque movement" (p. 36), I built my argument on the social and political position of matriarchy as an institution that is inhabited and cherished by displaced Syrian women.[5].

I approached the notion of agency by looking at the ways displaced Syrian women may "devise their own formations of agency within the circumstances of their own situation" (Schaefer 2019, p. 57). I used the role of motherhood as an example. Although the role of motherhood may reinforce oppressive social and patriarchal norms, matriarchy – as an institution –nevertheless can provide women with the opportunity to acquire maternal control in their domestic spheres. In transnational contexts, in which Syrian families have been or are being ravaged by war, many Syrian women may pave their way through life by acquiring security and dominance through their matriarchal roles. Therefore, one should be aware that "what may appear to be a case of deplorable passivity and docility from a progressive point of view, may actually be a form of agency" (Mahmoud 2005, p. 15). Building on Mahmoud's thoughts, Schaefer (2019) suggested that, in order to avoid "pluralizing agency," we ought to resist "focusing on individual agency as good in itself" (p. 57). But what does that really imply?

To reflect on these ideas formulated above, I refer back to Mahmoud's case study. The mosque movement in Cairo developed as "a response to the perception that religious knowledge – as a means of structuring daily conduct –

---

5   In her ethnographic case study, she looked at the act of Islamic veiling and the forms of piety and Islamic revival women practiced in the "historically male-centered character of mosques and Islamic pedagogy" (Mahmoud 2006, p. 34).

had become increasingly marginalized under modern structures of secular governance" (Mahmoud, 2005, p. 4). When Egypt was being ruled by the military regime of Husni Mubarak – a U.S. backed government with secularist policy – the country witnessed a growth in a popular secular opposition. The rivalry between the Islamic and the secular was more than religious entities resisting a secular way of life. This tension was primarily political, as the elite ruling class of Mubarak was enforcing liberal secular values on economically oppressed Egyptians, the same demographic group of Egyptians who participated in the mosque movement – namely, the female preachers at the mosque as religious bodies. Here, "the return to Islamism is, in part, an expression of defiance, an embodied gesture in a global affective economy that develops the dignity of the religious bodies involved" (Schaefer 2019, p. 60).

Thus, "the need to assert dignity or to repudiate shame" becomes the driving factor and a motivational force behind the affective self-labor of the female preachers in the mosque movement. Mahmoud (2005) examined the participants' emotional states and how they were cultivating the virtues of shyness and modesty. She found that:

> "Among the mosque participants, individual efforts towards self-realization are aimed not so much at discovering one's 'true' desires and feelings, or at establishing a personal relationship with God, but at honing one's rational and emotional capacities so as to approximate the exemplary model of the pious self" (Mahmoud 2005, p. 31).

For instance, Mahmoud described one of her participants, Amal, as *not* naturally shy, but someone who put affective self-labor in cultivating shyness and modesty, as a way to practice *al-hayā* in the mosque movement.[6]. Amal said:

> "I realized that *al-hayā* was among the good deeds...., and given my natural lack of shyness... I had to make or create it first. I realized that making.... it yourself is not hypocrisy, and that eventually your inside learns to have *al-hayā* too" (Mahmoud 2005, p. 156)

This is how Mahmoud observed those repeated bodily acts as emotional capacities practiced by the participants to model the pious self.

Furthermore, Mahmoud affirmed that there is no universal model for agency and that feminist scholarship needs to provide the analytics to read

---

6   "To practice *al-hayā* means to be diffident, modest, and able to feel and enact shyness" (Mahmoud 2006, p. 51).

agency in multiple forms. Schaefer (2019) built his ideas about Mahmoud's approach by giving a further suggestion that "it is not the individual body that has agency, but the affects moving through the body" (p. 60). In other words, Mahmoud's participants became religious bodies – in the same sense that I may become a secular body – through the affects, emotions, and sensibilities that are cultivated and self-labored in their bodily performances. In other words, "they did not coolly select affects in order to become religious" (Schaefer 2019, p. 61), just like I do not casually choose to feel certain emotions and sensibilities in order to become secular. My secular self (as with the pious self) is shaped through repeated bodily acts that produce affective self-labor. Here, the repeated bodily acts with affective self-labor are a form of performativity. In this context, performativity does not exactly refer to Butler's understanding of doing or undoing gender through performance; rather, it is more closely related to Deleuzian understanding of *becoming*. It refers to the "individual and collective struggles to come to terms with events and intolerable conditions and to shake loose, to whatever degree possible, from determinants and definitions" (Deleuze 1995, Biehl and Locke 2010, p. 317). Hence, performativity is driven by struggle in this context.

Granted, the Syrian woman's experiences during the conflict are directly tied to her struggle. The news report analysis showed that the Syrian woman's visibility in the Arab television news was constructed through the dynamics of shame, dignity, and fear. In the reporting, their experiences during the conflict were shaped by her suffering and hardships. Building on these findings and theoretical approaches, how does the Syrian woman's struggle appear as instances or attempts to overthrow fear, reassert dignity, and negate shame?[7]

I reflect on this question by referring to the issue of high birth rates among the Syrian displaced communities and the notion of "sexual pleasure as a luxury."[8] A number of Lebanese newspaper articles discussed the soaring birth rates among the displaced Syrian population in Lebanon (Asharq Al-Awsat 2019; Lebanon 24 2019), and almost entirely linked these high birth rates to

---

7   Here I look at the experience of deposing fear, reasserting dignity, and negating shame as a performance that takes place in a plural form rather than a singular form, the same way Schaefer perceived Deleuze's *becoming* through a collective struggle rather than an individual struggle.

8   Rola Yasmine's talk during a panel discussion on "Sexual Rights and Human Rights: What is Sexual Pleasure?" held at the American University of Beirut in December 2017, https://www.youtube.com/watch?v=ASx9Xs21LYQ&t=3277s

unemployment and poverty (Jalkh 2016). Most of these media narratives neglected the fact that sexual intercourse is a basic human need and an accessi-
ble "form of free entertainment" available to all humans (Seghaier 2018). The
reoccurring question among NGOs, government institutions, and the Lebanese media outlets is: Why are the Syrian refugees conceiving so many children
while living in such precarious circumstances?

In 2016, the French-speaking Lebanese newspaper *L'Orient-Le Jour* revealed
that the annual number of births among the displaced Syrians in Lebanon was
40,000, with a population of over a million and a half in the host country. In
comparison, the number of births among Lebanese citizens in Lebanon stood
at around 70,000 per year, with a total Lebanese population of just 4 million.
The newspaper article linked these high birth rates among the displaced population to the lack of education, ignorance about contraception, early/child
marriage, and polygamy in Islam.[9] The article ended with a closing statement
on how the high number of births among the displaced population could perhaps be a sort of adverse reaction to war and death. It featured a statement
by a displaced Syrian woman in Lebanon who was asked by a social worker
about why she engages in sexual intercourse during her marriage when she
and her family live in such dire economic conditions. The Syrian woman's response was: "Life already has abused us enough with its share of injustice and
suffering. Why do they want to deprive us of our only remaining pleasure?"

In fact, this common media narrative, which criticizes the high birth rates
among marginalized social groups in Lebanon, did not start with the onset
of the Syrian conflict. It can be traced back to the outbreak of the Israeli-
Lebanese conflict, which lasted from 1970 until 2006. The narrative referred
to the high birth rates among the marginalized Lebanese Shia Muslims, who
had settled in Beirut after being displaced from their hometowns in South
Lebanon. This exodus was prompted by the ongoing massacres, such as the
shelling of Qana d by the Israeli Forces in April 1996 and other violent conflicts,
such as the July War in 2006 between Hezbollah and Israel. In the context of
the 2006 war in Lebanon, I have a poignant memory of my grandmother saying: "They are always killing us, and they almost took away my son, and here
I am, (...) other mothers like me will conceive ten more children for every son
the Israelis take from them!" My grandmother was a Lebanese woman from

---

9   The Islamic marital jurisprudence allows Muslim men to practice polygamy; it grants
     them the right to have up to four wives simultaneously.

South Lebanon who fled to Beirut with her family because of the ongoing conflict on the Israeli-Lebanese border. Her words somehow embodied a death-defying struggle stemming from the experience of violence, troubles, hardships, shame, and fear.

In this setting, many questions come to mind: How is sex among the poor and displaced populations portrayed? Does the media coverage of the high birth rate among displaced Syrian families imply that pleasure is not an entitlement of these communities because of their social status or economic class? Should sexual pleasure not exist among the impoverished? Is sexual intercourse among poor populations seen as something repulsive and immoral, as opposed to a natural form of human pleasure? Is sexual intercourse seen as a luxury of those who can afford to have children? Do the media sufficiently address how women do not have access to contraception, healthcare, as well as access to safe and affordable abortions in countries like Lebanon? Is the sexual intercourse of a displaced Syrian woman with her husband, which results in her pregnancy, seen as a submissive act of marital duty or as a technical act within a marriage, rather than a moment of embracing desire and intimacy?

But a more significant question in the context of this case study is: Is not the idea of building a family based on the idea of restoring dignity in the face of an oppressive power that has destroyed your family? Is it not a way of expelling shame and nurturing and sustaining dignity? In this context, shame is the result "of relatively high toxicity... it strikes deepest into the heart of man... it is felt as a sickness of the soul which leaves man naked, defeated, alienated, and lacking dignity" (Tomkins 1995, p. 148). On the other hand, dignity serves as 'psychological oxygen.' In this context, has dignity not become crucial to one's survival, a strong form of affect that functions as an emotional investment in the face of despair, overthrowing fear (the fear of death) and expelling shame?

In the following chapter, I summarize the main findings of this research project and contextualize them with older and recent literature on the topics.

9. From Dominant Media Frames to Spaces of Appearance

In this chapter, I reflect on the biases and blind spots that have appeared in reporting in the sociopolitical context of the Syrian conflict; I then link these to the ownership of the respective television stations. I summarize the dominant media frames that have appeared throughout the news reports analysis, and I reflect on the procedures of media reporting that have produced the media frames. I discuss how the figure of the Syrian woman in the television news appears as a stage for the mediated representation against the background of the geopolitical tensions during the Syrian conflict. In the last two sections, I summarize the main findings of the research project in the context of media logic, gender logic, and war logic, and I propose a feminist logic to the media representations by discussing the notion of 'spaces of appearance.'

9.1 Television Ownership: Biases and Blind Spots

Nikunen (2020) found that the groups of refugees in Europe who were interviewed about the European media covered the refugee 'crisis' in 2015 "shared this sense of frustration" with regard to "the gap between representations of refugees and their own experience of being a refugee." These groups found the news coverage repetitive, as it reported "the same stories over and over again, with sensationalism and a tendency to make errors" (Nikunen, 2020).

Granted, the decision-making process in the newsroom remains largely in the hands of the social elite. "Hegemonic and gender ideologies [are] repeatedly reproduced" in media representations, and thus "circulated in society and habitually accepted as 'truth'" (Georgiou 2012, p. 795). The way mainstream media represent minorities and marginalized groups, such as refugee women, is highly influenced by these factors.

The three Arab satellite television stations, *Al Jazeera*, *Al Arabiya*, and *Al Aan*, are owned by different government officials and political elites from Qatar, Saudi Arabia, and UAE respectively (Sakr, 2007; Najjar, 2018). This research project has demonstrated how news reports from these television stations similarly condemned human rights violations committed by the Syrian regime. The three stations embraced sensationalism[1] when reporting on the violent crimes committed by the Assad regime. At the same time, they also ignored the violence inflicted on Syrian women by the Syrian opposition groups that were fighting against the Syrian Arab Army.

This probably does not come as a surprise to the reader, as the governments of Qatar, Saudi Arabia, and the UAE are not only outspoken about their support for the Syrian opposition: they have also contributed to a proxy war in Syria by selling and providing weapons to armed groups fighting the Syrian regime. The *Financial Times* revealed in 2013 that Qatar was becoming the largest provider of arms to the various rebel groups in Syria, such as the al-Nusra front (Khalaf & Smith, 2013). Similarly, in 2017, an article on the *Al Jazeera* news website disclosed that "an investigative report by a Bulgarian journalist says Saudi Arabia and the UAE have supplied Eastern European-made weapons to armed groups in Syria [...] using different intermediaries and diplomatic cover to mask their points of origin and final destinations" (Al Jazeera News, 2017).

Television ownership and political context explain the editorial bias in the television reporting. The editorial bias in the coverage of the Syrian conflict becomes evident in *Al Jazeera's* news reporting, as previously discussed by several academic studies (Zayani, 2016), as well as in the news reporting by *Al Arabiya* and *Al Aan*; the latter two stations are "seen as a simulacrum of *Al Jazeera*" (Darwich, 2009, p. 132).

The television stations owned and controlled by the Syrian regime, *SANA*, *SAMA*, and *Syria Al-Ikhbariya*, have acted as a mouthpiece to the government policies and political agendas of the Syrian regime and the Baath Party and ignored Syrian women living in exile. Only Syrian women living in Assad-controlled parts of Syria appeared in the news reports, as they were portrayed through their roles of as servants and protectors of the nation. Similarly, *RT Arabic*, a television station controlled by the Russian state, omitted the figure of the Syrian woman living in exile in its reporting. The depictions by this station were limited to the 'positive' experiences of women inside Syria, such

---

1   This has been previously shown by Ayish, 2002; Falk, 2003; Gunter and Dickson, 2013.

as young Syrian women getting married to soldiers from the Syrian regime in a public ceremony in Aleppo. The editorial bias in *RT Arabic's* reporting is explained by Russia's political and military support of the Assad regime, on-going since the outbreak of the conflict in 2011, and Russia's direct military involvement in Syria that began in September 2015 (Tsvetkova & Zverev, 2016).

9.2   The Dominant Media Frames and the Procedures of Media Reporting

The research project found that the experiences of Syrian women during the conflict were depicted in five dominant media frames in the television news. These media frames were perpetuated in the news reports through seven different forms of media reporting. The table below illustrates these findings and categorizes them according to the four main concepts: *violence, vulnerability, resilience,* and *resistance.*

Table 10. Main findings: dominant media frames and procedures of media reporting

Main Concepts	Dominant Media Frames	Procedures of Media Reporting
Violence	Women as a source of shame	Circulation of shame
	Women as victims of their previous imprisonment	Stigmatizing the female victim
Vulnerability	Females as destined child brides	Dehumanization by misrecognized female desire
		Sentimental de-politization
Resilience	Women as the neoliberal subject	Strategic silencing
		Dehistoricization
Resistance	Women as mothers of the nation	Nationalizing the female body

One of the perpetuated media frames in the television coverage is the construction of former female Syrian prisoners as victims of shame and their previous imprisonment. The *circulation of shame* in the news reports is built on the figure of a Syrian woman, who is shamed for falling as a victim to gender-based violence at Syrian prisons and detainment centers. This dominant media frame contains sexist rhetoric that normalizes the *stigmatization of fe-*

male victims by portraying the former female prisoners as a source of societal shame.

Similarly, the television coverage of child brides showed repetitive frames of victimization. The news reports from *Al Jazeera*, *Al Aan*, and *Al Arabiya* exposed the increasing number of child marriages among displaced Syrian communities in Lebanon and Jordan. The media narrative sympathized with the vulnerable figures of child brides.

Numerical dehumanization of refugees is a common finding among scholars who have spoken about the "highly numerical representation of refugees' plight in Europe" in the mainstream media (Nikunen, 2020, p. 414). Although the news report analysis did not find any dominant media frames that *numerically* dehumanized the images of the displaced Syrian communities, a different type of dehumanization occurred in the news reports. The news presented the figure of the child bride as akin to the figure of *Homo Sacer*. A term coined by Agamben, "Homo Sacer, or the dehumanized, the misrecognized, is an individual who can be killed with impunity because, already in exile from the moral community, his life counts for nothing" (Agamben, 1998, p. 71-115, from Oliver 2010). In this media frame, the child bride's state of victimization and vulnerability are reaffirmed; the child brides' desire to lead a different life is portrayed as something unattainable, and marriage is her only way to survive in exile.

By showing the pitiful and tragic stories of child brides and close-up images of their families living in states of impoverishment, the media reporting aroused sympathy and understanding for the displaced Syrian communities. However, this emotional intimacy offered through the individualized stories of child marriages and the media narratives' tendency to sympathize with their suffering, led to the depoliticization of the child brides' plight. Nikunen (2020) found that this is also a common mechanism used by the European mainstream media's reporting on Europe's migration 'crisis.' She writes:

> "In terms of agency, news stories that evoke empathy and compassion often lean on representations of passive victimhood. In this way then, the benevolent, empathic discourses depict victims who are grateful, humble and explicitly vulnerable (Höijer, 2004; Ticktin, 2011: 186–7). This means that submission to the forces of chaos and exploitation, ill treatment and hard conditions seems to be inscribed in the figure of the victims and operate as a guarantee of their innocence" (Nikunen 2020, p. 415).

Johnson (2011) asserted these visual constructions function, on the one hand, as tools for "the mobilization of support behind humanitarian intervention and refugee work" (Johnson 2011, p. 1032) and, on the other hand, contribute significantly to how the observer sees and acknowledges the dynamics of refuge and asylum.

In the context of this research project, similar notions appear in two approaches of media reporting: *The dehumanization by the misrecognized female desire* and *sentimental de-politization*. These forms of media reporting depicted the displaced child brides as vulnerable, innocent, passive, submissive, and 'in need of saving' (see Mohanty 1984), thereby reinforcing "traditional gender assumptions" and denying these individuals "the capacity of political agency" (Johnson 2011).

In the case of the resilient displaced Syrian woman, the television news limited her visibility to her participation in vocational and cash-for-work programs funded by humanitarian organizations. These representations were constructed with two procedures of the media reporting: the procedure of *strategic silencing* and the procedure of *dehistorization*. Initially coined by anthropologist Liisa Malkki (1996) as "the architecture of silence," strategic silencing appears when the media headlines limit the narrative to the 'benevolent' humanitarian initiatives conducted by NGOs. The research showed that the media frames rarely showed any engagement with the female participants; rather, media attention was directed to the humanitarian initiatives. Moreover, by producing media headlines that fail to mention the contextual background of the Syrian conflict and the complex reasons why the displaced Syrian women had to seek exile, a form of dehistorization takes place. The strategic silencing appeared in the dehistorization that reduces the visibility of a displaced person to a 'philanthropic mode of power.' This form of visibility objectifies the subject as apolitical, poor, and passive. Under the umbrella of neoliberal ideals, the plight of displaced Syrian women again becomes depoliticized, but this time not with sentimentalism but with humanitarianism.

As for the concept of resistance in the television news, 'mothers of the nation' was the dominant media frame that appeared in the reports by the stations *SANA, SAMA*, and *Syria Al-Ikhbariya*. In this media frame, as a nation Syria appears as the motherland in which motherhood becomes a national service (Aghacy, 2009). The media frame of the 'mother of the nation' portrays the figure of the Syrian woman as a subject who resists opposition groups, which destabilize the ideology of nationhood perpetuated by the Ba'ath Party in news reports. Similar representations are discussed by Elizabeth Thompson (2000) in the context of "women and deviance in Syrian and Lebanese periodicals of the 1930s" during the French colonization of Lebanon and Syria (p. 220). Thompson (2000) characterized these stereotypical gender roles of 'the women of the nation' into two juxtaposed groups. The first group of women are *the Patriotic Mother* and *the Good Wife*, who "protect the nation, produce patriotic children, and marry" in the face of colonial power. The second group of women are *the Backward Woman* and *the Deviant*, who are "the highly sexed, aggressive women who were a danger to the nation itself" (Thompson, 2000, p. 222).

The representations of the second group of women – *the Backward Woman* and *the Deviant* –do not appear in the news reports. Nevertheless, the media reporting's constant affirmation of the importance of pursuing the roles and duties of the 'mothers of the nation' reveals how the media narrative is being utilized by its owners and authorities, which define the agenda for the news. In times of conflict, anxieties on maintaining the national and state identity –the "authentic" culture of the Ba'ath Party and nationhood in Assad Syria – appear in these mediated representations as *a site of struggle*. Thus, when the groups of Syrian women who participate in the armed and unarmed resistance in Syria are portrayed as beacons of stability in the face of change; in this context, "change is seen as a potential betrayal of one's culture, values, and language" (Aghacy, 2004, p. 2). A different approach is pursued in the media reporting: the figure of the Syrian woman becomes *nationalized* in the television news.

9.3   The Mediated Figure of the Syrian Woman at the Forefront of Geopolitical Tensions

In their study on the German print media's construction of Afghani women during the war in Afghanistan, Klaus and Kassel (2005) found that women were rarely depicted shaping their own lives. Instead, the media depictions of vulnerable women and children in refugee camps were generally used to evoke feelings of sympathy and pity in the reader. The media representation called for the "protection of the refugee women and their children" from the Taliban as a way to justify the armed intervention by the USA and its allies in Afghanistan (Klaus & Kassel, 2005, p. 346).

A more recent study by Amores, Arcila-Calderon and Gonzales-de-Garay (2020) found that journalistic photographs in Western European media between the year 2013 and 2017 underrepresented refugees while also portraying male and female refugees differently. The study showed that,

> "Female refugees were more frequently depicted as victims compared to male, while male refugees were more frequently depicted in burden or threat frames compared to female, so that in a more negative but also more active way" (Amores, Arcila- Calderón & Gonzalez-de-Garay, 2020).

Depicting refugees and displaced persons as a threat is a common and often repetitive media frame in the television coverage of migration and crisis (Nikunen, 2020). Although this dominant frame does not appear in any of the news reports analyzed for this research project, this does not mean that it does not exist within the context of the Syrian conflict.

In Europe, the arrival of a large influx of refugees in 2015 gave rise to both a humanitarian discourse and a securitization discourse in the European media. A study by Ricarda Drüeke and Elisabeth Klaus (2017) analyzed the Austrian media reporting of the arrival of refugees to Europe in 2015. The findings of the study showed that the refugees were portrayed

> "...as victims of war and terror when they reach the saving beaches of Europe, that is, when they are still far away. But as soon as they arrive in Austria, there are only few visual representations that frame the topic in a humanitarian way – instead, a threat and security frame dominates" (Drüeke & Klaus, 2017, p. 15).

This shift from the humanitarian discourse to the securitization discourse in Austria, and Europe in general, is best explained by the "normalization of nationalistic, xenophobic, and racist rhetoric that fear of change of any kind that can be constructed as a threat for 'us', an imagined homogeneous group of people in Europe" (Wodak, 2015, from Nikunen 2020, p. 417). Another study found that the media narratives that portray refugees as a threat in the European news are mostly projected towards "young men with dark skin" who are perceived as foreign elements that trespass spaces and disturb social order (Chouliaraki & Stolic, 2017).

While the shift in the media frames in the Austrian media took place once the refugees had physically entered Europe (Drüeke & Klaus, 2017), the shift in discourse in the context of Lebanon took place in a slightly different form. Between 2011 and 2014, a humanitarian discourse dominated the media depictions of Syrian refugees entering Lebanon. Initially, Syrians arriving in Lebanon were depicted as the next-door neighbors who were fleeing a war.

They were "portrayed both as brothers [and sisters] in need, deserving of the best intentions, and as a burden that weighs on the Lebanese state and its population" (Turbay, 2015, p. 17) −− given the fact that Lebanon is a country with dysfunctional and underfunded public services and failed infrastructure.

After the Syrian conflict had "spilled over into Lebanon, leading to gun battles and bombing, with major incidents ...of bomb attacks in Beirut," which also left the country with "economic strains as the number of Syrian refugees [...] reached over one million, or close to one-fifth of the population" (Kinninmont, 2014, p. 53), the political media discourse in the country started to show notions on securitization. In 2015, the Lebanese mainstream media started portraying the large number of displaced Syrians no longer as a burden but as a threat to Lebanon's delicate sectarian balance and its political, social, and economic stability (Turbay, 2015).

The news report analysis in this research showed that *Al Jazeera*, *Al Arabiya*, and *Al Aan* did adopt a humanitarian discourse in their reporting. However, no shift to the securitization discourse was noticeable in the news reports used as a sample for this case study, even though the reporting was specifically focused on the displaced Syrian communities, particularly displaced Syrian women in Lebanon. Nonetheless, this does not indicate that the shift did not take place in the general political discourse in the Arab Gulf States. An article by *Reuters* in 2015 reported on a political analyst from Kuwait, a wealthy Arab Gulf State that supported the radical Islamist opposition in Syria (Baxter, 2016), who "raised hackles by saying in a television interview [...] that [Syrian] refugees were better suited to poorer countries" such as Lebanon and Jordan, "failing to acknowledge the pledges of rich European countries like Germany to take in many thousands" (Bayoumy & Browning, 2015). The article also revealed how a government official from the UAE defended the Arab Gulf States' policies of not accepting any Syrian refugees into their countries,[2] by claiming that the proportion of foreigners to the locals was already overwhelming. An article by the *Washington Post* (2015) stated that "like European countries, Saudi Arabia and its neighbors also have fears over new arrivals taking jobs from citizens" (Tharoor, 2015).

These statements show that the notions of threat and securitization appeared in the general political discourses, as they implied that accepting Syrian refugees would result in their 'outnumbering the locals' and thus disturb

---

2   These affluent Gulf Arab States officially took in no Syrian refugees since the outbreak of the conflict in 2011 (Browning and Bayoumy 2015).

the delicate demographic balance in the countries (Bayoumy & Browning, 2015). While the news report analysis found that the humanitarian discourse showed 'immense sympathy' towards displaced Syrian women, these mediated representations juxtaposed with the immigration policies of Qatar, Saudi Arabia, and the UAE. Although the Arab Gulf States offered "collective donations under $1 billion (the United States has given four times that sum)" (Tharoor, 2015) in humanitarian aid to the Syrian refugee camps in Lebanon and Jordan, the conspicuous role the Arab Gulf States have played in the Syrian conflict by " funding and arming a constellation of rebel and Islamist factions fighting the regime of Syrian President Bashar al-Assad," places the countries in a partisan geopolitical position as they were clearly not "innocent bystanders" during the conflict (Tharoor, 2015).

Given these contextual factors, the displaced Syrian women came to be portrayed in public political discourses in the Arab Gulf States as the *other* Arab, one who is better suited to staying in economically-struggling Arab countries such as Lebanon and Jordan. The mechanism of 'othering' in the television reports by *Al Jazeera*, *Al Arabiya*, and *Al Aan* appears, as in the Austrian media, when the representations depict "political-geographic and geopolitical spaces" that situate the displaced communities "with other territories, places, or spaces, creating an imaginary geography, with images of landscapes and the people who populate them" (Drüeke, Klaus, & Moser, 2019, p.9). In Chapter 6, I analyzed such a space that was constructed in news reports as a 'heterotopian site' occupied by the urban poor. These depictions suggest that displaced Syrian communities will always remain outside those countries.

Thus, the "mechanisms of othering with frames of threat and management of masses" (Nikunen, 2020, p. 414) should be seen in conjunction with the procedure of dehistorization under the frame of the neoliberal subject and the procedure of nationalizing the female body under the frame of mothers of the nation. I explore the connection between the aforementioned procedures of media reporting and media frames below.

The news report analysis demonstrated how *SANA*, *SAMA*, and *Syria Al Ikhbariya* have placed the figure of the Syrian woman within an imagery of "the Syrian collective family." According to Wedeen (1999), these images are "established through endlessly repeated narratives of sacrifice and familial loyalty to Assad" (quoted from Haugbolle, 2008, p. 264). Haugbolle (2008) asserted that these images of nationhood, which are characterized by Ba'athist nationalist propaganda, are part of a greater political agenda that depict "the steadfastness (*al-sumud* الصمود)" and "the sacrifice (*al-tadhiya* التضحية)" of 'the people' as a way to "resist Zionism, Israel, and Western imperialism, salvage the Golan Heights, and unite "the Syrian people and the Arab and Muslim *umma*" (p. 264). These imageries of the Ba'ath party, which are "strongly influenced by Communist imaginaries of 'the people' [...] [and] that mostly focus on collective historical feats of the people, the party and the nation" (Haugbolle, 2008, p. 264) place the 'heroic' figure of the mother of the nation at the forefront of this ideological battle; the Syrian woman is expected to offer her "sacrifice for the greater good of the nation" (Wedeen, 1999).

Here, the media frame of the Syrian woman as 'the mother of the nation' is juxtaposed with the mediated representations of displaced Syrian women as the neoliberal subject, which is a dominant media frame perpetuated by television stations owned by opponents of the Syrian regime (such as the Arab Gulf States). Portrayed as part of the passive poor with a neglected history, the figure of the vulnerable displaced Syrian woman is 'othered' in the television media owned by the political elites of UAE, Qatar, and Saudi Arabia. These countries supported and funded the opposition groups that rebelled against the Ba'athist nationalist power in Syria. Hence, these mediated representations are part of two competing political agendas: the Ba'ath's political agenda to have the regime' retain its power in the region and the Arab Gulf State's political agenda to dismantle the Syrian regime.

Given all these factors, this research project perceives the media frames that have appeared in the news reports as a reflection of the geopolitical tensions during the Syrian conflict. These tensions could be traced to a resistance axis of two opposing sides that have fought in the Syrian conflict: the Assad Regime and its allies, i.e., Iran, Hezbollah, Russia and Hamas, a (geo)political alliance that opposes and fights "US and Israeli interests in the region" (Kinninmont, 2014, p. 52), on one hand, and the Arab Gulf States, who tend to take pro-western and anti-communist stands (Cordesman, 1988) and who have a strong Islamic (Sunni) national identity (Kéchichian, 2001, p.444), on the other hand.

Klaus and Kassel (2005) asserted that "war needs the dichotomy of friends and foes, of perpetrators and victims, of those who act and those who suffer" (p. 336). In this research project, the dichotomies depicted through the dominant media frames in the television news appear in the context of these geopolitical tensions. Moreover, although the meanings attached to the media frames of the different groups of Syrian women during the conflict are contextual and may shift in the future, I argue that these media frames are mediated instances that are always symptomatic of broader issues concerning nation-alism, neoliberalism, gender politics, conflict, and (geo)political tensions.

9.4   The Intersection of Media Logic, Gender Logic and War Logic in Television News Narratives

After discussing media ownership, procedures of media reporting, and dom-inant media frames in relation to the geopolitical tensions, I reflect on how the findings in the news report analysis underscore the interrelation of media logic, gender logic, and war logic.

In their study on the German print media's coverage of the war in Afghanistan, Elisabeth Klaus and Susanne Kassel (2005) demonstrated how media narratives on war and conflict are militarized in the mainstream media as a way to legitimize the warring parties' political and military interventions. This often has led "the mainstream media in times of war [to] regularly neglect their function of presenting a diversity of opinions and of criticizing and controlling the political and economic elite" (Klaus & Kassel 2005, p. 338). In this case, "the media logic on conflict and war leads to 'structural militarization' of the media discourse" (Dominikowski, 1993, quoted from Klaus & Kassel, 2005, p. 338).

The findings in this research project were similar, given that a 'struc-tural militarization' in the Arab television news has been identified. For in-stance, Assad's prosecution of Syrian women was heavily perpetuated in the news reports by *Al Jazeera*, *Al Arabiya*, and *Al Aan*. The depictions of former fe-male prisoners who had been abused in detention centers were used to reveal how 'the enemy', namely the Syrian regime, violated human rights. The same news reports ignored the honor killing and sexual assault incidents commit-ted against women in rebel-held Syria. The media discourse 'reduced the com-plexity' of these human rights violations, focusing instead on the particulari-ties of how the female victims were shamed and stigmatized for to their im-prisonment. This induces an emotional rather than an analytical response. By presenting the media content on the sexual violations and assault in the Assad prisons in a sensationalist manner, the experiences of the victims of gender-based violence were restricted to gender binary constructions and attested to only 'the enemy.'

Furthermore, because the content of media texts is always shaped by cul-tural and political factors and vice versa, Klaus and Kassel (2005) proposed to

"extend the concept of media logic[3] (the militarization of the media and journalism) with those of gender logic (the symbolic construction of male–female
dichotomy) and the logic of war (the legitimization of war through the construction of self and other)" (p. 335). In this research project, television images
generated through the lens of gender logic appear in the news reports published by the television stations that are politically leaning against the Syrian
regime, as well as in the news reports by the television stations that are owned
or controlled by the Syrian regime.

In the news reports by *Al Jazeera*, *Al Arabiya*, and *Al Aan*, different groups
of Syrian women were depicted as helpless victims, child brides, and desperate mothers destined to their vulnerable states and their own victimhood. In
the news reports by *Syria Al Ikhbariya*, *SANA*, and *SAMA*, the female fighters
in Syrian Arab Army were portrayed as the mothers serving the nation and
the motherland, and they were described by Asma'a Al Assad as 'the beautiful
ornamented flowers of Syria.' The stereotypical image of "the woman that has
to be protected by a husband and brave fighter," as established by Schießer
(2002) (from Klaus & Kassel 2005, p. 346), does not appear in the news reports. Nevertheless, the general depictions in the Arab television news still
placed the figure of the Syrian women in the context of traditional femininity.

As for the war logic, Klaus and Kassel (2005) found that "gender logic and
logic of war are closely entangled in the refugee question: the connotation of
women as weak, passive, and in need of protection mingles with a demand to
help the needy refugees and a condemnation of the evil 'other' who forced the
women to leave their homes" (p. 346). On the one hand, in the news reports by
Al Jazeera, *Al Arabiya*, and *Al Aan*, the condemnation of the evil 'other,' that is
the Syrian regime, appears in the news reports related to the context of violence, for example by perpetuating images of former female prisoners. On the
other hand, images of displaced Syrian women with missing husbands and
child brides are depicted as helpless victims living in shelters of failed infrastructure and as 'the needy refugees.' Such images appear in the news reports
related to the context of vulnerability. These two media frames – the evil 'other'
and 'the needy refugee' who requires help – are intermingled with images of
displaced women participating in vocational and cash-for-work programs.

By relying on a humanitarian discourse to show the viewer that the displaced Syrian women are 'being taken care of,' the television news re-estab-

---

3   The concept of media logic was initially introduced by Altheide and Snow (1979).

lished spatial and temporal distances between victims of war and the television audiences. In this context, the media narratives gave the displaced Syrian communities 'the celebration of abstract humanity.' Konstantinidou (2008) described this media tactic as "the celebration of the dignity of the passive victim," which, in return, "gives the imaginary community back its sense of power, wellbeing, and, essentially, its ability to speak for and on behalf of the unity of human beings and to look down upon others" (p. 163).

Consequently, the war logic prioritizes humanitarian initiatives over the political meaning of the plight of displaced Syrian women. Meanwhile, the dominant narratives in the television news indirectly spares the affluent Arab Gulf States the assumption of greater responsibility for their participation in the proxy war in Syria. In other words, the depictions of displaced Syrian women participating in humanitarian initiatives have the following connotation: The humanitarian aid programs and donations exist to support the vulnerable Syrian women in exile, hence there is no need to assume responsibility for offering resettlement sites for the displaced Syrian communities.

9.5   A Feminist Logic by Spaces of Appearance?

Elisabeth Klaus and Susanne Kassel (2005) posed relevant questions that fit the context of this book. For example, they asked: "What are the gender discourses into which the news coverage ties? Do women routinely have their voices heard in the news? Are there more than symbolic and fleeting references to the way they live their lives?" (p. 351). This research project reflected upon these questions by addressing the notion of agency among the different groups of Syrian women in relationship to their visibility in the Arab television news. This research has attempted to expand the gaze of media logic, gender logic and war logic by both criticizing and reimagining the television news narratives through a feminist logic.

By taking a turn towards moral philosophy and sociology, I have enabled myself as a media studies researcher to expose the existing structures of power in the television images, as well as interpret them in context of socioeconomic inequality and suffering. Furthermore, by delving into questions on agency, points of reflexivity, power relations, affects and emotions, the purpose of this book is not to discard the analysis of television representations all together. By stepping away from the representations and media frames analyzed in the television news, the book has attempted to break the silence in the media, and rediscover spaces for voices that could have been lost between the entanglement of media logic, gender logic, and war logic. Nikunen (2020) writes:

> "While it is important to understand how representations work and what kind of political and moral claims they make, research could be more proactive in finding the spaces of agency and voice, in listening to migrants and refugees. Such a move requires a step away from the representational analysis of mainstream media, the frames of victimization and fear, to expand the exploration towards voice and alternative 'spaces of appearance' (Arendt, 1998 [1958])" (p.418).

While there is little hope for the mainstream media to start offering a feminist logic in their reporting, in which contemplating, acknowledging and visualizing alternatives become a dominant part of the discourse in the news, meanwhile, I do not find it productive to conduct research that is solely immersed in exploring the hegemonic media practices. This can lead to inadvertently ignoring the voice and agency that exist in other media realms. Therefore, I would start by asking: Where can refugees, migrants, women, minorities, and any marginalized community gain a political voice, rather than be represented as 'objects of inquiry' in the media? Where do the 'spaces of appearance' that challenge hierarchies of representations and empower voices exist?

Drüeke, Klaus, and Moser (2019) explored spaces of identity in press photographs and artistic representations of refugees and migration in Austria. They stated that hegemonic production of meaning is rarely challenged in mainstream media images of refugees and migrants. In contrast, they found that 'a counter-hegemonic image discourse' is more likely to appear in the "ambivalent and irritating representations" that are produced in contemporary artistic practices (Drüeke, Klaus, & Moser, 2019). They found that:

> "Art can 'infiltrate' or emphasize content that remains hidden in media discourses, for example, by addressing the causes of flight, multifaceted identities, the emphasis on flight as a self-determined act or freedom of movement for all. At the moment of reception, art can open up spaces of in-between and trigger productive uncertainties that – at its best – set in motion differentiated processes of reflection on identities and their constructions" (Drüeke, Klaus & Moser, 2019, p. 21).

While art can be a significant site for spaces of appearance, social media contexts where civil society protests, and grassroots movements are channeled are also spaces where hierarchies of representation can be undone and voices are enabled (Butler, 2015).

Throughout the discourse analysis of Arab television news, this research project showed that the experience of the subaltern is linked fundamentally to problems of social justice (see Mohanty, 2003; Stevenson, 2014). Thus, it is up to us, as researchers and as feminists, to seek methods in communication studies and other interdisciplinary fields that not only identify injustices in society, but also enable the subaltern to speak in dialogue, collaboration, and mutuality.

10. Concluding Remarks

This work investigated the relationship between the notion of agency and the Arab television media's representation of the experiences of displaced women during war and conflict. Its aim was to examine how the concepts of *violence, vulnerability, resilience,* and *resistance* were represented in the dominant media discourses. I explored how dominant media narratives driven by elitist ideals and humanitarian thinking impact the television media frames in news reports. Different experiences of displaced Syrian women during the recent conflict in Syria were chosen as a case study. The Syrian conflict has been covered extensively by many Arab television stations with diversified media ownership structures and different socio-political agendas. The displaced Syrian communities have witnessed many changes and continue to be drastically impacted by the conflict. At the same time, different Arab television stations have constructed the ever-changing gender realities experienced by different displaced Syrian women in the news. These factors rendered the case study challenging.

I began contextualizing the case study within current and previous debates concerning power, neoliberal ideals, gender politics in the context of displacement, exile, and the female body during war and conflict. The account then shifted to reflect on the experience of displaced Syrian women during the Syrian conflict in recent news reports published between 2013 and 2018 by seven different television stations, *Al Aan, Al Jazeera, Al Arabiya, SANA, SAMA, Syria Al Ikhbariyah,* and *RT Arabic.*

By employing a critical discourse analysis, I examined 32 news reports. The research found that the mediated representations in the television news could be traced based on five main dominant media frames:

(a) Women as a source of shame
(b) Women as victims of their previous imprisonment
(c) Females as destined child brides

(d) Women as the neoliberal subject

(e) Women as mothers of the nation

These media frames were constructed by seven different procedures of media reporting:

(a) The circulation of shame

(b) Stigmatizing the female victim

(c) De-humanization by misrecognized female desire

(d) Sentimental de-politization

(e) Strategic silencing

(f) De-historicization

(g) Nationalizing the female body

Throughout the news report analysis, I found that dominant media narratives in the television reporting at times were shaped by an elitist discourse and, at other times, by a humanitarian one. The sociopolitical views and the media ownership of the television station played a role in creating biases and blind spots in the news. In the television reporting, certain groups of Syrian women were rendered virtually invisible while others became hyper visible. I also found that a neoliberal agenda in the television news had influenced the mediated representations of the experiences of Syrian women in exile, as the depictions of their state of victimhood and vulnerability carried absent alternatives and hidden consequences.

Furthermore, the research showed that the agentive attempts by different groups of displaced Syrian women were either glorified, misconstrued, or left unrecognized by the dominant media narratives. I argued that the visibility of different groups of Syrian women and how their experiences were framed in the news should also be considered in the context of the geopolitical tensions in the Arab region. While the media frames in the Arab television news may shift and change in the future – depending on different context, sociopolitical views and media ownership structures – the mediated representations should always be read as *symptomatic* to broader issues around nationalism, neoliberalism, gender politics, conflict, and (geo)political tensions.

This research project has several limitations that hopefully will be tackled in future studies on gender, conflict, and media. The research design ignored other Arab and non-Syrian women who are also suffering from violent conflict, and there are also other groups of displaced Syrian women who did not appear in the news reports analyzed in this research's case study. For instance, throughout the sampling process, I found only one news report – by *Al Jazeera* – that depicted displaced Syrian women doing sex work in Lebanon as source income while in exile. These groups of women inhabit distinct socioeconomic realities that ought to be examined in future research.

Furthermore, this research analyzed news reports published within a narrow time period, the years between 2013-2018. The Syrian conflict consists of ongoing series of violent events that may continue or end unexpectedly. Although the research project analyzed news reports from seven different Arab television stations that have different sociopolitical views and media ownership structures, it nevertheless overlooked the television reporting produced by Kurdish militias and ISIS, which are both major actors in the Syrian conflict. Because I have no knowledge in the Kurdish language, I was not be able to analyze the content on Rojava TV. I also did not have any online public access to ISIS television station on Nilesat.

This project can be developed in many different ways. As previously mentioned, the research was limited to analyzing the encoding stage of the message; thus, the examination of the decoding of the public spectacle in the news is one route to take this further this research project. Journalistic coverage of distant suffering has been widely examined in academic studies, particularly with respect to how Western audiences decode news from mainstream media reporting on global crises. There is very little literature on how audiences in the Arab world decode such messages, particularly from Arabic speaking media outlets covering war and conflict. Pruce (2019) asserted that media content on distant suffering during war, conflict and crises, is:

> "...likely to include media products of human rights and humanitarian organizations. Similar considerations apply to news outlets and NGOs: What are our duties? To what ethical codes are we bound? What is effective in galvanizing the audience? Technology institutionalizes this debate at the intersection of emotion, communication, and politics by insisting that audiences wrestle with their obligations to suffering strangers. But what about the relationship among television viewers? If we all watch the same event at the same time through the same medium, do we become greater than the sum of our component parts? Is an audience truly a citizenry?" (p. 78).

So, when audiences act as transnational witnesses of victims of war and conflict, does the decoded message produce a sense of responsibility in the viewer, a sort of reaction prompting the need to act?

The findings in this research project reflected on how viewers consume spectacles of graphic images portraying distant suffering, whilst the perpetuated media messages perpetuated have contributed to providing cultural products of neoliberal capitalism. Therefore, the important question here is: What do these graphic images of distant suffering tell the viewers, particularly viewers who are members of advocacy groups and human rights communities, Pruce (2019) asks, and how does "transnational citizen advocacy in a social world structured and saturated by visuality" develop (p. 79)?

In today's digital media age, the viewer has wide access to information and is constantly witnessing human rights abuses and violations through videos, as well as satellite image, which are being circulated and disseminated faster and with greater influence than in the past. Thus, another question to address here would be: What do these technological capabilities have to offer viewers, particularly members of human rights groups? Is being aware of human rights abuses and spreading an awareness of human rights abuses sufficient to stop such abuses? And, if the viewer is transformed into "a mere spectator" of those violations, how can collective action emerge from simply bearing witness to the graphic images being circulated?

Another major finding showed that the narrative in news reports prioritized the role humanitarian initiatives play in tackling the plight of displaced Syrian women, without giving focusing on the political significance of suffering in exile. In this context, the news reporting celebrated the dignity of the victim by relying heavily on a humanitarian discourse to encode the message. Thus, it would be fruitful to further explore how such news reports are decoded by the viewer. What happens when the viewer establishes a relationship with the victims by seeing them suffer? What happens when the news celebrates the dignity of the victims by exposing the humanitarian initiatives that have taken place? Does the viewer feel relieved, and, if so, is the plight of the victim depoliticized in the eyes of the viewer? Another way to explore the decoding of the message is to ask what effects the spectacle of poverty, crisis, war, and catastrophe produce among the viewers? Can compassion "paradoxically prove to be an emotion that spares those feeling it from having to take more demanding action?" (Fassin, 2012, p. 180).

After providing a list of questions that serve as insights for future research, I close this chapter by reasserting the importance of spaces of appearance. With the rise of the human rights crises in the Global South and the deterioration of refugees and migrant rights across the world (Stevenson 2014; Rheindorf & Wodak 2017; Hollenbach 2019), "the ability to take part in political debates and discussions of justice" (Agamben, 2000) becomes increasingly fundamental to the issue of inequality.

"There is no doubt that the fragmentation of media spaces (with personal media and social media, for example)" and "the diffusion of communication technologies has benefited" displaced communities, refugees, and "other dispersed groups" (Georgiou, 2012, p. 794). Nonetheless, the digital divide or "the uneven distribution of information and communication technologies in society" (Schweitzer, 2008), along with the growing difficulty of gaining refugee status and the lack of access to membership in society, is leaving the most vulnerable groups in society with increased difficulty to take part of the debates on injustice and inequality. Granted, these groups continue to suffer from the expansion of "surplus humanity" (Ticktin, 2010; Robinson & Baker, 2019).

Examining biases in media coverage will always remain significant in the field of communications studies. Nonetheless, it is also crucial to recognize how particular methodological approaches may hinder our ability to engage with and listen to the subaltern and identify their agency. Instead of "repeating the power relations inscribed in the epistemological practices of Western social-scientific research" (Nikunen, 2020), we need to prioritize methodological choices that enable researchers to explore the spaces of appearance; spaces where the subaltern is "voicing their interests" and providing "alternative sets of representations against hegemonic ones" (Georgiou, 2012, p. 794).

Bibliography

Abirafeh, L., & Nassif, G. (2018). Ending Child Marriage in Lebanon: Films like 'Nour' Can Make a Difference. The Conversation. Retrieved from https://theconversation.com/ending-child-marriage-in-lebanon-films-like-nour-can-make-a-difference-92458.

Abou-Raad, M. (2018). Vocational Programs for Refugee Women: More than Sewing Classes? Retrieved April 28, 2019, from http://iwsaw.lau.edu.lb/publications/documents/OPS 3_Abou-Raad_FINAL 2018 .pdf

Abuelnaga, S. (2018). "I'm Not a Mother, Therefore I Don't Exist". Kohl: a Journal for Body and Gender Research, 4(2): 197-204. (Last accessed on 07 June 2019). Available at: https://kohljournal.press/im-not-mother.

Agamben, G. (1998). *Homo Sacer: Sovereign power and bare life*. Stanford University Press.

Agamben, G. (2000). Means without end: Notes on politics. Minneapolis, MN: University of Minnesota Press.

Aghacy, S. (2004). What about masculinity? *Al-Raida Journal*. 21(104-105) 2-3.

Aghacy, S. (2009). *Masculine identity in the fiction of the Arab East since 1967*. Syracuse, N.Y.: Syracuse University Press.

Ahiska, M. (2016). Violence against Women in Turkey: Vulnerability, Sexuality, and Eros. In J. Butler, Z. Gambetti & L. Sabsay (eds.) *Vulnerability in Resistance* (pp. 211–235). Durham and London: Duke University Press. doi: 10.1215/9780822373490-011

Al Hayari, M. (2017, November 3). Jordan is solving its water crisis by training women as plumbers. Retrieved from https://apolitical.co/solution_article/jordan-solving-water-crisis-training-women-plumbers/.

Alhayek, K. (2015). Untold Stories of Syrian Women Surviving War. *Syria Studies*, 7(1), 1–30. Retrieved from https://ojs.st-andrews.ac.uk/index.php/syria/article/view/1066

Ali, S. (2007) 'Introduction: Feminism and Postcolonial: Knowledge/Politics. *Ethnic and Racial Studies*. 30,191-212.

Alkhaled, S. (2018). The Resilience of a Syrian Woman and Her Family Through Refugee Entrepreneurship in Jordan. *Refugee Entrepreneurship*, 241–253. doi: 10.1007/978-3-319-92534-9_17

Al Jazeera. (2017, August 27). Report: Saudi, UAE weapons end up with armed groups. Retrieved from https://www.aljazeera.com/news/2017/08/saudi-arabia-uae-implicated-arms-transfers-170827115154085.html

Alous, Y. (2017, January 18). Skin-Deep Only: Troubling Hypocrisies in the Ba'ath Party's Approach to Women's Rights and Secularism in Syria. Retrieved June, 2019, from https://lb.boell.org/en/2017/01/18/skin-deep-only-troubling-hypocrisies-baath-partys-approach-womens-rights-and-secularism

Almezaini, K. S., & Rickli, J. (2016). *The small Gulf states: Foreign and security policies before and after the Arab Spring*. Routledge: Taylor & Francis.

Alsaba, K.H. & Kapilashrami, A. (2016). Understanding women's experience of violence and the political economy of gender in conflict: the case of Syria. *An international journal on sexual and reproductive health and rights*, 47(24), 4-17

Altheide, D. L. & R. P. Snow (1979) *Media Logic*. Beverly Hills, CA: Sage.

Amores, J. J., Arcila-Calderón, C., & González-de-Garay, B. (2020). The gendered representation of refugees using visual frames in the main western European media. *Gender Issues*. doi:10.1007/s12147-020-09248-1

Arab, R. E., & Sagbakken, M. (2019). Child marriage of female Syrian refugees in Jordan and Lebanon: a literature review. Retrieved from https://www.tandfonline.com/doi/abs/10.1080/16549716.2019.1585709.

Arendt, H. (1958). *The human condition*. Chicago: University of Chicago Press.

Arendt, H. (1970). *On Violence*. Place of publication not identified: Harcourt Brace Javanovich.

Arendt, H. (1998 [1958]). *The human condition*. Chicago: Chicago University Press.

Arenfeldt, P., & Golley, N. A.-H. (2012). *Mapping Arab Womens Movements: a Century of Transformations from Within*. Place of publication not identified: American University of Cairo Press.

Asaf, Y. (2017). Syrian Women and the Refugee Crisis: Surviving the Conflict, Building Peace, and Taking New Gender Roles. *Social Sciences*, 6(110). doi:oi:10.3390/socsci6030110

Asharq Al-Awsat. (2019, September 9). ‮ن...لبنان‬ ‮في نييرورسلا ديلاوم‬. ‮تسهيلات وهلع ميدفارغومفيضوش نوؤش نييئجاللا تووقت ةدايز‬ ‮تسجيهلم ةياهن علاإا‬ . Asharq Al-Awsat. https://bit.ly/3evxzEq

Atlantic Council's Digital Forensic Research Lab. (2018). Question that: RT'S military mission. Retrieved April 09, 2021, from https://medium.com/dfr lab/question-that-rts-military-mission-4c4bd9f72c88

Ayish, M. (2002) Political communication on Arab world television: Evolving patterns. *Political Communication*, 19, 137–54.

Ayoub, J., & Abou Jaoude, E. (2018). Lebanon's Scapegoating of Refugees Did Not Start With Syrians, but With Palestinians · Global Voices. Retrieved November 11, 2019, from https://globalvoices.org/2018/02/01/lebanons-s capegoating-of-refugees-did-not-start-with-syrians-but-with-palestinia ns/.

Bartels, S. A., & Michael, S., Roupetz, S., (2018). Making sense of child, early and forced marriage among Syrian refugee girls: a mixed methods study in Lebanon. *BMJ Global Health*.

Batha, E., & Thomson Reuters Foundation. (2013). Syrian war causing 'honour killings', child marriages - doctor. Retrieved from http://news.trust.org// item/20131204182854-8hegf/

Bayoumy, Y., & Browning, N. (2015, September 6). In rich Gulf Arab states, some feel shamed by refugee response. Retrieved from https://www.reut ers.com/article/us-europe-migrants-gulf/in-rich-gulf-arab-states-some- feel-shamed-by-refugee-response-idUSKCN0R60H620150906

Baxter, K. (2016). Kuwait, political violence and the Syrian War. *Australian Journal of International Affairs*, 71(2), 128-145. doi:10.1080/10357718.2016.1210081

Beals, E. (2016). Wheat as a Weapon of War in Syria. Retrieved from https://w ww.vice.com/en_us/article/jpka5k/wheat-as-a-weapon-of-war-in-syria.

Benkler, Y., Roberts, H, & Faris, R. (2018). Network Propaganda: Manipulation, Disinformation, and Radicalization in American Politics. New York: Oxford University Press.

Biehl, J., & Locke, P. (2010). Deleuze and the Anthropology of Becoming. *Current Anthropology*, 51(3), 317–351. doi: 10.1086/651466

Bielby, C. (2012). Violent Women in Print: Representations in the West German Print Media of the 1960s and 1970s. NY: Camden House.

Blommaert, J., & Bulcaen, C. (2000). Critical Discourse Analysis. *Annual Review of Anthropology*, 29, 447–466. doi: 10.1146/annurev.anthro.29.1.447

Bourbeau, P. & Ryan, C. (2017). Resilience, resistance, infrapolitics and enmeshment. European Journal of International Relations. Retrieved May

27, 2018, from http://journals.sagepub.com/doi/abs/10.1177/135406611769
2031

Bracke, S. (2016). Bouncing Back: Vulnerability and Resistance in Times of
Resilience. In J. Butler, Z. Gambetti & L. Sabsay (eds.), *Vulnerability in resistance*, 52-75. Durham, NC: Duke University Press

Bunch, M. (2017). Julia Kristeva, Disability, and the Singularity of Vulnerability. *Journal of Literary & Cultural Disability Studies* 11(2), 133-150. https://www
.muse.jhu.edu/article/664477.

Burguieres, M.K., (1990). Feminist Approaches to Peace: Another Step for
Peace Studies. *Millennium: Journal of International Studies*, 19(1), 1-18.

Butler, J. (1990). *Gender Trouble: Feminism and the Subversion of Identity*. New
York: Routledge.

Butler, J. (1997). *"Excitable speech": a politics of the performative*. New York: Routledge.

Butler, J. (1997). *The Psychic Life of Power: Theories in subjection*. Stanford, Calif:
Stanford University Press.

Butler, J. (2003) Violence, Mourning, Politics, Studies in Gender and Sexuality, 4:1, 9-37, DOI: 10.1080/15240650409349213

Butler, J. (2003). *Giving an Account of Oneself: a Critique of Ethical Violence*. Assen:
Van Gorcum.

Butler, J. (2004). *Precarious life: The powers of mourning and violence*. London:
Verso.

Butler, J. (2004). *Undoing gender*. New York: Routledge.

Butler, J. (2005). *Giving an account of oneself*. New York: Fordham University
Press.

Butler, J. (2009). *Frames of war: when is life grievable?* London: Verso.

Butler, J. (2015). *Notes toward a performative theory of assembly*. Cambridge, MA:
Harvard University Press.

Butler, J. (2016). Rethinking vulnerability and resistance. In J. Butler, Z. Gambetti & L. Sabsay (eds.), *Vulnerability in resistance*, 12–27. Durham, NC:
Duke University Press.

Butler, J., Gambetti, Z., & Sabsay, L. (2016). *Vulnerability in resistance*. Durham
and London: Duke University Press.

Cablegate (2012), "Ideological and Ownership Trends In The Saudi Media".
11 May 2009. Archived from the original on 16 January 2013. Retrieved 1
May 2012.

Calabresi, G., & Bobbitt, P. (1978). *Tragic Choices*. New York: W.W. Norton &
Company, 1978.

Carrie, S., & Alomar, A. (2018). 'They see no shame': 'honour' killing video shows plight of Syrian women. Retrieved from https://www.theguardian .com/global-development/2018/nov/12/they-see-no-shame-honour-killin g-video-shows-plight-of-syrian-women.

Chapman, M.W. (7 October 2016). "ISIS Genocide of Yazidis: 'Girls As Young as 9 Were Raped, As Were Pregnant Women'". CNS News. Retrieved 14 Nov 2019.

Charles, L., & Denman, K. (2012). ""Every knot has someone to undo it." Using the Capabilities Approach as a lens to view the status of women leading up to the Arab Spring in Syria". *Journal of International Women's Studies.* **13**(5): 195–211.

Charap, S., Treyger, E., & Geist, E. (2019, October 31). Understanding Russia's intervention in Syria. Retrieved April 09, 2021, from https://www.rand.o rg/pubs/research_reports/RR3180.html

Chouliaraki, L. (2013). *The ironic spectator: solidarity in the age of post-humanitarianism.* Cambridge, UK: Polity Press.

Chouliaraki, L., & Stolic, T. (2017). Rethinking media responsibility in the refugee 'crisis': A visual typology of European news. *Media, Culture & Society*, 39(8): 1162-1177.

Cordesman, A. H. (1988). *The Gulf and the west: Strategic relations and military realities.* Routledge.

Couldry, N. (2000). *The Place of Media Power: Pilgrims and Witnesses of the MediaAge.* London: Routledge

Clare, S. (2009). Agency, Signification, and Temporality. *Hypatia*, 24(4), 50–62. doi: 10.1111/j.1527-2001.2009.01057.x

Cornish, C. (2018, November 22). Building lives: The Charity that Gives Lebanon's Hidden Refugees a Home. Retrieved January 15, 2019, from h ttps://www.ft.com/content/b27283ce-ed29-11e8-8180-9cf212677a57

Cvetkovich, A. (2012). *Depression: A Public Feeling.* Durham, NC: Duke University Press.

Daily Sabah. (2019). Syrian Woman Recalls Regime Torture, Condition of Women in Prisons. Retrieved from https://www.dailysabah.com/politics /2019/06/27/syrian-woman-recalls-regime-torture-condition-of-women-in-prisons.

Darwich, A. (2009). *Social semiotics of Arabic satellite television: Beyond the glamour.* Melbourne: Writescope Publishers.

Deleuze, G. (1995). Negotiations, 1972–1990. New York: Columbia University Press

Discourse Analysis Part 1: Discursive Psychology (May 6, 2015) YouTube video, added by Graham R Gibbs [Online]. Available at https://www.youtube.co m/watch?v=F5rEy1lbvlw

Dominikowski, T. (1993) 'Massen'medien und Massen krieg. Historische An-näherungen eine unfriedliche Symbiose', in M. Löffelholz (ed.) *Krieg als Medienereignis. Grundlagen und Perspektiven der Krisenkommunikation*, pp. 33–48. Opladen:Westdeutscher Verlag.

Doraï, K., & Piraud-Fournet, P. (2018). *From Tent to Makeshift Housing: A Case Study of a Syrian Refugee in Zaatari Camp (Jordan)*. M. Fawaz, A. Gharbieh, M. Harb and D. Salamé. Refugees as City-Makers, American University of Beirut (Issam Fares Institute, Social Justice and the City Program), pp.136-139, 2018, 978-9953-586-39-7. halshs-01871781

Doraï, M.K. (2010, December 10). *Palestinian Refugee Camps in Lebanon*. Migra-tion, mobility and the urbanization process. Retrieved from https://halsh s.archives-ouvertes.fr/halshs-00545433

Drüeke, R., Klaus, E., & Moser, A. (2019). Spaces of identity in the con-text of media images and artistic representations of refugees and mi-gration in Austria. *European Journal of Cultural Studies*, 136754941988604. doi:10.1177/1367549419886044

Drüeke, R., & Klaus, E. (2017, May 29). *"Us" and "The others". Pictures of refugess in the Austrian print media*. Retrieved from Televizion website: https://ww w.researchgate.net/publication/317278613_Us_and_The_Others_Pictures _of_Refugess_in_the_Austrian_Print_Media

Dunham, J. (2011, September 14). Syrian TV station accuses Al Jazeera of fab-ricating uprising. Retrieved from https://thelede.blogs.nytimes.com/2011 /09/14/syrian-tv-station-accuses-al-jazeera-of-fabricating-uprising/

Dupuy, K. & Rustad, S. A. (2018). *Trends in Armed Conflict, 1946–2017*, Conflict Trends, 5. Oslo: PRIO.

Enloe, C. (1993). *The Morning After: Sexual Politics at the End of the Cold War*, Uni-versity of California Press, Berkeley.

Enloe, C. (2000). *Maneuvers: The International Politics of Militarizing Women's Lives*, University of California Press, Berkeley.

Fairclough, N. (1992). Discourse and Text: Linguistic and Intertextual Anal-ysis within Discourse Analysis. *Discourse & Society, 3*(2), 193–217. doi: 10.1177/0957926592003002004

Fairclough, N. (1996). A reply to Henry Widdowson's 'Discourse analysis: a critical view'. Language and Literature, 5(1), 49-56.

Fairclough, N. (2001). The discourse of New Labour: Critical Discourse Analysis.

Fairclough, N. (2001). The discourse of New Labour: Critical Discourse Analysis. In M.

Fairclough, N. (2003). *Analysing discourse: textual analysis for social research*. Routledge.

Falk, W. (18 April 2003) The impact of Al-Jazeera. *The Week Magazine*, p. 11.

Fanack. (2019). No Action from Lebanese Government as Financial Collapse Looms. Retrieved from https://fanack.com/lebanon/economy/no-action-from-lebanese-government-as-financial-collapse-looms/

Fassin, D. (2012). *Humanitarian reason: A moral history of the present times*. Berkeley: University of California Press.

Foucault, M. (1969). The Archeology of knowledge. London: Routledge.

Foucault, M. (1975). *Discipline and Punish: The Birth of the Prison*. New York: Pantheon Books.

Foucault, M. (1980). Power/ Knowledge: Selected Interviews and Other Writings 1972-1977. Ed. Colin Gordon. NewYork : Pantheon

Foucault, M. (1982). The Subject and Power. *Chicago Journals, 8*(4), 777–795. Retrieved from http://www.jstor.org/stable/1343197 .

Foucault, M. (1984). "The Ethics of the Concern for Self as a Practice of Freedom", in *Essential Works of Foucault 1954-1984, Volume 1: Ethics, Subjectivity and Truth*, ed. Paul Rabinow (1997), 292.

Foucault, M. (1984). "What is Called 'Punishing?'", in Essential Works of Foucault, Volume 3: Power, ed. James D. Faubion (2001), 386.

Foucault, M., & Gordon, C. (1980). Power/knowledge: Selected interviews and other writings, 1972-1977. New York: Pantheon Books.

Foucault, M. (1976). The History of Sexuality, Vol. 1: An Introduction. New York: Vintage Books.

Foucault, M. (1984). *Of Other Spaces*. The John Hopkins University Press, 16(1), 22-27

Freedman, J., Nurcan Baklacıoğlu, N. Ö, & Kivilcim, Z. (2017). *A Gendered Approach to the Syrian Refugee Crisis*. Routledge.

Freedom House. (2010). *Women's Rights in the Middle East and North Africa 2010 – Syria*. Available at: https://www.refworld.org/docid/4b99011dc.htm l [accessed 23 October 2019]

George, A. (2003). Syria: Neither bread nor freedom. London: Zed Books.

Georgis, D. (2013). Thinking past pride: Queer Arab shame in Bareed Mista3Jil. *International Journal of Middle East Studies, 45*, 233-251.

Georgiou, M. (2012). Gender, migration and the media. Ethnic and Racial Studies, 35(5), 791-799. doi:10.4324/9781315873220

Georgiou, M. (2018). Does the subaltern speak? Migrant voices in digital Europe. *Popular Communication*, 16(1): 45–57.

Grandi, F., Mansour, K., & Holloway, K. (2018, November 01). Dignity and displaced Syrians in Lebanon. Retrieved September 15, 2020, from https://www.odi.org/publications/11236-dignity-and-displaced-syrians-lebanon

Graham R Gibbs. (2015, May 6). *Discourse Analysis Part 2: Foucauldian Approaches* [Video file]. Retrieved from https://www.youtube.com/watch?v=E_ffCsQx2Cg

Gunter, B., & Dickinson, J. R. (2013). *News Media in the Arab World: a Study of 10 Arab and Muslim Countries*. Continuum International Publishing Group, Limited.

Hall, S. (1992). The West and the rest: Discourse and power. In Stuart Hall & Bram Gieben (Eds.), *Formations of modernity* (pp. 275-320). Cambridge: Polity Press/Open University.

Hall, S. (1997). The Television Discourse; Encoding and decoding. Reprinted in A.Gray, & J. McGuigan (Eds.). Studies in Culture: An Introductory Reader. (pp, 28- 34).

Hall, S. (1974). Media Power: The Double Bind. Journal of Communication, 4(1), pp. 19–26.

Halldorsson, H. (2017, January 23). Syrian Children Forced to Quit School, Marry Early to Survive. Retrieved January 15, 2019, from https://www.unicef.org/stories/syrian-children-forced-quit-school-marry-early-survive

Haugbolle, S. (2008). Imprisonment, truth telling and historical memory in Syria. *Mediterranean Politics*, 13(2), 261-276. doi:10.1080/13629390802127646

Herald Sun. (2012). Syrian TV station attacked, 7 staffers die. (2012, June 27). *Herald Sun*. doi:https://www.heraldsun.com.au/archive/news/dead-in-attack-on-syria-tv/news-story/0ea22183599a21d252a4f6c60b1af92a

Herwig, R. (2017): Strategies of Resistance of Syrian Female Refugees in Şanlıurfa. In: movements. Journal for Critical Migration and Border Regime Studies 3 (2). URL: http://movements-journal.org/issues/05.turkey/12.herwig--strategies-resistance-syrian-female-refugees.html

Hilhorst, D. (2018). Classical humanitarianism and resilience humanitarianism: making sense of two brands of humanitarian action. *Journal of International Humanitarian Action*, 3(1). doi: 10.1186/s41018-018-0043-6

Hilton, D. (2017, December 22). The Shifting Role of Women in Syria's Economy. Retrieved March 3, 2020, from https://timep.org/syrias-women/economy/the-shifting-role-of-women-in-syrias-economy/

Hirsch, M. (2016). Vulnerable Times. In J. Butler, Z. Gambetti & L. Sabsay (eds.), *Vulnerability in resistance* In *Vulnerability in Resistance* (pp. 76–96). Durham and London: Duke University Press.

Hollenbach, D. S. (2019). *Humanity in crisis: Ethical and religious response to refugees*. Georgetown University Press.

House, R. (2009). *Childhood, Well-being, and a Therapeutic Ethos*. London: Karnac Books.

Höijer, B. (2004). Discourse of global compassion: The audience and media reporting of human suffering. *Media, Culture & Society*, 26(4): 513–531.

Høvring, R. (2019, February 11). What you need to know about Syrian child marriage. Retrieved March 6, 2020, from https://www.nrc.no/perspectives/2019/what-you-need-to-know-about-syrian-child-marriage

Human Rights Watch. (2019). Lebanon: Syrian Refugee Shelters Demolished. Retrieved from https://www.hrw.org/news/2019/07/05/lebanon-syrian-refugee-shelters-demolished

Independent. (2018, November 17). The brutality of the Syrian regime must be told. Retrieved March 6, 2020, from https://www.independent.co.uk/news/long_reads/syria-civil-war-detention-brutality-death-toll-prison-assad-regime-a8626071.html

Jalkh, J. (2016, August 29). Polygamie et mariages précoces derrière le taux de natalité galopant parmi les réfugiés syriens – L'Orient-Le Jour. Retrieved from http://www.lorientlejour.com/article/1004345/polygamie-et-mariages-precoces-derriere-le-taux-de-natalite-galopant-parmi-les-refugies-syriens.html

Jawad, R. (2015, September 25). Why are the Gulf States so reluctant to take in refugees?. Retrieved from https://theconversation.com/why-are-the-gulf-states-so-reluctant-to-take-in-refugees-47394

Johnson, H. (2011) Click to Donate: visual images, constructing victims and imagining the female refugee, Third World Quarterly, 32:6, 1015-1037, DOI: 10.1080/01436597.2011.586235

Kajjo, S. (2017, January 31). Syrian Regime Forms All-female Military Force in Kurdish Heartland. Retrieved February 28, 2020, from https://www.voanews.com/extremism-watch/syrian-regime-forms-all-female-military-force-kurdish-heartland

Kechichian, J. (2001). *Iran, Iraq and the Arab Gulf states*. Springer.

Kelly, L. (2000). 'Disabusing the Definition of Domestic Abuse: How WomenBatter Men and the Role of the Feminist State', Fla. St. U. L. Rev. Morrissey, 2003

Kenney, K. (2009). *Visual Communication Research Designs*. Florence: Taylor and Francis.

Khaddour, K. (2015). "The Assad Regime's Hold on the Syrian State." Carnegie Middle East Center. Accessed November 18, 2019. https://carnegie-mec .org/2015/07/08/assad-regime-s-hold-on-syrian-state/id3k?mkt_tok=3R kMMJWWfF9wsRogu6%2FKZKXonjHpfsX76eouX6%2Bg38431UFwdcjKP mjr1YYHS8t0aPyQAgobGp5I5FEIQ7XYTLB2t60MWA%3D%3D.

Khalaf, R., Asad, R., & Tawil, R. (2016). Women in Emerging Syrian Media: A Critical Discourse Analysis. *The Stichting Female Journalists Network*, 1–72. Retrieved from http://www.sfjn.org/research-en.pdf

Khalaf, R., & Smith, A. F. (2013, May 16). *Qatar Bankrolls Syrian Revolt With Cash And Arms - FT.Com*. [online] Financial Times. Retrieved from URL: <http ://ig-legacy.ft.com/content/86e3f28e-be3a-11e2-bb35-00144feab7de> [Accessed 1 July 2020].

Khiabany, G. (2016). Refugee crisis, imperialism and pitiless wars on the poor. Media, Culture & Society, 38(5), 755–762. doi:10.1177/0163443716655093

Kinninmont, J. (2014). *The Syria Conflict and the Geopolitics of the Region*. Retrieved from IEMed. Mediterranean Yearbook website: https://www.iem ed.org/observatori/arees-danalisi/arxius-adjunts/anuari/anuari-2014/Ki nninmont_Syria_Conflict_geopolitics_region__IEMed_yearbook_2014_E N.pdf

Klaus, E., & Kassel, S. (2005). The veil as a means of legitimization. *Journalism: Theory, Practice & Criticism*, 6(3), 335-355. doi:10.1177/1464884905054064

Kohl Journal. (2019). Shereen Abuelnaga. Retrieved from https://kohljournal. press/authors/shereen-abuelnaga

Konstantinidou, C. (2008). The spectacle of suffering and death: the photographic representation of war in Greek newspapers. *Visual Communication*, 7(2), 143–169. doi: 10.1177/1470357208088756

Kotef, H., & Amir, M. (2011). Between Imaginary Lines Violence and its Justifications at the Military Checkpoints in Occupied Palestine. *SAGE Theory,Culture & Society*, 28(1), 55-80.

Kraidy, M. M. (2002) Arab satellite television between regionalization and globalization. *Global Media Journal*, 1(1), www.reposi-tory.upenn.edu/asc_papers/186

Kraidy, M. M. (1998) Satellite broadcasting from Lebanon: Prospects and perils. *Transnational Broadcasting Studies*, 1, www.tbsjournals.org

Kristeva, J. (2014). Liberty, Equality, Fraternity, and…Vulnerability. Trans. J Herman. *Women's Studies Quarterly* 38.12 (2010): 251–68.

Lazar, M. (2007). Feminist Critical Discourse Analysis: Articulating a Feminist Discourse Praxis. *Critical Discourse Studies* 4 (2), pp.141-164.

Lebanon 24. (2019, September 9). أزمة المواليد السوريين في لبنان... ارقام تغيير ديمغرافي وتغيرة كبيرة. Lebanon 24. https://bit.ly/3esIBdp

Leduc, S. (2015, April 2). Assad's female fighters: Progress or propaganda? Retrieved January 7, 2020, Retrieved from https://www.france24.com/en/20150402-syria-women-soldiers-assad-army-propaganda.

Lefebvre, H. (1970). *La Revolution Urbaine*. Bussiere, Saint-Amand (Cher), France: Editions Gallimard.

Long, P., & Wall, T. (2009). *Media Studies: texts, production, context*. New York: ROUTLEDGE.

Love, H. (2009). Feeling backwards: Loss and the politics of queer history. Cambridge: Harvard University Press.Marsi, F. (2017, October 18). Amid War, Women Are Starting to Make a Mark on Syrian Politics. Retrieved from https://www.newsdeeply.com/syria/articles/2017/10/17/amid-war-women-are-starting-to-make-a-mark-on-syrian-politics

Macdonald, A. (2016). Assad's women soldiers complain of sexual harassment. Retrieved from https://www.middleeasteye.net/fr/news/syrian-female-soldiers-1908652801.

Mahmoud, S. (2005). *Politics of piety: the islamic revival and the feminist subject*. Princeton: Princeton University Press.

Mahmoud, S. (2006). Feminist Theory, Agency, and the Liberatory Subject: Some Reflections on the Islamic Revival in Egypt. Temenos - Nordic Journal of Comparative Religion, 42(1). doi: 10.33356/temenos.4633

Majalla. (2012). The Media War in Syria. Retrieved 10 July, 2018, from http://eng.majalla.com/2012/10/article55234370/the-media-war-in-syria

Makki, R. (2014, May 24). Protecting women and girls' dignity is a life-saving need. IFRC Beirut. URL: https://www.ifrc.org/fr/nouvelles/nouvelles/middle-east-and-north-africa/lebanon/protecting-women-and-girls-dignity-is-a-life-saving-need-66028/

Malkki, L. (1995). *Purity and exile: Violence, memory and national cosmology among Hutu refugees in Tanzania*. Chicago: University of Chicago Press.

Malkki, L. (1996). Speechless emissaries: Refugees, humanitarianism, and dehistoricization. *Cultural Anthropology*, 11(3): 377–404.

Mansbach, D. (2009). Normalizing violence: from military checkpoints to 'terminals' in the occupied territories, Journal of Power, 2(1), 255-273

Marcuse, H. (1955). *Eros and civilization: A Philosophical Inquiry into Freud.* Boston, Massachusetts: Routledge.

Martínez, J. C., & Eng, B. (2017). Struggling to Perform the State: The Politics of Bread in the Syrian Civil War. *International Political Sociology.* doi: 10.1093/ips/olw026

Maze, J. (2018). Towards an Analytic of Violence: Foucault, Arendt & Power. *Foucault Studies,* 120–145. doi: 10.22439/fs.v0i25.5577

Meyer, C. O., Sangar, E., & Michaels, E. (2017). How do non-governmental organizations influence media coverage of conflict? The case of the Syrian conflict, 2011–2014. *Media, War & Conflict,* 11(1), 149–171. doi: 10.1177/1750635217727309

Mitchell, T. (2002). *Rule of Experts: Egypt, Techno-Politics, Modernity.* Berkeley, CA: Univ. of California Press.

Mohanty, C. T. (1984). Under western eyes: Feminist scholarship and colonial discourses. *boundary 2,* 12(3), 333. doi:10.2307/302821

Mohanty, C. (2003). 'Under western eyes' revisited: Feminist solidarity through anticapitalist struggles. *Signs: Journal of Women in Culture and Society,* 28(2): 499–535.

Moreiras, A. (2010), "Infrapolitical Literature. Hispanism and the Border." CR: The New Centennial Review 10:2 (pp.183-204).

Morrissey, B. (2003). *When Women Kill Questions of Agency and Subjectivity.* Abingdon, Oxon: Taylor and Francis.

Moser, C. & Clark, F. (eds). (2001), Victims, Perpetrators or Actors? Gender, Armed Conflict and Political Violence (London: Zed Books).

Mourad, S. (2020, August 16). Aftershock. Retrieved August 31, 2020 from www.rustedradishes.com/aftershock/?fb-clid= IwAR3sKPe_S5ESA1pM3z0G-cy_Gmy4fjpvpwsmVWaulDWrGvkogn-JuGmj McZk

Najem, C. T. (2016). *Can the prisoner speak? An ideological and visual analysis of prisons in Lebanese television news* (Unpublished doctoral dissertation). American University of Beirut. Retrieved April 21, 20201 from www.semanticscholar.org/paper/Can-the-prisoner-speak-%3A-an-ideological-and-visual-Najem/cda71f1917a0ce40b95d91d28a7d92ce792776c8

Najjar, O. A. (2018, December 23). Al Arabiya. Retrieved March 6, 2020, from https://www.britannica.com/topic/Al-Arabiya

Neocleous, M. (2013). Resisting Resilience. Radical Philosophy. https://www.r adicalphilosophy.com/commentary/resisting-resilience

Nikunen, K. (2020). Breaking the silence: From Representations of victims and threat towards spaces of voice. *The SAGE Handbook of Media and Migration*, 411-423. doi:10.4135/9781526476982.n41

Nikunen, K. (2019) Once a refugee: selfie activism, visualized citizenship and the space of appearance, Popular Communication, 17:2, 154-170, DOI: 10.1080/15405702.2018.1527336

Oliver, K. (2007). *Women as Weapons of War*. Columbia University Press.

Oliver, S. (2010). Dehumanization: Perceiving the Body as (In)Human. In P. Kaufmann, H. Kuch, C. Neuhaeuser, & E. Webster (Eds.), *Humiliation, degradation, dehumanization: Human dignity violated* (pp. 85-97). Springer Science & Business Media.

Ong-Van-Cung, K. S. (2011). Critique and Subjectivation: Foucault and Butler on the Subject, 49(1), 148. doi: 10.3917/amx.049.0148

Pavlik, J. V. (2019). *Digital technology and the future of broadcasting: global perspectives*. New York: Routledge.

Pine, L. (2017). Creating Conformity: The Training of Girls in the Bund Deutscher Mädel. *Sage Journals: European History Quarterly*, 143-162. doi:10.4324/9781315248271-8

Porter, L. (2016). Shamed and Abandoned: The Fate of Syria's Female Ex-Inmates. Retrieved from https://www.newsdeeply.com/syria/articles/201 6/12/22/shamed-and-abandoned-the-fate-of-syrias-female-ex-inmates .

Pruce, J. R. (2019). *The mass appeal of human rights*. Cham, Switzerland: Palgrave Macmillan.

Ramadan, A. (2012). "Spatialising the Refugee Camp." Transactions of the Institute of British Geographers. doi:10.1111/j.1475-5661.2012.00509.x.

Ramadan, A. (2012). *Spatialising the Refugee Camp*. Transactions of the Institute of British Geographers. doi:10.1111/j.1475-5661.2012.00509.x.

Reliefweb. (2019). UNHCR Jordan Factsheet - February 2019 - Jordan. Retrieved from https://reliefweb.int/report/jordan/unhcr-jordan-factsheet-february-2019.

Rheindorf, M., & Wodak, R. (2017). Borders, fences, and limits — Protecting Austria from refugees:Metadiscursive negotiation of meaning in the current refugee crisis. Journal of Immigrant &Refugee Studies, 16(1–2), 15–38 doi:10.1080/15562948.2017.1302032

Richter-Devroe, S. (2011). Palestinian women's everyday resistance: Between normality and nor- malisation. *Journal of International Women's Studies* 12(3): 32–46.

Robinson, W.I & Yousef K. Baker, Y.K. (2019): Savage Inequalities: Capitalist Crisis and Surplus Humanity, International Critical Thought, DOI: 10.1080/21598282.2019.1649171

Rogers, P. (2012, June 14). Syria, the Proxy War. Retrieved March 6, 2020, from https://www.globalpolicy.org/security-council/index-of-countries-on-the-security-council-agenda/general-issues/51693-syria-the-proxy-war.html

RT Arabic. (2019, May 26). Retrieved from https://en.wikipedia.org/wiki/RT_Arabic

RT News. (2012, March 12). Al Jazeera exodus: Channel losing staff over 'bias'. Retrieved March 6, 2020, from https://www.rt.com/news/al-jazeera-loses-staff-335/

Sakr, N. (2007). *Arab television today*. Place of publication not identified: I.B. Tauris.

Sakr, N. (2007). *Arab media and political renewal: Community, legitimacy and public life*. London: I. B. Tauris.

Sama TV. (2018, December 20). Retrieved from https://en.wikipedia.org/wiki/Sama_TV

Sanyal, R. (2018). *Managing through ad hoc measures: Syrian refugees and the politics of waiting in Lebanon*. Political Geography, 66, 67–75. doi: 10.1016/j.polgeo.2018.08.015

Schaefer, D. O. (2019). *The evolution of affect theory the humanities, the sciences, and the study of power*. Cambridge: Cambridge University Press.

Schießer, S. (2002) 'Gender, Medien und Milit¨ar: Zur Konstruktion weiblicher Stereotypein der Darstellung von Soldatinnen in den Printmedien der Bundeswehr', 25(61): 47–61.

Schuring, S. (2014, April). Mothers of the Nation: The Ambiguous Role of Nazi Women in Third Reich. Lake Forest College Publications. Retrieved from https://publications.lakeforest.edu/masters_theses/1/

Seghaier, R. (2018, December 24). Poverty Porn and Reproductive Injustice: A Review of Capernaum. Retrieved January 15, 2019, from https://kohljournal.press/poverty-porn

Sjoberg, L., & Gentry, C. E. (2013). *Mothers, monsters, whores: womens violence in global politics*. London: Zed Books.

Sparre, S. L. (2008). Educated Women in Syria: Servants of the State, or Nurturers of the Family? Critique: Critical Middle Eastern Studies, 17(1), 3-20. doi:10.1080/10669920701862468

Spivak, G. C. (2010). *Can the Subaltern Speak: Reflections on the History of an Idea.*

Stables, G. (2003) 'Justifying Kosovo: Representations of Gendered Violence and U.S. Military Intervention', *Critical Studies in Mass Communication* 20(1): 92–115.

Stevenson, N. (2014). Human(e) rights and the cosmopolitan imagination: Questions of human dignity and cultural identity. *Cultural Sociology*, 8(2): 180–196

Succar, R. (2014, December 26). Harvard Arab Alumni Association. Retrieved from https://www.youtube.com/watch?v=39hAf4CWJsA

Schweitzer, E. J. (2008). Digital divide. In *Encyclopedia Britannica*. Retrieved from https://www.britannica.com/topic/digital-divide

Syrian Arab News Agency. (2019, February 24). Retrieved from https://en.wikipedia.org/wiki/Syrian_Arab_News_Agency

Syrian News Channel. (2018, June 20). Retrieved from https://en.wikipedia.org/wiki/Syrian_News_Channel

Szanto, E. (2016). Depicting Victims, Heroines, and Pawns in the Syrian Uprising . *Project Muse* , 12(3), 306-322

Tharoor, I. (2015, September 4). The Arab world's wealthiest nations are doing next to nothing for Syria's refugees. Retrieved from https://www.washingtonpost.com/news/worldviews/wp/2015/09/04/the-arab-worlds-wealthiest-nations-are-doing-next-to-nothing-for-syrias-refugees/

Tadros, M. (2016). Understanding Politically Motivated Sexual Assault in Protest Spaces: Evidence from Egypt (March 2011 to June 2013). *SAGE, Social & Legal Studies*, 25(1), 93-110.

The Economist. (2019). Politicians are stoking anti-refugee sentiment in Lebanon. Retrieved from https://www.economist.com/middle-east-and-africa/2019/08/22/politicians-are-stoking-anti-refugee-sentiment-in-lebanon.

Thomson Reuters Foundation. (2013). Syrian war causing 'honour killings', child marriages - doctor. Retrieved from http://news.trust.org//item/20131204182854-8hegf/

Thompson, E. (2000). *Colonial citizens*. New York: Columbia University Press.

Ticktin, M. (2011). Casualties of care: Immigration and the politics of humanitarianism inFrance. Berkeley: University of California Press.

Tomkins, S. (1995). *Shame and Its Sisters: A Silvan Tomkins Reader*. Eve Kosofsky Sedgwick and Adam Frank, eds. Durham, NC: Duke University Press.

Tsvetkova, M., and Zverev, A. (2016, November 3). Ghost soldiers: The russians secretly dying for the Kremlin in Syria. Retrieved from https://www.reut ers.com/article/us-mideast-crisis-syria-russia-insight-idUSKBN12Y0M6

Tuchman, G. (1978). *Making News: A Study in the Construction of Reality*. New York: The Free Press

Turbay, M. G. (2015). *The 'politics of representation': Syrian refugees in the official discourse in Lebanon (2011-2015)* (Master's thesis). Retrieved from ProQuest Dissertations and Theses Global.

Tuysuz, G. (2011). Syrian men promise to marry women who were raped. Retrieved from https://www.washingtonpost.com/world/middle-east/sy rian-men-promise-to-marry-women-who-were-raped/2011/06/20/AG6s O1cH_story.html.

UN Career. (2019). Persevere: Promoting Economic Resilience of Syrian Women-terms of Reference for Contract of Conduct Baseline Assessment. UN CAREER. URL: https://uncareer.net/vacancy/persevere-promoting-e conomic-resilience-syrian-women-terms-r-221063

UNHCR. (2013). *Joint Assessment for Syrian Refugees in Alexandria, Egypt*. Geneva: UNHCR

UNHCR. (2018). "Syria Emergency." Retrieved from http://www.unhcr.org/e n-us/syria-emergency.html

UNIFEM. (2007, January). Women and the People's Assembly in the Syrian Arab Republic. Retrieved June, 2019, from https://www.refworld.org/doci d/46cadac70.html

Unmüßig, B. (2016, August 3). Syria: Systematic Torture and Sexualized Violence: Gunda-Werner-Institut. Retrieved from https://www.gwi-boell.de/ en/2016/08/03/syria-systematic-torture-and-sexualized-violence

Usta, J., Masterson, A. R., & Farver, J. M. (2016). Violence Against Displaced Syrian Women in Lebanon. *Journal of Interpersonal Violence*, 1–13. doi:10.1177/0886260516670881

Van Dijk, T. A. (1983). Discourse analysis: Its development and application to the structure of news. Journal of Communication, Spring. 20-43.

Van Dijk, T. (2001). Multidisciplinary CDA. In R. Wodak, & M. Meyer (Eds.), *Methods of critical discourse analysis*. SAGE Publications: Great Britain.

Vulnerability. (2021). In *Merriam-Webster.com*. Retrieved April 23, 2021, from h ttps://www.merriam-webster.com/dictionary/vulnerability

Web.archive.org. (2011). Syrian Arab news agency - SANA - Syria: Syria news:. Retrieved from https://web.archive.org/web/20120103102945/www.sana. sy/eng/article/27.ht

Weiss, B. (2018, July 23). Slavoj Žižek and Violence. Retrieved May 28, 2020, from https://notevenpast.org/slavoi-zizek-and-violence/

WITW. (2016). 20 Syrian women reportedly chose suicide over being raped. Retrieved from https://womenintheworld.com/2016/12/13/20-syrian-wo men-reportedly-chose-suicide-over-being-raped/.

Wedeen, L. (1999) Ambiguities of Domination – Politics, Rhetoric, and Symbols in Contemporary Syria (Chicago: The University of Chicago Press).

Wodak, R. (2015). *The politics of fear: What right-wing populist discourses mean.* London, UK: SAGE

Wodak, R. (1995). Critical Linguistics and Critical Discourse Analysis. *Handbook of Pragmatics,* 204–210. doi: 10.1075/hop.m.cri1

Yuval-Davis, N. (1997). *Gender and Nation.* New York: Sage.

Zachs, F. (2013). Muḥammad Jamīl Bayhum and the Woman Question. *Welt Des Islams,* 53(1), 50–75. doi: 10.1163/15700607-0003a0003

Zayani, M. (2016). Al Jazeera's Complex Legacy: Thresholds for an Unconventional Media Player from the Global South. *International Journal of Communication, 10,* 3554–3569. Retrieved from file:///C:/Users/elzei/Downloads/4815-21239-1-PB.pdf

Žižek S. (2008). *Violence six sideways reflections.* New York (N.Y.): Picador.

Žižek, S. (2002). *Welcome to the desert of the real!: five essays on September 11 and related dates.* London; New York: Verso

Zureik, R. (2012). *Food, Farming, and Freedom: Sowing the Arab Spring.* Charlottesville, VA: Just World Books.

Cultural Studies

Gabriele Klein
Pina Bausch's Dance Theater
Company, Artistic Practices and Reception

2020, 440 p., pb., col. ill.
29,99 € (DE), 978-3-8376-5055-6
E-Book:
PDF: 29,99 € (DE), ISBN 978-3-8394-5055-0

Elisa Ganivet
Border Wall Aesthetics
Artworks in Border Spaces

2019, 250 p., hardcover, ill.
79,99 € (DE), 978-3-8376-4777-8
E-Book:
PDF: 79,99 € (DE), ISBN 978-3-8394-4777-2

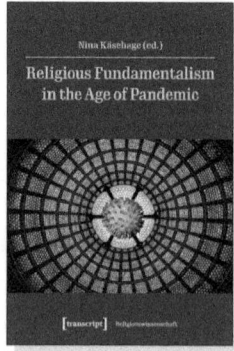

Nina Käsehage (ed.)
**Religious Fundamentalism
in the Age of Pandemic**

April 2021, 278 p., pb., col. ill.
37,00 € (DE), 978-3-8376-5485-1
E-Book: available as free open access publication
PDF: ISBN 978-3-8394-5485-5

**All print, e-book and open access versions of the titles in our list
are available in our online shop www.transcript-publishing.com**

Cultural Studies

Ivana Pilic, Anne Wiederhold-Daryanavard (eds.)
Art Practices in the Migration Society
Transcultural Strategies in Action
at Brunnenpassage in Vienna

March 2021, 244 p., pb.
29,00 € (DE), 978-3-8376-5620-6
E-Book:
PDF: 25,99 € (DE), ISBN 978-3-8394-5620-0

German A. Duarte, Justin Michael Battin (eds.)
Reading »Black Mirror«
Insights into Technology and the Post-Media Condition

January 2021, 334 p., pb.
32,00 € (DE), 978-3-8376-5232-1
E-Book:
PDF: 31,99 € (DE), ISBN 978-3-8394-5232-5

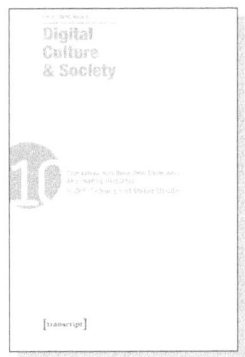

Cindy Kohtala, Yana Boeva, Peter Troxler (eds.)
Digital Culture & Society (DCS)
Vol. 6, Issue 1/2020 –
Alternative Histories in DIY Cultures and Maker Utopias

February 2021, 214 p., pb., ill.
29,99 € (DE), 978-3-8376-4955-0
E-Book:
PDF: 29,99 € (DE), ISBN 978-3-8394-4955-4

**All print, e-book and open access versions of the titles in our list
are available in our online shop www.transcript-publishing.com**

GPSR Authorized Representative: Easy Access System Europe, Mustamäe tee
50, 10621 Tallinn, Estonia, gpsr.requests@easproject.com

www.ingramcontent.com/pod-product-compliance
Lightning Source LLC
Chambersburg PA
CBHW061744120626
46550CB00005B/1882